SACRED WELLS

SACRED WELLS

A STUDY IN THE HISTORY, MEANING, AND MYTHOLOGY OF HOLY WELLS & WATERS

2nd Edition

Gary R. Varner

Algora Publishing
New York

Library of Congress Cataloging-in-Publication Data —

Varner, Gary R.
   Sacred wells: a study in the history, meaning, and mythology of holy wells & waters
/ Gary R. Varner. — 2nd ed.
      p. cm.
   Includes bibliographical references and index.
   ISBN 978-0-87586-717-5 (soft cover : alk. paper) — ISBN 978-0-87586-718-2 (hard
cover: alk. paper) — ISBN 978-0-87586-719-9 (e-book) 1. Holy wells. 2. Holy water. I.
Title.
   GR690.V37 2009
   265—dc22
                        2009011274

Front cover: 19th-Century Well Surrounded by Cow Parsley
© Roger Wilmshurst; Frank Lane Picture Agency/CORBIS, ca. 1965–1995

Printed in the United States

This book is dedicated to those researchers devoted to the understanding and preservation of traditional holy sites around the world. In particular I would like to thank Katy Jordan and Alison Maloney for their kindness and for providing information to me that I would not otherwise have found. In addition the research of Richard Pederick, Mara Freeman, Stephen Buckly, Graham Jones, Patrick Logan, Dr. Madelein Gray and innumerable others continues to enrich our knowledge and understanding of ancient traditions, religion, history and legends. Most importantly, they have unveiled even more mystery which waits for our understanding.

This book is for my parents, Robert and Edith Varner, and for Ellen Lissard, a good friend and a true inspiration.

Acknowledgements

There are many books on holy wells, most having to do with specific localities or specific wells. This is one of a few books on holy wells and sacred waters to be written from a global perspective. Obviously, I have not been able to visit all of the wells mentioned herein — only a few. But all of them offer intense mystical feelings of unseen powers. I have cited all my references in footnotes and in the bibliography at the end of the book. Any of the works by Nigel Pennick, Janet and Colin Bord, Ronald Hutton and Miranda Green are valuable for an historical synthesis, and Ralph Merrifield's *The Archaeology of Ritual and Magic* is an excellent treatise on the history of votive offerings and the continuation of traditions from Pagan through contemporary Christian times. Older works such as those by Hardy, Hope, Trevelyan and MacKenzie are extremely valuable for their 19th century views of paganism, religious traditions and mythology.

Because discovery is constant, the findings and conclusions reached in this work are only momentary. Any errors or omissions are, of course, mine.

I would like to offer specific thanks to Jamie George, *guide extraordinaire*, for his expertise and humor while showing my family and me many of the sacred wells located in Cornwall discussed in this book; Emma "Bobcat" Restall Orr, co-chief druid of The British Druid Order for her kindness and suggestion that a book on holy wells was sorely needed; Rick Adams, Maidu healer, for his time and kind help in my research on Maidu and pre-Maidu traditions, as well as the many helpful people I met on my travels over the years to Great Britain, Yucatan, the American Southwest and Northern California.

"Springs have held, down to the present day, the name of holy things, and are objects of veneration, having the repute of healing the sick; as for example, the springs of the Prophetic Nymphs, of Apollo, and of Juturna." — Sextus Julius Frontinus in *The Water Supply of the City of Rome*, AD 97.

Holy Wells "are not only opposed in their nature and tendency to every precept of the moral law and of the Christian religion, but are so many stains upon the character of a civilized and even nominally Christian people, and consequently a disgrace to the age and the country in which we live..." — Philip Dixon Hardy in *The Holy Wells of Ireland*, 1840

"There is an interesting Swedish superstition, that the old pagan gods, when worsted by Christianity, took refuge in the rivers, where they still dwell." — Robert Charles Hope in *The Legendary Lore of the Holy Wells of England*, 1893

"No religious place in Ireland can be without a holy well." — attributed to Rev. C. Otway, 1894

"What once were the Celtic equivalents of the Greek 'fountains of the nymphs ' were consecrated as 'holy wells'" — Charles Squire in *Celtic Myths & Legends*

"The feelings of the faithful in believing that the Deity has a partiality for wells and fountains is the survival of an ancient superstition, perhaps one might say the most ancient superstition in the world." — T. Sharper Knowlson in *The Origins of Popular Superstition and Customs*, 1910

"Wells and springs are often said to represent the spiritual womb of the Earth and to heal, confer wisdom, or grant wishes...and...are often alleged to provide openings to the underworld..." — Brian Leigh Molyneaux in *The Sacred Earth*, 1995

"Continuity is demonstrated by the ancient, enduring sanctity of many of the great religious centers. It is illustrated...by the prehistoric holy wells which are found beneath such cathedrals as York, Winchester, Carlisle, and Ely and at innumerable parish churches." — John Michell in *Sacred England*, 1996

PREFACE TO THE ALGORA EDITION

Sacred Wells was originally published in 2002. Since that time, I have visited a large number of additional sacred sites, including those associated with Native American rock art, gargoyle-embellished cathedrals, sacred landscapes and, of course, sacred wells. I have written a number of books having to do with folklore, mythology, the environment and the history of religion since *Sacred Wells* was first published. However, I continue to travel back to the subject of holy wells and waters and when Algora Publishing gave me an opportunity to expanded and reissue *Sacred Wells* in this present volume, I couldn't resist.

Much of our mythic environment is forgotten, discarded or abused. The thirst for coal and oil, for land for housing developments and business parks, and the desire to control the few wild rivers to harness energy, consistently degrades our habitat and the habitat of the wild animals that continue to struggle to survive. It also destroys much of the landscape that, for a variety of reasons, has a special meaning for various people, some of that revealed in ancient tales that used to be told. Now, many of the mysterious locations our ancestors held in awe are forgotten. I am pleased to reissue *Sacred Wells* so that these sacred places and their legends will continue to be known to those who may wish to learn from them and perhaps even travel to them to experience their special nature for themselves.

I would like to express my thanks to good friends Ricky and Holger Jordan, editors of the German journal *Magister Botanicus,* for their kind permission to include some of their beautiful photographs taken of several holy wells in Cornwall, England, which appear only in this expanded edition of *Sacred Wells.* All other photographs were taken by the author.

— Gary R. Varner, 2009

TABLE OF CONTENTS

Introduction

Sacred wells are recognized around the world, in nearly every culture and in every age. Long associated with feminine, divine power they are also seen as places of healing, magick,[1] wisdom and sources to the Other World. Some believe that these wells were originally created to bring the moon and its powers to the earth, at least in its reflection. Water from these holy wells was believed to have the intrinsic value of fertility and life, and thereby love and sexuality. In many cultures, and for untold centuries, it has been believed that Holy wells are inhabited, or at least guarded, by nymphs and faeries. Holy wells are also contradictory. Traditions have held that they are life giving, they grant wishes, they heal, they foretell the future but also that they may take life, apply curses, and serve as residences for lost souls and supernatural mischief-makers.

Over the years, most holy wells have been renamed after Christian saints but in many cases the ancient practices associated with them continue. Thousands of people still flock to Lourdes and other sacred sites for healing. Votive offerings are still left in secret at many out-of-the-way locations throughout Great Britain and Europe. Today some scholars are questioning the origin of these holy wells. Were they really venerated by our pagan ancestors? Are they purely the creation of the Christian era? Ronald Hutton noted in his work, *The Pagan Religions of the Ancient British Isles*, that "not a single structure, not even a basin or retaining wall, can be convincingly dated back to the early Middle Ages, let alone to pre-Christian times."[2] It is acknowledged that many, if not most, structures constructed

---

1 I use the word "*magick*" to denote the difference between the use of ritual to change one's present reality and "stage magic" which is simple trickery.

2 Hutton, Ronald. *The Pagan Religions of the Ancient British Isles: Their Nature and Legacy*. Oxford: Blackwell Publishers, 1993, 167

around these water sources were created in Christian ages along with the associated linking to a particular saint.[1] The early Church assigned Christian names to specific wells in an effort to remove traces of pagan usage. The study of the particular saints who had wells dedicated to them is an interesting one. There are over 200 wells named for St. Helen in Britain but it is likely that the original term for these wells was *hael*, meaning "omen." "St. Alkelda's" well in Middleham is an obvious reworking of the Old Norse words *halig kelda* ("hal kelda"), meaning a spring of living waters. However, far too many myths and legends tie particular wells to pagan gods and goddesses to discount the pagan origin of many of these sites. These wells were considered sacred long before the followers of the new religion of Christianity placed walls and other structures over them. In addition, many wells, springs, rivers and lakes have ancient offerings in their depths indicating a pre-Christian origin. Richard Muir, in his book *The National Trust Guide to Prehistoric and Roman Britain*, wrote: "It seems very likely that the multitude of early Christian holy wells are an inheritance resulting from the Christianization of much older pagan holy places."[2] What is most important, however, is how these monuments affect us today. Do we find an important archetypal link in our concept of what is holy and divine through these wells? Do we find ourselves at peace when we visit these areas? Do we find physical relief of our aches and illnesses by partaking of the waters?

Springs and wells are archetypal symbols of life, fertility and vitality. The Irish have a legend of the Well of Knowledge and, in fact, wells have been regarded as having a special wisdom that can be obtained through their waters. The underground sources of the life giving waters have naturally attracted a religious significance for those living around them. These sources of life (also described as avenues to the underworld) have special guardians in the forms of nymphs, faeries and other mystical beasts and beings.

The United States does not have "holy wells" as they are known in Europe. Modern America does not have the history or traditions associated with long periods of habitation by a single, widespread culture with an intimate relationship with the Earth. The cultures of Native Americans are diverse and their populations are and were located over a widespread geographic area. In a broad sense, these cultures do share a belief in a special relationship with nature and the mystical or divine and there are many areas, including springs and rivers, which were and are still held sacred by the indigenous peoples of America.

---

1 See Jeremy Hart, "Holy Wells and Other Holy Places" in *The Living Spring Journal*, Issue #1, May 2000)

2 Muir, Richard and Humphrey Welfare. *The National Trust Guide to Prehistoric and Roman Britain*. London: George Philip/The National Trust & The National Trust for Scotland 1983, 166

Thus the United States does have many magickal places, but they are not as well known or documented as those in Europe and Great Britain in particular. Some Native American sacred sites are discussed in detail in Chapter 2.

It is the personal relationship that each of us has with the Earth which creates sacred space. The sacred sites discussed in this book have been considered special for hundreds and thousands of years. But one individual, or a few, recognized them originally as places of wonder and power. We can do the same even if we live in a country that has not had the linear history that Great Britain and Europe have had. If you know an area that is meaningful to you, that feels powerful and mystical, then you have connected with the sense of spirit and have begun the process of creating a sacred place.

This book will examine the ancient roots of the mythology and spirituality that is associated with holy wells and the religious conflicts that surround them. In addition, the contemporary religious rites practiced at various sacred wells that date back to prehistoric times will be examined.

CHAPTER 1. THE SACRED WELL IN ANCIENT HISTORY

Wells and springs are essentially the same thing. They are sites where water "springs" or "wells" out of the ground and originate in subterranean water sources. All of the sacred wells around the world meet this definition. These holy water sources create springs, pools or fountains of water, many having strange and miraculous properties attributed to them. In later years many of these pools had stone walls built around them that resulted in the well characterization we visualize today. Like lakes and rivers, these water sources were thought to be divine in origin and most were associated with particular goddesses and gods. Wells are usually considered feminine but there are also indications that particular gods were also connected to wells. Ancient Celtic literature gives credence that the Celts believed that the gods themselves created wells.

Marija Gimbutas noted, "the cult of wells and thermal springs, especially those at the source or larger streams and rivers, cannot be separated from the cult of the life-dispensing Goddess."[1] While many of Gimbutas' conclusions are now viewed as being erroneous, her views do inspire discussion and many tend to be based upon reasonable assumptions. Gimbutas also believed that the "cup marks" found so often pecked in stones around the world, including those in North America made by Native Americans, are symbolic wells. Rainwater was collected in these cupolas and was thought to have curative powers. Gimbutas wrote that prehistoric wells and cupolas were both "symbols of the centrally concentrated Goddess life force."[2] Alev Croutier, in her book *Taking the Waters*, wrote that "wells and cupmarks became interchangeable, both being symbols of the centrally con-

---

1 Gimbutas, Marija. *The Language of the Goddess.* NY: Harper Collins Publishers, 1991, 43
2 Ibid., 61

centrated goddess life force. Early civilizations often attributed healing powers to the rainwater that collected in these hollows...Cupmarks found throughout Europe still retain some of their symbolic significance in the peasant subculture."[1] These cupmarks are also common among American Indian sites. Many areas of concentrated cupolas (or "pit and groove" as archaeologists refer to them) appear in central California and Alberta, Canada. While archaeologists have not been able to determine any meaning to these stone cupolas, many have curvilinear meandering lines pecked into the rock as well. These meandering lines are normally associated with prehistoric symbolism of rivers and streams. Cupolas are a common artistic motif on megaliths in Brittany. Many are found along with carvings of footprints, breasts and meandering lines. "Rain rocks" were common among the Northern California Indian tribes and consisted of boulders with pecked conical pits, incised grooves and, in a few cases, carved designs representative of bear feet. Native Shamans were able to control weather, including rain and the severity of the rainfall, by including these rocks in ritual.[2]

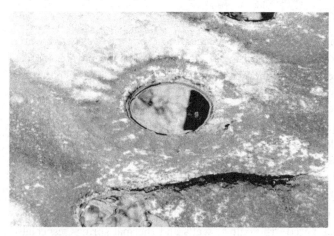

Photo 1: Maidu cupola, Northern California

Cup-holes are also found near sacred wells in Ireland and Scotland. Like the cup-basins located in bedrock areas of North America, those also found in rock outcroppings in Ireland and Scotland were regarded as "wells" because they held water. Some of these cup-holes were thought to have healing powers for warts and others, in Scotland, were believed to cure barrenness.

There is some agreement among both modern and traditional historians that the creation of the sacred well in a religious vein began at the same time as the erection of the megalithic monuments in Europe and Great Britain. Gimbutas remarked that "sometimes a well, not a stone pillar, is found in the middle of a stone circle."[3] In fact, stone circles usually contained a spring, or "well," or had a cause-

---

1 Croutier, Alev Lytle. *Taking the Waters.* New York: Abbeville Press 1992, 66

2 Heizer, Robert F. "Sacred Rain Rocks of Northern California," in *Reports of the University of California Archaeological Survey, No. 20,* March 16, 1953, 33-38

3 Gimbutas, op. cit., 311

way that led to a nearby river. James Bonwick wrote in 1894 that the custom of well worship originated "with the erection of stone circles."[1] Reportedly, the more than 900 stone circles still existing in Britain today are located near river valleys or low-lying water. In Wales, over 60 megalith-well combinations exist with the possibility of several more as many of the standing stones have been destroyed over the years.[2] The standing stones may have been symbolic trees.[3] The symbolism of the standing stone-well relationship is obvious. The age-old womb-phallus fertility meaning is apparent. Another view of the megalith-water association proposed by Brian Molyneaux is that of a more utilitarian function:

> The hope of an afterlife is clearly expressed in the design and location of some burial chambers. Oval burial mounds built 2,000 years ago in what is now the Central African Republic, and topped by standing stones, are sited near springs so that the dead would never be far from water.[4]

Old Testament writings commonly refer to *masseboth*, or sacred pillars erected either in honor of dead ancestors or to particular deities. The ancient Israelites, prior to their monotheistic period, worshipped not only Yahweh but also a female consort called Ashtoreth, also known as Astarte, the ancient goddess.[5] So far, 142 such sites have been found in the southern Negev and eastern Sinai deserts dating back to the 11,000 BCE. While no water associations have been identified with these complexes, a common usage does appear to exist among all of the various megalithic sites in the world. Offerings, including sacrifices, were commonly made to these sacred pillars as they were in other locations around the world.[6] Due to the ever-changing nature of deserts, it is also possible that these early ritual sites did have a water connection at one time. A megalithic circle dating back 7,000 years located in the Nubian Desert 500 miles south of Cairo, at times was partially submerged by the seasonal monsoon rains and more than likely was used to mark the onset of the rainy season. Other, larger, megalithic structures, some up to 20 feet in length and weighing as much as 20 tons, have been found on a coastal plain in western Yemen and have been dated from 2400 and 1800 BCE Again a water association is seen.

The Hupa Indians of Northern California venerated standing stones as well and referred to them as the "story people." Many of these stones were situated in

---

1 Bonwick, James. *Irish Druids and Old Irish Religions*, New York: Barnes & Noble Books, 1986, 244 (a reprint of the 1894 edition)

2 Jones, Francis. *The Holy Wells of Wales.* Cardiff: University of Wales Press, 1954 15-18

3 Bauschatz, Paul C. *The Well and the Tree: World and Time in Early Germanic Culture.* Amherst: The University of Massachusetts Press, 1982, 26

4 Molyneaux, Brian Leigh. *The Sacred Earth: Spirits of the Landscape, Ancient Alignments and Sacred Sites, Creation and Fertility.* Boston: Little, Brown and Company, 1995, 136

5 Varner, Gary R. *The Gods of Man: Gods of Nature God of War.* Morrisville: Lulu Press Inc. 2007, 72

6 Avner, Uzi. "Sacred Stones in the Desert," in *Biblical Archaeology Review*, Vol. 27, May-June 2001, 30-41

rows. Heizer reported that "when frosts come in the fall...a man or a virgin takes a basket of water with incense root and washes all these stones, praying, as he does it, that gentle rain may come and that the frost may go away."[1]

Many legends pertaining to sacred wells and standing stones indicate that a close relationship between the two in religious symbolism existed in our past. Wittelstone (or Wissel Stone) in Gloucestershire is said to walk down to Our Lady's Well to drink of the water when it hears the Stow clock chime. In Londonderry County, according to R.C. Skyring Walters,[2] pilgrims would travel to a holy well where they would place pieces of cloth in the nearby bushes and then visit a large standing stone in the Roe River. There they would bathe and walk around the stone, bowing and praying to it. They then went on to a local church where they held a ceremony to be followed by returning to the stone and again walking around it. Was this perhaps the survival of an ancient ritual?

Miranda Green, however, wrote, "the tradition of endowing wells with supernatural powers is at its commonest immediately before the Roman period."[3] Due to the large amount of sacred wells in Britain (an estimated 3,000 in Ireland alone) with spiritual-healing qualities, it seems unlikely that holy wells were a new phenomenon of the time. Wells with religious connotations are evident on the continent dating back to the Late Bronze Age and there are signs that such wells were in use for ritual purposes in England. A 110-foot-deep well near Stonehenge, with associated offerings, appears to have been completed contemporaneously with the final stages of the megalithic site (around 1900 BCE or 4,000 years ago).

A second century BCE ritual site near Stuttgart, Germany, consisted of a deep well in a square enclosure with oak animal carvings left as offerings. Another holy water site in Germany is the salt springs near the River Saale. Tacitus records a great battle that was fought at this spot for the rights to the holy spring. He wrote that men believed that their prayers would be heard here more than other places because the sacred spring was close to heaven.

One example of a sacred well with a continuous history of use is that of St. Helen's Well in Yorkshire. Archaeological fieldwork has found a large amount of Roman and Mediaeval pottery near this well in addition to numerous fragments of worked flint from the Neolithic. Another is that at Grand in Gaul that was used in Celtic, Romano-Celtic and Romano-Christian times. The Celts honored the god Grannos, the Romano-Celts honored Apollo-Grannos and then it became dedicated to St. Libaire.

A recent discovery in Wales indicates that a huge, 85-acre temple complex existed with continuous use for 4,700 years — right up until the advancing Roman

1 Heizer, op. cit., 34

2 Walters, R. C. Skyring. *The Ancient Wells, Springs, and Holy Wells of Gloucestershire*. Bristol: St. Stephen's Press, 1928, 53

3 Green, Miranda. *The Gods of the Celts.* Gloucestershire: Allan Sutton Publishing, Ltd., 1997, 145

armies violated it. Constructed of 1400 oak obelisks 23 feet high, the oval shaped complex stretched over an area of one and one-half miles — over 30 times larger than Stonehenge. Archaeologists believe that the focal point of the complex was a natural spring and shrine area. And, like many other ancient religious sites, the entryway was oriented toward the sunset on the summer solstice.[1] The nature of the site with the shrine, spring and the oval shape of the complex itself indicate that this was a site dedicated to a goddess.

The long reach of Celtic culture and religion can be seen in Denmark where many of the ancient churches have sacred groves and holy wells associated with them. At many of these sites are also found relief carvings of stone heads that are representative of the ancient Celtic head cult discussed elsewhere. Some holy wells are found at Rorkaer, Vestervig in northern Jutland and at Bramminge. The holy well at Rorkaer is located in a field called Heliggaard-Fenner, which means "enclosure of holy water."[2] An island in Norway called the "bath of Njord" was sacred to Njord, the God of Ships. The lake, which surrounded the island, was also sacred to this god who was the father of the Norse gods Freyr and Freyja. Njord controlled the seas and the winds. The goddess Nerthus was said to bathe her wagon each year in a sacred lake.[3]

Until recently, it was assumed that the Bronze Age people of Britain, three thousand years ago, preferred to bury their dead in barrows atop hills and ridges. However, it now appears that they more often used barrows on the lower slopes of hills close to springs, lakes and rivers. Only those barrows now found on the upper slopes of hills and ridges have survived the years of agricultural disruption. Burial shrines such as West Kennet Long Barrow and others were placed near water sources as part of "a cosmological plan that was widely understood and accepted."[4] Such a plan incorporated the ritual landscape and the inherent mythology associated with it to provide a "point of contact" with the spirit world. Votive offerings to sacred waters, including wells, springs, rivers and lakes, were, according to Ronald Hutton, "an important regional tradition of the pre-Roman British."[5] The Druids certainly revered the springs and waterways and more than likely utilized them in some form of baptism as part of a naming ceremony. While we are familiar with the sacred groves used by the Druids, it is not common knowledge that each grove would also have a lake or holy well at the center that served as the goddesses' home. The Romans, in particular, paid homage to

1 Keys, David. "4,700 year-old Oak temple found in Wales," in *The Independent*, November 26, 2000

2 Ross, Anne and Don Robins. *The Life and Death of a Druid Prince*. New York: Summit Books 1989, 161

3 Davidson, H.R. Ellis. *Gods and Myths of the Viking Age*. New York: Bell Publishing Company 1964, 132

4 Field, David. "Bury the dead in a sacred landscape," in *British Archaeology*, Issue 43, April 1999

5 Hutton, Ronald. *The Pagan Religions of the Ancient British Isles: Their Nature and Legacy*. Oxford: Blackwell Publishers Ltd., 1991, 230

sacred waters. *Aquae Arnemetiae* in Derbyshire was dedicated to the "waters of the Goddess of the grove" and temples were constructed over several ponds and springs in Essex, Wiltshire, Bath and Kent.

Court Well in Oxfordshire was known specifically for its ability to cure eye ailments and there is some indication that this well was once associated with the Germanic-Norse god Woden (or Odin). Woden, it should be remembered, was a healer and sacrificed one of his eyes so that he could drink from Mimir's Well, which was a well of knowledge. Mimir was the guardian of the well of knowledge, living next to the sacred spring under the World Tree. Some versions of the myth say that Woden severed Mimir's head in battle, visiting the well to converse with the head each day. Another well that in ancient times had been called Woden's Well is a well in Wanswell located in Gloucestershire. Undoubtedly other and more numerous wells were also associated with the Norse god throughout Britain. Brian Branston wrote in his book *The Lost Gods of England* "that the Angles, Saxons and Jutes were practicing heathens during their first five generations in England...they worshipped at least four divinities, Woden, Thunor, Tiw and Frig, they had temples, images of the gods and priests.

"The temples...appear to have been simple rectangular ridge-roofed structures set up in forest clearings possibly in association with sacred groves or a venerated tree and a holy well."[1]

Many of the Norse countries were not converted to Christianity until long after the rest of Europe. In the 16th century, the Prussians were still very pagan and, according to Davidson, "writers who visited them described sacred woods in which they made sacrifices and sacred springs in which Christians were not allowed to approach."[2]

While not wells per se, there are many deep ritual shafts in Britain that mirror wells in that they were given similar votive offerings and religious significance. The shaft mentioned previously, which is situated near Stonehenge, contained ropes and buckets that may indicate that at one time it did contain water. It has been suggested that these shafts were a first step toward the creation of holy wells. Many of these ritual pits, or shafts, were dug as deep as the water table. The pits may have been representative of "a channel to the underworld."[3] Some of the items found at the bottom of these shafts include antlers, trees soaked in blood, carvings, etc. Miranda Green notes that these shafts, or pits, appear to be most common in southeastern Britain in the late Iron Age. Some are located in Wilsford and Swanwick dating from the Bronze Age, which indicates a long-standing tradition. There is some indication that human and animal sacrifices were made at these sites as well.[4]

1 Branston, Brian. *The Lost Gods of England*. New York: Oxford University Press 1974, 55
2 Davidson, op. cit., 87
3 MacAnTsaoir, Iain. "Sacred Precincts, The Nemeds." *Clannada na Gadelica*, 1999
4 Green, op. cit., 20

An upright skeleton of a man with his spear found in a shaft in Scotland, as well as that of a dwarf found in another, may indicate that these individuals were guardians of these "channels to the underworld." In Norse pagan belief, dwarfs were thought to take the form of stags during daylight hours. As the Stag was a representation of the god Cernunnos, it is possible that the skeleton of the dwarf found represented an individual with shamanic powers. Skeletons found buried upright have also been found in County Meath and County Mayo in Ireland. Mackenzie noted that heroes killed in battle were buried in a standing position, sometimes in full battle gear and facing the land of the enemy.[1] Other, deeper shafts have been found in Bavaria (up to 40 meters deep) and central France — all with offerings in place.

The remains of 52 individuals, children as well as older adults of both sexes have been found in a "sump" in a marsh area in Levanluhta, Finland.[2] Evidence indicates that these individuals were sacrificial offerings along with birds, cows, horses and a wide variety of precious metal objects such as a bronze cauldron, arm-rings and brooches. This site in Finland is very similar to other sacrificial sites discussed in Chapter 4.

A sacrifice to holy wells was a universal act, from the human sacrifices in the sacred cenotés of Yucatan and Arizona, and similar finds in Europe and Great Britain, to animal sacrifices in other areas of the world. In fact, one of the gods of ancient Egypt, Apis, was represented as a bull and was ritually drowned in one of the sacred wells of the Nile. Apis was the avatar of Osiris — the god of renewal that wells also signify.

In Sardinia, one of the most important "cults" dating back to the Bronze Age is that of sacred wells. Wells and springs at Abini-Teti, S. Vittoria-Serri and Sos Malavidos-Orani contained votive offerings of bronze objects (including figurines), jewelry and miscellaneous imported objects. It is believed that many of these sacred wells and springs, which were normally associated with villages, served as religious and political centers.

Similar to the sacred cave sanctuaries in Yucatan, discussed later in this work, is the Cave of Psychro near Lyttos, Crete. The cave consists of a large upper chamber sloping 200 feet to a pool, with several hallways shooting off into the rock. A large roughly cut stone altar approximately three feet tall with various small cups, vases and lamps is prominently displayed near the pool. In the upper chamber, several iron weapons (swords, knives and axes) as well as iron bracelets were found. Small bronze figurines and masks were located in the lower levels. Skulls of oxen, goats, sheep, deer, pigs and dogs have been recovered from the

1 Mackenzie, Donald A. *Pre-Columbian America: Myths and Legends.* London: Senate 1996, 157 (A reprint of the 1923 edition published by The Gresham Publishing Company Ltd., London)

2 Kivikoski, Ella. *Ancient Peoples and Places: Finland.* New York: Frederick A. Praeger 1967, 127

pool itself, which is a common find among the sacred wells and waterways in Great Britain and Europe.

According to Willetts, this Middle Minoan site was "presumably...a cult of the Minoan Goddess." One of the votive objects found here was a bronze tablet depicting the goddess and the sacred tree in association with a moon-crescent and horns.[1]

The sacredness of water, especially from springs and wells, has a universal appeal. Many of our myths denote the pathway to the Underworld as through an underground river (the River Styx is one, Lake Avernus is another). Other myths and legends such as the Arthurian legends depict lakes and waterways as sacred points exiting between the Otherworld and the physical world we know. Legends of Otherworld Beings who reside in wells, and in strange happenings that occur near sacred wells, all point to a primeval connectedness between humankind and the spirit world through these portals. Both healing and deadly, generating life and taking it away, a source for knowledge and a place where knowledge is hidden, sacred wells are a metaphor for our world and our existence in it; they are the "reservoir of all the possibilities of existence...they are at once purifying and regenerating."[2]

Certain wells and springs were regarded so highly for their sacredness that they became part of the inauguration of kings. The Brennemans in their 1981 survey of inauguration sites in Celtic Ireland found that "at or near every inauguration complex we located a spring, usually now in use by Catholic Christians...the king or chieftain, then, was married to the goddess of the place...through ritual acts at the well."[3]

Sacred wells continue to exist and to offer humans a source for comfort and healing as well as a link through the dim past to another realm of existence. John Messenger, in his ethnographic study of a small, scantily inhabited island off Ireland, wrote:

> The sacred well, probably appropriated from the Druids 15 centuries ago, still attracts the folk and occasionally pilgrims from Inis Thiar and other islands...It was customary until about ten years ago for those who came to pray here to attach bits of cloth, rosaries, or sacred objects obtained from holy places of pilgrimage on the mainland and abroad, but this practice was halted by the clergy as smacking of paganism. Now it is visited for religious purposes mostly by small groups on Sunday afternoon...who come to pray for the good fortune...

Messenger wrote that the water in the well was not considered holy but the virtue of drinking from it was the same:

---

1 Willetts, R.F. *Cretan Cults and Festivals.* Westport: Greenwood Press, Publishers 1962, 145
2 Eliade, Mircea. *The Sacred & the Profane: The Nature of Religion.* San Diego: Harcourt Brace & Company, 1959, 130-131
3 Brenneman, Walter L. & Mary G. *Crossing the Circle at the Holy Wells of Ireland.* Charlottesville: University Press of Virginia 1995, 36

"...if it is drunk during prayer, it is believed to be especially efficacious for curing sterility, among other afflictions. In this century, a partially blind islander is believed to have regained his sight after paying nine visits to the well on successive Sundays, and miraculous cures from earlier times are reported."[1]

The extreme age of humankind's reverence for sacred wells and waterways cannot be fully appreciated because we still do not know how far back in time such observances go. It can be assumed, due to the nature of sites already discovered in Europe dating to the Neolithic as well as universal myths that include sacred water sites that humankind's relationship with these areas has been continuous since the perception that we coexist with nature, which is mysterious in itself.

It would be a mistake to say that all holy wells have been revered throughout time, from pagan days to the modern, in a continuous time line. In fact, there is no true way to prove or disprove a continuous usage. Katy Jordan [2] has broken down the likely possibilities of well histories thusly:

- Wells which may once have been venerated by pagans, then were no longer venerated, then venerated by Christians
- Wells once venerated by pagans, then venerated by Christians (no gap in veneration)
- Wells not venerated by anyone, coming into Christian veneration later
- Wells venerated by pagans, then by nobody

However, in a broader sense we can say that the veneration of wells and other sacred waters has been and will be a continuous part of our collective souls. The rich story of sacred wells continues to evolve in today's world with few minor changes.

1 Messenger, John C. *Inis Beag: Isle of Ireland.* New York: Holt, Rinehart and Winston, Case Studies in Cultural Anthropology 1969, 97
2 Jordan, Katy. *Wells-And-Spas@JISCMAIL.AC.UK* June 22, 2001

Chapter 2. Spotlight on Sacred Wells

The various wells discussed in this section are a small representative of those found around the world. By no means is this an exhaustive treatment of sacred wells but rather a detailed look at some of the sacred wells and springs located in Britain, France, India and the United States. A more detailed account of those wells considered to be healing wells is given in Chapter 6.

An extensive gazetteer is located in Chapter 13 and is broken out by type of well (such as healing, wishing, etc.), description, and location. It is doubtful if any reference work will contain all of the sacred wells of the world, and it is not the intent to do so in this work.

The Chalice Well, Glastonbury

One of the most famous sacred wells in the world is that of Chalice Well in Glastonbury, England. Steeped in the mystical legends of Arthur and the Lady of the Lake, Chalice Well is situated a short distance from Glastonbury Abbey and the Tor. Together the area makes up the legendary Isle of Avalon. Until the 5th century, the sea typically flooded the flat lands surrounding Glastonbury creating a flat, glass-like lake, which lapped at the edges of the Tor. At the time of Arthur Glastonbury was, indeed, the Isle of Avalon. Before Arthur's day, Avalon was sacred to the prehistoric "lake people" who buried their dead on the Isle. It is easy to see how the early name for Avalon, Ynys-witrin, meaning the "Isle of Glass," was created. Glastonbury itself means "Glass-town-borough." The flat, inland sea would have appeared as smooth glass to those sailing to the Isle.

During the 1st to the 10th centuries, first the Romans and then the Christian monks from the abbey, undertook the huge task of digging drainage ditches and building sea walls to keep the water from flowing back into the valley. Canals were dug to allow ships to sail practically right up to the abbey and even today a continuous effort must be made to drain the land least the sea again reclaim it.

The abbey itself was said to have been larger than the present Westminster Abbey in London and the fame of Glastonbury was spoken of as the Second Rome. During Henry VIII's reign, the abbey was dissolved and the last abbot, Richard Whiting, was hanged from the Tor tower. Over the years, private citizens obtained the abbey and the majestic buildings were torn down, little by little, to provide building stone for the city. In 1907, the abbey ruins were advertised for sale as part of the nearby nunnery. Described as "interesting ruins in the back" a wealthy lady from the United States set off for the auction. Her intent was to have the ruins cut up and reassembled in the United States. It was fortunate that her train was delayed long enough for the Church of England to buy it at a great price (£36,000) and it has remained more or less untouched.

The Chalice Well is said to be the resting place of the Holy Grail. Stories of Jesus visiting the area with his uncle, Joseph of Arimathea abound. In fact, Joseph supposedly founded the first Christian church in Britain at Glastonbury and the ruins of the present Glastonbury abbey now occupy the location. After Jesus' execution, Joseph and other followers are said to have returned to Glastonbury with the Holy Grail, which was placed under the well area where the blood red waters spring.

The Holy Grail though is older than Christianity. The Chalice, the Grail, is symbolic of the cauldron of plenty and the Cup of Knowledge of Celtic lore, as well as mythology from many other ancient cultures. The famous magician and astrologer of Elizabeth I, John Dee, proclaimed the Chalice Well to have the powers of youth and health.

THE TOR

The Tor is a huge whale-shaped hill that juts up from the flat plain of Glastonbury. The ruins of the tower of St. Michael's Church stand at its peak. Prior to the church being constructed, the Tor was sacred to the Neolithic residents and then the Druids. A labyrinth pathway circles around the Tor to the top. It is estimated that it takes over three hours to walk the labyrinthine path. Some researchers believe that the labyrinth is Neolithic in age and that standing stones once existed at the top of the Tor in ages past.[1] It is easy to visualize a procession of Druids progressing up the pathway. At the beginning of the pathway is a large white boulder called "The Living Rock." This rock vibrates to the touch and becomes energized at dawn and sunset each day. The Living Rock also marks the entranceway to the Underworld. On my visit to the Tor, my guide suggested that I touch the Living Rock, which I did — before he told me that it was the entranceway to the Underworld Kingdom of Gwynn ap Nudd. Luckily, the en-

---

1 Mann, Nicholas R. *The Isle of Avalon.* St. Paul: Llewellyn Publications, 1996, 101

tranceway remained closed! Undoubtedly the Tor was a place of ritual long before the Christian presence. The Tor is a short distance on foot to the Chalice Well and the White Spring.

Ancient Celtic mythology places the entranceway to the Underworld Realm of Annwn, guarded by the Wild Huntsman Gwynn ap Nudd, at the Tor. It is interesting that Celtic mythology describes the dogs and the horses of the Wild Hunt as being red and white and that the clothes and furnishings of the Underworld beings as also being red and white. The waters of the Chalice Well run blood red due to the heavy iron content and nearby the waters of the nearby White Spring are clear. The construction of St. Michael's Church was an attempt to neutralize the pagan spirituality of the site — as well as to banish the Underworld Kingdom guarded by Gwynn ap Nudd.

Photo 2: The Living Rock

The Druids and the Chalice Well

The Chalice Well site has had a continuous history of religious use. The well is part of a beautiful garden area that has several old yew trees. The practice of planting yews is pre-Christian and, in fact, an 1800-year-old yew stump has been found near the well and it is probable that the well was part of a sacred grove in Druidic times. There is also evidence that an oak avenue led through the grove to the well and on to the Tor. Two oaks, estimated to be more than 2000 years old, still survive as part of the original oak avenue.

The Celtic belief that the Underworld was home to the Cauldron of Plenty and that wells and springs were entryways to the Underworld would have been verified at the Chalice Well. Not only healing, the red waters represented the menstrual blood flow of the goddess which is constant and never failing. To the Christians who absorbed the legends surrounding the Sacred Well of Glastonbury, the red water is symbolic of the blood of Jesus.

THE WELL TODAY

The beautiful surroundings of the well today exhibit many natural connections with the goddess. The red water symbolizing the earth's fertility as well as a yew tree, which has grown in the form of a vulva near the well, are just two of the evident symbols. Ancient ocean fossils litter the ground as well as the remains of the sacred grove of the Druids. In addition, the well is on the important Michael and Mary ley lines that run from Cornwall and traverse through the well, abbey and the Tor as they head off to the large stone circle at Avebury.

Since the Neolithic times, Chalice Well has produced 25,000 gallons of water a day, without fail, even during serious droughts. The water is a steady 52 degrees. The healing qualities of the water, according to the Chalice Well Trust, are "not in its mineral content but in a subtle vibratory force that is released when the water leaves its subterranean home and interacts with the forces of earth, air and light above ground."[1]

Chalice Well continues to entice thousands of pilgrims each year with its healing waters and rich history.

Photo 3: The Chalice Well

GLASTONBURY'S WHITE SPRING

Located a short walk away on Wellhouse Lane, almost "across the street" from Chalice Well, Glastonbury hosts another sacred spring called White Spring. An archaeological excavation conducted in 1961 found that White Spring had been used for hundreds and possibly thousands of years. Straffon noted that White Spring was probably the principal source of water for the Romano-British and Anglo-Saxon settlements that existed on the Tor.[2]

Today the spring is situated within an old stone building that, at one time, was the reservoir for all of Glastonbury. Erected in 1870, the reservoir provided clean water for the town during a cholera epidemic. Originally, the White Spring bubbled up from a hidden grotto underneath the Tor, mixing with other red springs and producing waters with similar healing powers to that of Chalice

1 Anon. *The Chalice Well*. Glastonbury: Chalice Well Trust, n/d.
2 Straffon, Cheryl. *The Earth Goddess: Celtic and Pagan Legacy of the Landscape*. London: Blanford 1997, 92

Well. White Spring is a mixture of the red and white waters sacred to the area but, because the White Spring water is calcium carbonate rather than iron, lacks the strong iron taste of the Chalice Well. While the waters mix the Chalice Well and its blood red water and the White Spring with its clear stream are, and have always been, two separate and special springs. They have been compared to the Ying/Yang being male and female, red and white — complimentary to each but also sacred in their own right. Unfortunately, when the reservoir was constructed the "enchanted leafy grotto"[1] was destroyed. Inside, the spring flows over a stonewall and winds across the stone floor. Nearby a clootie tree is festooned with strips of cloth and ribbons — a continued practice of leaving offerings at sacred and healing waters.

Photo 4: Clootie Tree

When I visited White Spring, I was pleasantly surprised to see that a pipe had been laid to the street allowing the spring water to flow beside the wall enclosing the Chalice Well, giving pilgrims and residents the opportunity to obtain the healing water of White Spring twenty-four hours a day. The rate of flow for White Spring varies throughout the year with an average output of 15,000 gallons a day.

As discussed earlier, the Tor is the legendary home of Gwynn ap Nudd, Lord of the Underworld. The White Spring emerges from under the Tor and leaves a white calcium carbonate deposit around its source. Nicholas Mann and Kathy Jones both suggests that a natural cavern over two hundred feet within the Tor

---

1 Jones, Kathy. *In the Nature of Avalon: Goddess Pilgrimages in Glastonbury's Sacred Landscape.* Glastonbury: Ariadne Publications 2000, 60

hillside where the White Spring originates may be the source for the legend of the entryway to the Underworld kingdom of Gwynn ap Nudd.[1] Springs and wells have been regarded as passageways between the physical world of humans and the spirit world of the dead, faeries and other denizens of the Underworld — this is a belief found in traditions around the world. As Mann wrote, "the cave at the White Springs is the emergence place of the psychic potential that lies at once within the world and within consciousness."[2]

Since the construction of the reservoir building over the spring, this magickal spot has lost much of its natural appeal even though the old reservoir building has a charm and character of its own. The grotto is gone but the spring continues to pour forth. When I was last at the White Spring a café was in operation in the old stone building and the water, considered to be a healing and nourishing liquid, was being sold in bottles. Recently I have learned that the reservoir building with the White Spring has closed its retail operations and has been boarded up with a "for let" sign posted. In the past, the water of the White Spring and the Chalice Well ran together in an alchemical balance of red and white streams. Today there is some interest in tearing down the structures that "restrict and divide" the two water sources, so that they again will run freely. However, as one individual wisely remarked, "I'm not sure that demolition of the wellhouse is desirable. What is 'restoration' but an attempt to restore something to a condition at a particular time in the past? Who is to decide which time? Many would like to see the building itself 'restored'...Let's find a way of opening the doors so that the place can be filled with light again..."[3] The Chalice Springs and the White Springs have always been separate and apart, even though their waters may have merged underground to create that balance of yin and yang, so the theory that the reservoir and the nearby street have restricted and divided the waters is incorrect. As Sally Griffyn writes, "the White Spring is considered to be a fertility site, with the white waters representing the waters of ovulation."[4]

St. Madron's Well, Cornwall

St. Madron, a saint who is said to have died on June 20th, the summer solstice, probably did not exist. "Madron" may have been of Irish origin *Medrhan* or *Maternus*,[5] meaning "mother" or *Madron*, or *Modron*, Old Celtic/Welsh meaning "Earth Mother" — the goddess also referred to as The Mother of Fates, the Spinner of the Threads of Life, the Provider, and the Creatrix. In Britain, Modron is also known as Morgan, Queen of the Otherworld. Morgan is a great healer and

---

1 Mann, Nicholas R. *The Isle of Avalon: Sacred Mysteries of Arthur and Glastonbury Tor.* St. Paul: Llewellyn Publications 1996, 142 and Jones, op. cit., 63

2 Ibid., 150

3 David, Philip. *Wells-And-Spas@JISCMAIL.AC.UK* August 4, 2001

4 Griffyn, Sally. *Sacred Journeys: Stone Circles & Pagan Paths.* London: Kyle Cathie Limited 2000, 144

5 Potter, Chesca. "Madron Well: 'the Mother Well'" in *The Source*, Issue #5, July 1986

protector of holy springs. She is part of a triad of the Triple Goddess with sculptures of her in the Triple Goddess form found all over Britain, most always near wells. As in most other sites of pagan origin, the ancient names have been altered in the process of assimilating pagan deities and transforming them into models acceptable to Christianity.

Photo 5: St. Madron's Well

There are approximately 100 holy wells in Cornwall and St. Madron's is one of the most well known, located just a few miles outside of Penzance (the "Jews' Market" — associated with Joseph of Arimathea). A fifteen-minute walk through a heavily ferned and treed wood, the well is located inside the ruins of a small chapel, which was constructed over it during the early Christian era. At best, the small chapel could have held 10–12 people and more than likely was used only by one or two people at a time. The structure today consists of four walls about 4 feet high, 8 feet wide, and approximately 12 feet long. The roof is missing, but the baptistery is still intact. The well opening is at one end to the right of the stone seat. When I visited St. Madron's in September 2000, the well had dried up. This was the first time in memory that the well had been dry. Information received three months later indicated that the flow had once again been established, but no reason yet has been forthcoming for its sudden dry spell. An explanation usually given when a holy well dries up is that it had been desecrated and moved to another location on its own volition or had transferred its holiness to a nearby tree.

St. Madron's has been called "one of the earliest sites of the Age of the Saints."[1] During the English Civil War (1642–1651) Puritan fanatics destroyed the chapel, however the well itself is still well preserved.

St. Madron's, as well as many of the other sacred wells in the world, has some notoriety for its healing powers. The most famous healing at St. Madron's was that of John Trelill, who had been crippled for 16 years, until he bathed in the waters of the well and was cured. This healing occurred in 1640. As part of the healing ritual, pilgrims would leave a strip of cloth, or ribbon on a nearby tree or bush so that the spirit of the well would perform a healing act upon it. Some of the ribbons and cloth I saw were red in color, symbolic of the plague of the modern era — AIDS. The view that clooties may transfer one's disease to the host tree is found in a variety of cultures; however, another view is that those who

---

1 Michell, John. *Sacred England.* Glastonbury: Gothic Image Publications, 1996, 192

have been healed have left these tokens to the well's spirits in gratitude. This practice is still very much alive today and this author saw such offerings at St. Madron, Sancreed and St. Nectan's Falls. Such votive offerings will be discussed in a subsequent chapter.

Along with the healing qualities of St. Madron's, the well was also a site for young maidens to visit to wish for a sweetheart. These young women also dropped offerings in the form of bent pins and other items into the well. The practice of dropping pins into the water was said to provide a means to divine the future.[1] It was said that the "uneasy, the impatient, the fearful, the jealous, and the superstitious, resort to learn their future destiny from the unconscious water" of St. Madron's.[2] An article in the November 18, 1854, issue of *Notes and Queries* concerning St. Nun's Well[3] gives another reason for the offerings of pins:

> In the basin of the well may be found a great number of pins, thrown in by those who have visited it out of curiosity, or to avail themselves of the virtues of its waters. I was anxious to know the meaning the peasantry attached to this strange custom, and on asking a man at work near the spot, was told that it was done "to get the good will of the piskies," who after the tribute of a pin not only ceased to mislead them, but render fortunate the operations of husbandry.

Inside the chapel ruins is a stone seat or, as some have referred to it, an altar. The seat is along one wall to the left of the well opening. Mara Freeman proposed a very interesting theory in her article *Sacred Waters, Holy Wells* [4] that St. Madron's was not only a healing well but also a "dream-temple." Evidently, many sacred wells have a mild, radioactive quality, which makes many people drowsy and actually fall into a deep sleep while visiting the wells. During this time dreams occur, many of a divinatory form. According to Freeman the altar, or dream-seat at St. Madron's, "was customarily used for dream-incubation purposes."[5] This practice of soliciting sacred dreams appears to have been a replacement for the ageless oracles normally consulted at sacred wells prior to the arrival of Christianity. Such foretelling appears to be consistent with the characterization of sacred wells as being Wells of Wisdom. Earth scientist Paul Devereux noted that dream-temples occurred in 300 locations in the Mediterranean area in Greco-

---

1 Straffon, Cheryl. *The Earth Goddess: Celtic and Pagan Legacy of the Landscape.* London: Blanford, 1997, 72

2 Hope, Robert Charles. *The Legendary Lore of the Holy Wells of England.* London: Elliott Stock 1893, 10 (Facsimile reprint by Llanerch Publishers, Felinfach Wales 2000)

3 Anon. "St. Nun's Well, Etc.: With A Notice of Some Remains of Ancient Well Worship," in *Notes and Queries.* Nov. 18, 1854, 397

4 Freeman, Mara. "Sacred Waters, Holy Wells," in *Parabola*, Volume XX, Number 1, Spring 1995, 53

5 Ibid.

Roman times and that a dream-temple dedicated to the god Nodens[1] was built at Lydney near Gloucester in England. Devereux wrote:

> All dream temples were located at major water sources. The patient would bathe in and drink the waters, then incubate a dream in special cells known as abatons...Ideally, the dream would reveal instructions from the god how the illness was to be dealt with, or, in some traditions, the 'Temple Sleep' was considered healing in its own right.[2]

Photo 6: "Dream Seat" at St. Madron's

"Incubation" was also practiced at certain wells in Wales. Nigel Pennick defines "incubation" as "an ancient technique of psychological transformation and healing through sleep"[3] which, depending on the well required an individual to sleep in a special place associated with the well's presiding spirit.

The size of the "chapel" is such that this site could very well have been a "dream-temple" used for healing and for its oracular powers. Hope noted that the "altar" or "bed" at St. Madron's was used by "impotent folk" to recline on "when they came to try the cold-water cure."[4]

---

1 Noden was a healer God, and father of Gwynn ap Nudd. Noden's symbolic form was that of the dog. Dogs were regularly sacrificed and interred in sacred wells as will be discussed later.

2 Devereux, Paul. *Earth Memory: Sacred Sites — Doorways into Earth's Mysteries*. St. Paul: Llewellyn Publications, 1992, 255-256

3 Pennick, Nigel. *Celtic Sacred Landscapes*. London: Thames and Hudson, 1996, 72

4 Hope, op. cit., 11

Photo 7: An 1856 drawing of Madron's Well showing the "dream seat" on the left.

A story in the March 1858 issue of *Blackwood's Edinbugh Magazine* reported that a "worthy clergyman who had reason to reprove his parishioners for resorting, in a very superstitious frame of mind, to a certain St. Maddron's Well. One day it happened that he met a woman returning from this well with a bottle of the precious water in her hand. He lectured her gravely on her superstition; but it seems that the old woman, perceiving that he himself was not altogether right, persuaded him to taste the water, and 'it cured him of the colic.' After this the repute of St. Maddron's well might very fairly survive for another century."[1]

It has indeed survived for another century and more!

When I visited St. Madron's the pathway was very muddy which made walking rather hazardous. The two or three ancient steps, which led me through the dark tunnels of growth also led to a "faerie glen" that exists along the pathway. It is said that the Otherworld guardians frequent the glen and can be seen at certain times if one is willing to take the time to wait for their appearance.

St. Nectan's Falls, Tintagel

Tintagel itself is a place of mystery. The legendary birthplace of Arthur, the location of Merlin's Cave, and the seat of mystical learning, Tintagel is also home of the Rocky Valley labyrinth carvings dating back to 1400 BCE, indicating that this location has been regarded as sacred for over three thousand years. The labyrinth carving faces the quiet Trevillitt River that flows within a few feet of it, indicating perhaps that the site was a shrine dedicated to the goddess of the waters.

---

1 Anon. "Sullivan on Cumberland," in *Blackwood's Edinburgh Magazine*, Vol. 83, March 1858, 352

Photo 8: Tintagel Maze

Another sacred spot near Tintagel is St. Nectan's Glen. It is from here, according to legend, that Arthur's knights set off in search of the Holy Grail. The official story of St. Nectan's is that the saint settled in the area around 500 CE and built a small sanctuary beside the Trevillitt River above the beautiful waterfall still flowing today. The good saint also built a bell tower behind the sanctuary and rang a silver bell that was hung there to warn sailors from the treacherous coastal rocks. Having visited St. Nectan's, it is difficult to see how anyone could have clearly seen the coast from this location.

As St. Nectan approached death he prophesied the return to "the older, simpler faith" — it is not known if he was referring to the "Old Religion" of the pagans or simply the original form of Christianity. St. Nectan was buried in an oaken chest with a chalice and other object of veneration. According to legend, the waters of the fall were diverted for the digging of the grave and then were diverted back again to their present, natural course, flowing over the grave.

St. Nectan's Glen is situated in a gorgeous forest along a very long path and up rock-cut steps, which are at least 1500 years old. When I visited there, I continually expected to see Pan walking through the ferns with the other woodland spirits. Researcher Paul Broadhurst wrote, "many tales speak of unearthly chanting, laughter and ethereal figures gliding through the thickly-wooded dell."[1] The waterfall basin is steeped in the legends of faeries, ancient guardians of sacred wells.

In this instance, the term "well" must be clarified — for there is nothing that looks like a "well." However, in the old sense, *wella, wielle* or *waella,* the Old English word for "well," means any natural spring or moving water. *Holy or sacred wells* are recognized for their spiritual and/or healing properties.

---

1   Broadhurst, Paul. *Tintagel and the Arthurian Mythos.* Launceton: Pendragon Press, 1992, 179

Photo 9: St. Nectan's Falls

Like St. Madron — that "unknown" saint named after the goddess, St. Nectan was also a pre-Christian deity. "Nectan," a Pictish man's name, is a derivative spelling of "Nechtan," who was a water god known as The Daghda — or the "good god." "Nechtan" also means to wash, to be clean, pure and white. [1] Ellis notes that Nechtan "had a well which was called the Well of Segais" or "Conlai's Well." This well had nine hazel trees of wisdom which grew over it and caused the waters of the well to bubble in "mystic inspiration" as the hazel nuts fell into the well.[2] Only The Daghda/Nechtan and his attendant cupbearers were allowed to draw water from the well.

The waterfall at St. Nectan's is approximately 60 feet in height, emptying into a 20-foot deep basin. The rock formation making up the fall is spectacular. The force of the falls has broken out one section of rock producing an amazing feature, which has been described as "water spring(ing) forth from an opening to the body of the goddess."[3] Here again the waters are said to be healing and are watched over by a population of faeries. Many African legends speak of water deities residing in waterfalls that made ill children healthy and the Japanese waterfall god Fudo was also said to

---

1   Ellis, Peter Berresford. *The Druids.* Grand Rapids: Wm. B. Eerdmans Publishing Company, 1995, 134
2   Ibid.
3   Jones, Kathy. *The Ancient British Goddess: Her Myths, Legends and Sacred Sites.* Glastonbury: Ariadne Publications, 1991, 19

cure blindness.[1] In Icelandic legend, it was believed that by standing under or behind a waterfall one could remain protected from evil spirits. The 13th century Orkney Bishop Bjarni Kolbeinsson was said to complain about "heathens who grow wise under waterfalls."[2]

Pieces of cloth and ribbon, as well as food offerings and coins, are left in the trees and on the rock ledges near the falls for the water spirits. One visitor stated that the offerings were "ritual garbage" but I believe that she was very incorrect in her assessment. Offerings such as these have been part of the heritage of sacred wells since ancient times and the on-going practice of leaving offerings continues to links us to that past.

Photo 10: Coins are often inserted into tree limbs at St. Nectan's by pilgrims as offerings to the water spirits. (Photo courtesy of Ricky and Holger Jordan)

The waters from St. Nectan's falls flow into a large shallow pool, which is thought to be healing. I walked barefoot across the pool and found relief for two very sore feet. The water then flows over a stone lip and into a ravine, finally reaching the coast near Tintagel Castle.

1 Andrews, Tamra. *A Dictionary of Nature Myths:Legends of the Earth, Sea, and Sky*. Oxford: Oxford University Press 1998, 222

2 Simpson, Jacqueline, trans. *Legends of Icelandic Magicians*. Cambridge: D.S. Brewer Ltd., for the Folklore Society 1975, 101

St. Keyne's Well

St. Keyne's Well is another found in the beautiful Cornish woods, not far from the River Looe. It is said that five ancient trees grew from a single root at the top of the well, an oak, a Cornish elm, an ash-tree, and a willow. By the 1890s only the elm and one ash-tree remained, the others had been blown down in a storm in 1703. An 18th century account of the well described the site:

> ...a spring rising under a tree of a most strange condition: for beyinge but one bodie it beareth the branches of four kinds — oke, ashe, elme, and withye. This Kayne is sayde to be a woman Saynte, of whome it taketh its name; but it better resembleth Kayne, the devil, who had the shape of a man, the name of an apostle, the quallytee of a trayter, and the hands of a bryber.[1]

St. Keyne (461–505 CE), according to lore, was a "holy and beautiful virgin of British royal blood" being the daughter of the Prince of Brecknockshire.[2] She came from a large family of saints. Her father had 26 children. Accounts of the family state that anywhere from 16 to 25 of the children, mostly girls, became saints. She was also the aunt of Sts. David and Cadock of Wales. Tradition says the as a small child Keyne would often shine like the sun. While living in the dangerous world of the 5th century she reportedly was able to travel about the country, performing miracles and healing the sick because of her great inner and outer beauty.

Photo 11: St. Keyne's Well (Photo courtesy Ricky and Holger Jordan)

1 Quoted in *The Holy Well & The Water of Life*, by R.A. Courtney. Penzance: Beare & Son 1916, 31.
2 He has also been said to have been a Welsh King by the name of Brychan.

On one of her trips taken in 490 CE, she journeyed to St. Michael's Mount in Cornwall as part of a pilgrimage. She stayed for some time and became so loved by the residents that she was induced to remain far longer than she had intended. While there, she visited a local well and, according to traditional lore, placed a spell upon the well that whoever drank from the water, or sat in a naturally occurring rock "chair" nearby, either a husband or wife, would become master in their wedded life. Evidently getting to the rock chair was no easy feat so only the most deserving would receive the blessing. Another well, near Liskeard, also in Cornwall, received the same spell from St. Keyne.

One day her nephew, St. Cadock, visited Keyne and struck his staff in the earth which resulted in a bubbling spring. St. Keyne gave the holy water site to the residents who dedicated the nearby church in her name.[1]

Cadock[2] persuaded Keyne to return to Wales with him and she settled near Abergavenny, where she also has a well dedicated to her. One of the miracles attributed to her was the turning of snakes in her homeland into fossilized ammonites.

The legends surrounding St. Keyne contain many elements that make up the background of Christian saints in Britain including the miraculous removal of snakes (a sure symbol of evil), sticking a staff into the earth to unleash healing waters, the performing of miracles and great mystical beauty.

It is said that when St. Keyne died at the ripe old age of 44, a column of fire appeared over her body and two angels carried her body to heaven.

St. Piran's Holy Well

Not far from the magickal St. Nectan's Glen is another holy well. Near the small village of Trethevey, approximately 1–2 miles up an ancient roadway is the small, slate-stone "pyramid" that marks St. Piran's well. An iron gate bars the opening to the well, which now feeds into modern water pipes, an old iron cross is perched at the top of the monument. St. Piran's, "and the whole valley that leads down to the sea must be one of the most haunted as well as one of the most strangely beautiful in Cornwall."[3]

Who was St. Piran? St. Piran supposedly came from Ireland; his father may have been Prince Dywel ap Erbin of the Royal House of Dumnonia. St. Piran was a busy man in his early years, having founded six monasteries in Ireland, and a church in Cardiff, Wales. Legend has it that St. Piran, in advanced age, was captured by local Irish pagans who were jealous of his ability to heal, tied to a millstone and tossed into the ocean in a horrendous storm. However, much to the

1 Hope, Robert Charles. *The Legendary Lore of the Holy Wells of England.* London: Elliot Stock 1893, 15.

2 Cadock would, in time, become both King and Abbot over southeast Wales.

3 Broadhurst, Paul. "Secret Shrines: Strange Happenings a Stone's Throw From Tintagel," in *The Source*, Issue 7, May 1987

pagans' amazement, the millstone floated and Piran used it to sail to Cornwall where he founded a small oratory.

This legend of the floating stone is similar to many told in Ireland. One of these is that of St. Boec who sailed to Brittany from Carn parish in County Wexford on a stone. When the saint landed near Penmarch, the stone sailed back to Ireland. Supposedly, a piece of the floating stone still rests in a cemetery in Brittany and bears the imprint of the saint's head. It is said that individuals seeking a cure for fever can find it by placing their heads on this stone.[1]

St. Piran is remembered mostly for discovering tin in Cornwall and because of this has become Cornwall's patron saint. St. Piran reportedly lived to be 206 years of age. Relics of St. Piran included his head kept in Exeter Cathedral until 1433. The head and other relics now reside in the Parish Church of Perranzabulo. Celtic head veneration was an important aspect to Celtic Spirituality. Heads were often taken in battle and preserved — it being believed that the soul and intelligence still resided in the skulls after death. The separation of Piran's head from his body and the preservation of it as a relic is a survival of ancient head veneration.[2] Arthurian legend has it that St. Piran became chaplain to King Arthur. Piran is credited with bringing Christianity to Cornwall in the 6th or 7th century. An ancient stone cross called St. Piran's Cross stands in Cornwall at Perranzabulo and may be one of the oldest Celtic crosses in Cornwall.

Photo 12: St. Piran's Well

1 Logan, Patrick. *The Holy Wells of Ireland.* Buckinghamshire: Colin Smythe 1980, 105
2 Pennick, Nigel. *Celtic Sacred Landscapes.* London: Thames and Hudson, 1996, 175

Why St. Piran's Well is regarded as holy is unknown, although some accounts state that St. Piran's Well was famed in earlier days for its ability to cure rickets.[1] Legends of his life state that he was "fond of drink and met his end falling down a well." It may be that the holy well bearing his name is the same which ended his life. Offerings were not seen at the well when I visited the area although there is some history for the offerings of bent pins that are discussed in Chapter 4.

March 5th is celebrated as St. Piran's Day throughout Cornwall with festivities, processions and plays drawing large crowds.

SANCREED

Only four miles from Penzance, Sancreed is a holy well situated in a most unusual location. The well is approximately ¼ mile west of the ancient[2] Sancreed Church on the adjacent property of the Glebe Farm, where pigs are raised. Sancreed, or rather "St. Creed" (also known as St. Credan), is supposedly named after another long forgotten Christian saint. One legend is that the saint accidentally killed his father and "in contrition," became a swineherd. This is interesting in that the well is today located on a pig farm. Pigs, in Celtic mythology, are associated with the Otherworld, and swineherds "often represent an initiation into the mysteries of the dark goddess."[3]

Regarded by many as "the most spiritual place in Cornwall"[4] and described by some as "weirdly prehistoric,"[5] the well can be reached by walking down a flight of stone stairs into the small cavern of the well itself. Covered with moss, the rock walls of the well are festooned with offerings of candles, food and small images of the goddess (a statue of Merlin had been placed carefully inside the well when this author visited the site).

Photo 13: A statue of Merlin given as a votive offering at Sancreed Well

A modern Celtic cross has been placed nearby, the trees above and around the well are covered with the cloth,

1 Radford, E. and M.A. *Encyclopaedia of Supestitions.* New York: The Philosophical Library 1949, 256

2 While the church is much older, records date to 1559 for marriages and 1566 for baptisms performed here.

3 Straffon, Cheryl. *The Earth Goddess: Celtic Pagan Legacy of the Landscape.* London: Blanford, 1997, 86

4 Michell, John. *Sacred England.* Glastonbury: Gothic Image Publications, 1996, 191

5 Broadhurst, Paul. "Holy Well or Holy Grail ? The Mystic Quest in Cornwall," in *The Source,* Issue #4, March 1986

and ribbon votive offerings seen at the other sacred wells of Cornwall attesting to the healing sought here. The Church of Sancreed has an old cemetery with several 6th century Celtic Crosses depicting the unusual image of the crucified child Jesus. This site was originally an old Celtic sanctuary. The age of this well cannot be accurately determined but the antiquity is such that the identity of the saint for which it was named has been lost.

Photo 14: Entrance to Sancreed's Holy Well (photo courtesy Rickey & Holger Jordan)

Like Madron's Well, Sancreed also has the power to induce sleep. Paul Devereux wrote, "I have actually seen every person in a group of 15 people enter a deep, languid state here, or fall completely asleep! It is a place to sleep; to have the Dream of Earth."[1] Devereux measured the radiation emanating from Sancreed and determined that the well radiated 200% more radia-

tion than the background radiation.

Photo 15: Brightly colored ribbons adorn Sancreed's Clootie tree (photo courtesy Rickey & Holger Jordan)

St. Euny's Well

One mile west of Sancreed is St. Euny's Well, named after a sixth century Irishman. St. Euny's sister was St. Ia and his brother St. Erc who, it is said, died on Samhain (the Celtic New Year and a time when the "veil" between the Otherworld and ours is

---

1 Devereux, Paul. *Places of Power: Secret Energies at Ancient Sites: A Guide to Observed or Measured Phenomena.* London: Blandford 1990, 157

at its thinnest) in the 6th century. But, St. Euny's is also the site of a Neolithic village occupied up to the 1st century BCE. The well is said to have miraculous waters, which have   cured eye diseases, heal wounds and sores, and "children's diseases." Divination is also one of the practices at this well. Like Sancreed, the well is reached through a series of steps down into the earth.

Photo 16: Entrance to St. Euny's Well (photo courtesy Rickey & Holger Jordan)

In order to be cured an individual must adhere to activities performed at strict times. One must visit and wash in the well water either on the last day of the year or on the first three Wednesdays in May. Hope noted, "children suffering from mesenteric disease should be dipped three times in Chapel Uny 'widdershynnes', and widdershynnes' dragged three times

around the well."[1]

Obviously, this has pre-Christian connotations. "Widdershins" is the counterclockwise motion used in many pagan dances and contemporary folk-dances that represent the direction of the moon. A legend concerning the opening of a faery hill requires walking around the hill three times in the widdershins direction.[2]

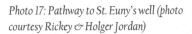

Photo 17: Pathway to St. Euny's well (photo courtesy Rickey & Holger Jordan)

1 Hope, Robert Charles. *The Legendary Lore of the Holy Wells of England.* London: Elliot Stock 1893, 14 (A facsimile reprint by Llanerch Publishers, Felinfach Wales, 2000)

2 Walker, Barbara G. *The Women's Encyclopedia of Myths and Secrets.* Edison: Castle Books, 1983, 1076

St. Bridgid's Well, Ireland

St. Bridgid, also known as Bride, Brighid and Bridgit, is second only in popularity to St. Patrick among the Irish. Her wells are found throughout Ireland and whether she is a saint, a pagan goddess or a mixture of both, she continues to be venerated by millions. The First of February, the date of the pagan festival of Imbolc, which marks the beginning spring, is also the Feast day of St. Bridgid.

According to Church history, Bridgid was born in Fochard (also spelled Forchart and Faughart), in Ulster, not long after Christian missionaries visited Ireland. St. Patrick baptized her parents and she received her religious training from the nephew of St. Patrick, St. Mel and established a female religious community at Kildare. St. Mel conferred abbatial authority upon her and she became the first abbot in Ireland. At Kildare she is said to have started a center for learning and arts and her school was renowned for its illuminated manuscripts. She is said to have been buried with St. Patrick and St. Columba but Henry VIII destroyed the burial shrine during the Reformation. Only her head is now kept in Lisbon in the Church of the Jesuits.[1]

Bridgid as pagan goddess was a deity of fire but also of water. Many of her wells are known to be effective against eye diseases. Bridgid's connection with eyes is based in a legend that she plucked her eyes out and threw them at a suitor but regained her sight when she washed out the sockets in one of her sacred wells. However, the sight she regained most likely was that of inner-sight, of wisdom and knowledge. Pilgrims though, seek relief from blindness and other physical ailments.

The goddess Bridgid represents the Maiden, Mother, and Crone aspect of the Great goddess and was regarded as the goddess of crafts, knowledge, healing, fire and water. Bridgid was also patroness of poetry, an important aspect of Druidry in the bard class. St. Bridgid is a many-faceted personality. A carving on the 12th century St. Michael's Tower at Glastonbury Tor shows St. Bridgid milking her cow. Both the goddess and the saint are associated with fertility, both human and animal, and in lambing. Imbolc, St. Bridgid's feast day, means "ewe's milk." The goddess Bridgid is known as a Cow Mother, the Great Goddess who "nurtures the whole universe" — the Mother of All. She is the shepherdess of humans and of farm animals and is closely associated with dairy products, cattle and sheep. Dairy products were so connected with St. Bridgid that milk was poured out in oblation to her and butter thrown into the well water at Balla. In Irish legend, a great white, red-eared cow, one of the denizens of the Otherworld, raised the

---

1   At least it was in 1864 when Rev. Alban Butler wrote *The Lives of the Fathers, Martyrs and Other Principal Saints*, published by D.& J. Sadlier & Company

goddess Bridgid.[1] The hundreds of St. Bridgid Wells located throughout Ireland are named after the many "St. Bridgids." Pennick and others believe these numerous St. Bridgid's reflect the many disciples of the original St. Bridgid of Kildare who were followers of the Great Goddess and later converted to Christianity.[2] The "creation" of St. Bridgid from her original existence as a goddess was, according to Pennick, "a remarkable accommodation of polytheism in a monotheistic framework, permitting the continuation of women's mysteries under the aegis of patriarchal monotheism."[3]

The place of St. Bridgid's birth, Fouchart in County Kildare, is a shrine complex that is also the source of St. Bridgid's Stream. The posts and wire that surround the well are festooned with cloth offerings — as are many of the other trees and bushes which are near the other shrines at Fouchart.

The "cult" surrounding St. Bridgid has become so large in Ireland that other patron saints have been pushed aside with the feast days of St. Bridgid the only ones now honored. As Logan noted, the "cult of St. Bridgid was long established in the twelfth century..."[4] In 650 CE, *The Life of St. Brighid*, written by Cogitosus, relates many of her attributes that were thinly disguised characteristics of the pagan goddess. Her Christian origins are directly tied to the Druids (one was her father), which also links her past to that of the pagan Celts. Bridgid was perhaps the most important of the Celtic deities. Kildare, the place of Bridgid's birth, is also a connection to the pagan past as Kildare is derived from the Gaelic *Cill Dara*, or Church of the Oak Tree.[5] Kildare was most likely an important Druid center in Ireland dedicated to the goddess Bridgid and has continued its holy role today as an important Christian center. Catholic legend in the Hebrides relates how St. Bridgid was the midwife or foster mother of Jesus and that she helped to deliver him in the manger at Bethlehem. At that time, according to the legend, she placed three drops of sacred spring water on his head.[6] This is an obvious mixture of Christian and Celtic myth. In Celtic myth, the Son of Light (Bel or Belenos) is anointed with three drops of sacred water, which gave him wisdom.[7]

St. Bridgid's powers were absolute in the protection of her shrine at Kildare. One man who attempted to cross over the hedge surrounding the sacred fire immediately became lame. Another who attempted to blow the flame out went mad

---

1   Brenneman, Walter L. and Mary G. *Crossing the Circle at the Holy Wells of Ireland*. Charlottesville: University Press of Virginia 1995, 97

2   Pennick, Nigel. *Celtic Sacred Landscapes*. London: Thames and Hudson 1996, 173

3   Ibid.

4   Logan, Patrick. *The Holy Wells of Ireland*. Buckinghamshire: Colin Smythe 1980, 37

5   Straffon, Cheryl. *The Earth Goddess: Celtic and Pagan Legacy of the Landscape*. London: Blandford 1977, 195

6   This is highly unlikely as Church history records her birth during the 6th century CE.

7   Stewart, R.J. *Celtic Gods Celtic Goddesses*. London: Blandford 1990, 98

and drank water incessantly until "he burst in the middle and died."[1] Reportedly, even though cattle grazed the pastures around the shrine each day until not a blade of grass was left, the next morning there was always lush carpet of grass waiting for the cattle's return.

One of St. Bridgid's Wells is located at Sligo. This well is one of the numerous moving wells that will be discussed in Chapter 5. Bonwick noted in his book, *Irish Druids and Old Irish Religions*, that when pilgrims visit the well "the bushes (nearby) are draped with offerings, and the procession must move round as the sun moves, like the heathen did at the same spot so long ago."[2] Today, the well at Sligo is in a state of "atrophy." An ancient stone pillar, which had incised ogham marks and a sun-swastika carved into its surface, has been removed and pilgrimages have fairly ceased since 1959.[3]

Likewise, St. Bridgid's Well at Kildare has waned in its popularity. The Brennemans wrote that there is no longer a "pattern" at the well even though the nearby Father Moore's Well has maintained a systematic ritual. The power at St. Bridgid's well have also atrophied and become dormant, according to the Brennemans, because "her power has been closed off from the people by a transparent shield. She has become a transcendent power manifest through an imposed neatness and order, more in the sense of a garden than as the powers of nature displaying themselves on their own terms."[4] However, a new vitality appears to be taking place through the metamorphosis of Bridgid into the personage of Mary, Mother of Jesus. While the names change, the original powers of the sacred wells remain and are believed to act through the ancient Mother Goddess as they always have.

LOURDES

It is natural, when we think of holy wells, that Lourdes comes to mind. Since 1858, thousands of pilgrims travel to Lourdes, France each year to visit the holy waters seeking a cure for various afflictions.

Located in a small village of 17,000 people in the foothills of the Pyrenees, the "miraculous spring" was discovered by 14-year-old Bernadette Soubirous at the direction of the Virgin Mary on February 11, 1858. According to Bernadette herself, she was directed by the Virgin to a Grotto under an overhang of rock, near the River Gave:

> "...the Lady said to me in a serious but friendly voice — 'Go, drink and
> wash in the fountain'. As I did not know where this fountain was, and as
> I did not think the matter important, I went towards the Gave. The Lady

---

1 Gerald of Wales. *The History and Topography of Ireland*. Translated by John O'Meara. London: Penguin Books 1982, 88

2 Bonwick, James. *Irish Druids and Old Irish Religions*. New York: Barnes & Noble, Inc. 1986, a reprint of the 1894 edition, 241

3 Brenneman, op. cit 102

4 Ibid.,101

called me back and signed to me with Her finger to go under the Grotto to the left; I obeyed but I did not see any water. Not knowing where to get it from, I scratched the earth and the water came. I let it get a little clear of the mud then I drank and washed."[1]

Similar legends are found among Native American traditions. The Iroquois myth of "The Healing Waters" speaks of Nekumonta, a good man, who sees all of his family stricken by a dreadful disease, dying one by one until only his beloved wife remains. The woodland creatures plea for the intervention of the Great Manitou who tells Nekumonta to dig for a healing spring. Taking a flint blade, Nekumonta scrapes and digs until he uncovers a miraculous spring. He first bathes in the healing waters and becomes refreshed and then he bathes his wife who falls into a peaceful sleep, to awaken cured.[2]

It is interesting to note that when the water first appeared, Bernadette scooped up three handfuls of the water and threw them away before she drank. She reported that the Lady made her ask three times about her name before she was told whom the apparition was. The sacred number three is prominent in most religions as representative of the Trinity or Triad. Soon it was noticed that Bernadette's "scratching" had produced a "ribbon" of water flowing from the rock.

At first the local officials and Church hierarchy closed the grotto and dismantled the first crude attempts of a shrine until miracles began to happen. As Ruth Cranston wrote in her book, *The Miracle of Lourdes:*

> A blind man who washed his eyes in the spring water regained his sight. A mother...dipped her dying child in the waters, and the child not only lived but became well and robust for the first time.[3]

Researchers analyzing the water have found that it has chlorides of soda, lime, magnesia, bicarbonates of lime, silicates, aluminum, oxide of iron, sulfate of lime, phosphates and organic matter — but nothing that would account for its reputation for healing. But, heal it does.

Jean Markale, in his book *The Great Goddess*, writes,

> It is impossible to doubt, even for an instant, the reality of the apparitions of Bernadette Soubirous. She saw something and, on the advice of what she saw, she made a spring burst forth at the entrance of a cave.... Lourdes is one of those lofty places where the Spirit breathes....It is an undeniable fact: Notre-Dame-de-Lourdes is the representation that the twentieth-century has made for itself of the Goddess of the Beginnings..."[4]

---

1 Catholic Online. "Ninth Apparition, Thursday 25 February 1858: Discovery of the Miraculous Spring," *www.catholic.org/mary/ninth/html.*
2 Ferguson, Gary. *The World's Great Nature Myths.* Falcon Publishing, Inc., 1996, 155-157
3 Cranston, Ruth. *The Miracle of Lourdes.* New York: Image Books 1988, 34
4 Markale, Jean. *The Great Goddess.* Translated from the French by Jody Gladding, Rochester: Inner Traditions 1999, 158

The Virgin Mary is another aspect of the Earth Mother and, as such, acts as pro-tectress of holy wells.[1]

This sacred site attracts more than three million pilgrims per year, usually on February 6th, which is regarded as the day of pilgrimage to Lourdes, to its healing waters. Approximately 2500 healings have been recorded since 1858. Of these 2500, the Catholic Church has deemed 66 "official miracles." One of the most famous of these is the case of Lydia Brosse, a Frenchwoman suffering from tubercular abscesses, who visited the shrine on October 9, 1930. At that time, she was bathed in the icy waters in the grotto and left cured the next day.[2] One of the most recent cures is that of Jean Pierre Bély who went to Lourdes as part of a pilgrimage in 1987 seeking relief from multiple sclerosis. According to a story in *The Irish Times*, Bély "went to confession and received the sacrament of the sick. He felt 'a sensation of cold, then a soft heat' going through his body. 'I then took my first steps, like a child that is learning to walk.'"[3] Like many of the sacred waters discussed in this book, Lourdes also is known for its ability to restore inner calm. As Father Pat Carroll wrote, "the phenomenon of inner peace is a reality almost more important that the physical cures which grab the attention of the world."[4]

THE WELLS OF ROME

Rome has the luck of being situated in an area overflowing with springs that allowed the ancient Romans to inhabit the area that would eventually become the basis of the Roman Empire. Sextus Julius Frontinus, Water Commissioner of the City of Rome, wrote in 97 CE, "springs have held, down to the present day, the name of holy things, and are objects of veneration, having the repute of heal-ing the sick; as for example, the springs of the Prophetic Nymphs (Camenae), of Apollo, and of Juturna."[5] These springs were located in the Egerian Valley near one of the city walls and were regarded as the dwelling-place of Nymphae. It was at the grottos of the spring of Egeria that a nymph made love to the second king of Rome, Numa Pompilius. He was inspired after his tryst to create his codex of laws. Frazer said that Numa was inspired by his "communion with her divinity" in the creation of the laws given by him to the Romans more so than by her beauty.[6] Near the springs of the Prophetic Nymphs a sacred grove existed as

---

1 Sheldrake, Rupert. *The Rebirth of Nature: The Greening of Science and God.* New York: Bantam Books 1991, 28

2 Harpur, James. *The Atlas of Sacred Places: Meeting Points of Heaven and Earth.* New York: Henry Holt and Company 1994, 219

3 Carroll, Father Pat. "Experiencing inner calm and cures at Lourdes," in *The Irish Times*, August 10, 1999

4 Ibid.

5 Frontinus, Sextus Julius. *The Water Supply of the City of Rome*, trans. By Clemens Herchel. Boston: New England Water Works Association 1973, 28

6 Frazer, Sir John. *The Golden Bough: A Study in Magic and Religion.* Hertfordshire: Words-worth Editions 1993, 4

---

was the case with many of the sacred springs of the Druids. The sacred springs located here were visited for their healing as well and were still believed to have curative powers into the late 19th century.

There is more to the legend of Numa and the Nymph than is apparent. Frazer notes that the "nuptials of Numa and Egeria" are reminiscent "of a sacred marriage which the old Roman kings regularly contracted with a goddess of vegetation and water for the purpose of enabling him to discharge his divine or magical functions."[1]

The spring of Juturna is also, in legend, the spring where the divine twins Castor and Pollux watered their horses after the battle of Lake Regillus in 496 BCE, which was the instrumental battle that gave the Roman empire its beginnings.[2]

The ancient Romans, as exhibited by their acts during their occupation of Britain, commonly placed objects of thanks in springs and wells. In 1852, the Jesuits had a "gang of masons" clear out the mouth of the sulfur springs called Aquae Apollinares. During their draining operation, the masons came upon four layers of brass, silver, gold and bronze coins dating from earliest days of the empire through the 4th century CE. At the very bottom of the spring mouth was found a thick layer, covered over with copper fragments, of polished stone knives, projectile points and other tools which indicate that this spring was held sacred from prehistoric times through the 4th century CE.[3]

The importance of the sacred spring assigned by the Romans can be adduced by the treatment given to them by the Roman officials. A separate administrative control of these sites existed apart from the control of the aqueducts, which, for the most part, supplied drinking water.

Sacred wells and springs were under the control of priests and Vestal Virgins. The Vestal Virgins were not allowed to drink water that had passed through the more modern lead pipes of the Roman system. The Vestal Virgins only used water from a marble tank situated in their temple that was filled daily from a sacred water source. These priestesses annually performed a ritual on the Ides of May, during the full moon, to ensure the continuous flow of sacred spring water. Neptune, the fierce god of the Oceans, was originally a god of springs and was regarded as a benign freshwater deity.

It is probable that well dressings, the custom most commonly associated with the English region of Derbyshire, originated with the Roman festival of Fontinalia. It was during Fontinalia that the Roman gods and spirits of the springs and wells were celebrated.

---

1 Ibid., 147
2 Ferguson, John. "Classical Greece and Rome," in *Legends of the World.* Edited by Richard Cavendish. New York: Barnes & Noble 1994, 168
3 Frontinus, op. cit, 108

LUMBINI, BIRTHPLACE OF BUDDHA

Situated in southwestern Nepal, approximately 250 kilometers from Katmandu is the Sacred Gardens of Lumbini where it is said that the Buddha was born either in 623 or 642 BCE, over 2600 years ago. According to Buddhist tradition, Maya Devi was on her way to her parent's home in Devadaha one May day when she stopped to rest under a sal tree. After bathing in a nearby pool, known as Puskarni, Maya Devi — a virgin, became impregnated and immediately fell into labor and gave birth to Prince Siddhartha Gautam — the future Buddha.

Lumbini is surrounded with ancient ruins. One is a stone pillar erected by Indian Emperor Ashoka in 249 BCE commemorating the birthplace of the Buddha. In 1895, a German archaeologist discovered the pillar after it had been forgotten for thousands of years. In 1996, archaeologists uncovered a "flawless" stone in the nearby river Ol, which was also the results of efforts made by the Emperor Ashoka. This stone was to mark the exact spot of the Buddha's birth. Like other sacred sites, such as in England's Tintagel where the footprint of Arthur is said to be found in rock, a footprint of the Emperor is also said to be imprinted in the stone.

Since the Buddha's birth the pool, where Maya Devi bathed, has become sacred to Buddhist pilgrims from around the world. Buddhist carvings at Lumbini depict the baby Buddha standing on a lotus petal with the gods Brahma and Indra showering him with water and lotus petals.

Lumbini has many aspects common in water lore and the mythology of gods. The lotus is a common symbol of the fertility and the resurrective powers of water.[1] The lotus also represents a divine birth "issuing unsullied from the muddy waters."[2] The erection of the stone pillar near the sacred pool is also a common feature of sacred wells and waterways throughout the world.[3]

THE HOLY SPRINGS AND WATER LORE OF ETHIOPIA

The comfort and healing provided by sacred wells is still sought today in many parts of the world. In Ethiopia, crowds assemble at the holy spring in Gondar every morning at six a.m. where deacons and priests from the Ba'ata church dispense holy water and blessings to treat, and cure, spiritual and physical ailments. It is believed that demons will "become agitated and...will shout through the

---

1 Andrews, Tamra. *A Dictionary of Nature Myths*. Oxford: Oxford University Press 1998,112

2 Cooper, J.C. *An Illustrated Encyclopaedia of Traditional Symbols*. London: Thames and Hudson 1978, 100

3 Additional information for this section was obtained from the following web sites: Holy Sites of Buddhism (*www.buddhanet.net/lumbini.htm*), Nepal Tourism Board www.welcomenepal.com/lumbini.html) and Lumbini (*www.catmando.com/com/travellers-nepal/lumbini.htm*)

mouth of the possessed" once the sacred water has been drunk.[1] For the equivalent of 50 cents, seven days of treatment may be received for such ailments as gastric problems, difficulty in walking, demons and other conditions such as pregnancy. The water from this holy spring purges the body of "impurities" as soon after the water is drunk it induces diarrhea and vomiting. The faith placed in the healing qualities of the spring is such that, according to researcher Rachel Chambers, "they believe that the cure they will find here will be more complete than any offered in the government hospitals in the city."[2]

The people living in the area around Gondar, in the northwestern part of Ethiopia, are of a group called the Qemant. The Qemant culture is an interesting mixture of Pagan, Christian, Arabic and Hebraic cultures. Priests and shamans administer the Qemant religion with the more important politico-religious positions being filled by the priest class. Prehistorically the Qemant are descendants of the Agaw and they continue many of the Agaw traditions including worshipping a sky god and recognizing personal spirits; genii loci; and sky spirits. While considered patriarchal, the sky god is believed by some to have a female consort who is "usually an earth goddess."[3] Other spirits recognized by the various Ethiopian sub-groups include the *eqqo* that are elemental spirits residing in trees and running water and the *agannint*, which the Amhara people believe are malevolent spirits living in water places. The River Omo is also the home of the water spirit *Talehe*.[4] The Amhara utilize sacred groves of trees, which, along with hills, single trees, and streams are thought to be the abodes of supernatural beings.[5] The Qemant continue to annually sacrifice a white bull or sheep to the genii loci that are sprits residing in the sacred groves and other holy geographic features. The Qemant also have personal spirits, which are regarded as their guardian angels that help to ensure well-being. Some of these spirits, however, are malevolent and cause sickness and hostility among the Qemant.[6] Although the Qemant rituals are far older than Christianity, annual fertility and rain-regulating ceremonies are held to coincide with Christian holidays. Both Muslim and Christian Ethiopians gather in huge numbers for the fertility rite observed at Lake Bishoftu, which include an animal sacrifice. Levine states that this ceremony is "a fertility rite of pagan...origin."[7]

---

1 Chambers, Rachel. "Ethiopia: Washing Away the Demons," in *BBC News*, October 18, 1999 (//news.bbc.co.uk)

2 Ibid.

3 Levine, Donald N. *Greater Ethiopia: The Evolution of a Multiethnic Society.* Chicago: The University of Chicago Press 1974, 47

4 Ibid., 48

5 Gamst, Frederick C. *The Qemant: A Pagan-Hebraic Peasantry of Ethiopia.* Case Studies in Cultural Anthropology. New York: Holt, Rinehart & Winston 1969, 30

6 Ibid., 50

7 Levine, op. cit., 44

One of the important ceremonies of the Qemant is held at the holy spring called *Enzayimarku*, located in Chelga approximately five miles west of Gondar. According to Gamst, "the miraculous waters of this spring are said to cure diseases and make barren women fertile. The ceremony centering on prayer and drinking of the water from the spring is on a Saturday and extends through Sunday night."[1]

Obviously, rain is an important part of Ethiopia's survival. A variety of rituals regulate rain and rainmaking to ensure enough but not too much rain is received for crops and animals. Among the Amarro people, the king places his right foot in a stream, the act is said to ensure rainfall.[2]

Ethiopia is a land rich in hot springs. There are over 100 springs in Addis Ababa at the commercial Filwoha springs facility. Other hot spring facilities are Bate, in Wollo, and Hagere Hiwot in Ambo.[3]

CENOTÉS & OTHER SACRED WATERS OF THE AMERICAS

While most of the sacred wells of the world are found in Europe, the native peoples of the America's also had holy wells. While not as well known as those in Britain and Europe, a few examples of sacred cenotés and other water features in North and South America are discussed here.

Photo 18: The Sacred Cenoté at Chichen-Itza

1 Gamst, op. cit., 96
2 Levine, op. cit., 52
3 Altman, Nathaniel. *Healing Springs: The Ultimate Guide to Taking the Waters.* Rochester: Healing Arts Press 2000, 248

Yucatan

One of the most famous is the Chichen-Itza Sacred Cenoté in remote Yucatan. An oval shaped opening in the earth 180 feet across and 60 feet below the lip of the rocky rims, this natural well has been used by the Maya to connect with the Otherworld for centuries. Located in an open area surrounded by the steaming jungle, the cenoté is of a dark green color with sheer white rock walls. Today the well is still open with no protection for the unfortunate pilgrim who happens to walk too close to the edge. In 1579, Charles V of Spain received a report from the mayor of Valladolid, located near the cenoté:

> The Lords and principal personages of the land has the custom, after sixty days of abstinence and fasting, of arriving by daybreak at the mouth of the Cenoté and throwing into it Indian women belonging to each of these lords and personages, at the same time telling these women to ask for their masters a year favorable to his particular needs and desires. The women being thrown in, unbound, fell into the water with great force and noise. At high noon, those that could, cried out loudly and ropes were let down to them. After the women came up, half dead, fires were built around them and copal was burned before them. When they recovered their senses, they said that below, there were many people of their nation, men and women, and that they had received them...the people responded to their queries concerning the good and bad year that was in store for their masters.[1]

According to Frederick Peterson,[2] the survival of these sacrificial victims was rare as evidenced by the rewards and honors bestowed upon those lucky few, including being made temporary ruler of certain geographic areas. Most of those chosen for sacrifice, however, were given up to the rain god during periods of drought.[3] The skeletons of several men, women and children have been recovered from the sacred cenoté at Chichen-Itza. There were all sacrificed during periods of drought to appease the rain god Chac (who is still worshipped by the Maya to this day). It was believed that Chac resided at the bottom of the cenoté, referred to as "The Well of God" (*Chen-ku*). Early Meso-Americanist Thomas Joyce wrote, in a somewhat contradictory manner from the report made to Charles V, that "at Chichen Itza human sacrifice was made to the sacred *cenote* (natural well), which was supposed to be a place of great sanctity. The victim was cast into the water with other offerings and was believed to emerge alive after three days had elapsed."[4] The Sacred Cenoté at Chichen-Itza was a destination for pilgrims who came to give offerings. Votive offerings of gold, jade, a turquoise "serpent mask," and other items were recovered from the Sacred Cenoté during the early

---

1 Tompkins, Peter. *Mysteries of the Mexican Pyramids.* New York: Harper & Row, 1976, 179

2 Peterson, Frederick. *Ancient Mexico.* New York: Capricorn Books 1962, 83

3 Krickenberg, Walter & et al. *Pre-Columbian American Religions.* New York: Holt, Rinehart and Winston 1968, 35

4 Joyce, Thomas A. *Mexican Archaeology: An Introduction to the Archaeology of the Mexican and Mayan Civilizations of Pre-Spanish America.* London: Philip Lee Warner 1920, 262

20th century by Edward H. Thompson. Thompson attempted to establish a link between the Mayans and the Lost Continent of Atlantis during his excavations. In addition, gold discs have been found which date to the 10th century with etchings of warfare and human sacrifice on their surfaces. Over the last hundred years more than 30,000 items of gold, copper, jade, pottery, fabric, human bones and wooden and stone artifacts have been recovered from the Well of God.[1] Other artifacts found in the Sacred Cenoté originated in central Mexico, Costa Rica and Panama.[2]

Photo 19: The cenoté water level is still 60 feet below the rim.

This particular cenoté may have been the most important pilgrimage site that existed in pre-conquest Yucatan. It has been suggested, "the great round surface of water may have been perceived as a giant mirror for divination and auguring."[3]

Certain hot springs were also regarded as being sacred to the indigenous peoples of Central and South America. According to Joyce, "the valley-dwellers of Michoacan around

1   Baldwin, Neil. *Legends of the Plumed Serpent: Biography of a Mexican God.* New York: Public Affairs 1998, 68
2   Krickenberg, op. cit., 72
3   Miller, Mary and Karl Taube. *An Illustrated Dictionary of the Gods and Symbols of Ancient Mexico and the Maya.* New York: Thames and Hudson 1993, 58

Pazcuaro revered a goddess of fertility and rain, named Cueravahperi, casting the hearts of her victims into certain hot springs which were supposed to give birth to the rain-clouds."[1]

John L. Stephens in his classic work of archaeological discovery, *Incidents of Travel in Yucatan*, described a mysterious cenoté he happened upon in a thick grove at Balankanché ("Hidden Throne"), on his 1841 expedition:

> ...it was a great circular cavity or opening in the earth, twenty or thirty feet deep...It was a wild-looking place, and had a fanciful, mysterious, and almost fearful appearance; for while in the grove all was close and sultry, and without a breath of air, and every leaf was still, within this cavity the branches and leaves were violently agitated, as if shaken by an invisible hand....on our first attempting to enter it the rush of the wind was so strong that it made us fall back gasping for breath....It was one of the marvels told us of this place, that it was impossible to enter after twelve o'clock.[2]

Stephens discovered a well-worn pathway around the cenoté leading to a stone block, which according to Stephens, "had been a great item in all the accounts, and was described as made by hand and highly polished." After descending through the passageways for some time, Stephens and his party finally came upon the well itself. The water, he wrote, "was in a deep, stony basin, running under a shelf of overhanging rock." Stephens believed that the well was the main source of water for a nearby ruined city located between Nohcacab and Uxmal. Due to the hand crafted stone altar and the various legends associated with the well, it would appear that the indigenous people had considered it sacred for hundreds of years. The admonishment to not enter the well after twelve o'clock is also one of many legends that are attached to sacred wells. Caves and still, standing water were all viewed as entryways to the Underworld by the Meso-Americans as they were among most other cultures. They were held sacred and were places of veneration, but they were also viewed with fear as they led to the world of the dead.

The cave shrine at Balankanché has still not been fully explored but many of the stone and wooden offerings, stoneware pots, incense burners and other offerings remain as they have since 860 CE. The most amazing aspect of this shrine is a huge, fused stalagmite-stalactite column, which rises from the caves' floor reaching the roof in an amazing likeness of a great tree — the representation of the Mayan World Tree.[3]

1 Joyce, op. cit., 37

2 Stephens, John L. *Incidents of Travel in Yucatan*. New York: Dover Publications, Inc. 1963 (A reprint of the Harper & Brothers 1848 edition), 213

3 Devereux, Paul. *The Sacred Place: The Ancient Origin of Holy and Mystical Sites*. London: Cassell & Company 2000, 95-96

Arizona

Another cenoté known for its religious importance is that of Montezuma's Well located southwest of Flagstaff, Arizona. This water filled limestone sinkhole is 368 feet across and 55 to 470 feet deep (depending on which authority is cited) that feeds 1,500,000 gallons of subterranean spring water daily into Beaver Creek. It is also the site of the emergence of Kamalopukwia, the grandmother spirit, and her grandson Sakaraka, the first of The People of the Yavapai. Like other sacred wells, these cenotés were also conduits between our physical world and the other worlds that are normally kept hidden from our eyes.

Photo 20: Montezuma's Well

Several cliff dwellings from 700 CE are situated around the well and were once occupied by Hohokam clans. These people were farmers and used the well water for crop irrigation until 1400 CE when environmental conditions forced the abandonment of the area. The first European visit of Montezuma's Well occurred in 1583 by Spanish explorers.[1] The well is still considered sacred by many of the neighboring tribes.

Attempts to identify the source of the well have been fruitless. No connection to any other source of water in the area has been made.

California

Besides the cenotés, other sacred water sources were also common among the indigenous peoples of America. In California, the Chumash Indians, living in the Santa Barbara and Channel Islands area, had several areas they considered holy.

---

1 Mays, Buddy. *Ancient Cities of the Southwest*. San Francisco: Chronicle Books 1982, 30

Las Animas Spring (*Animo* means "spirit"), three miles north of Point Conception, was believed to be the site where the souls of the deceased Chumash bathed.

Photo 21: Cliff dwellings around Montezuma's Well

Another sacred site for the Chumash was Point Humqaq; so holy was this area that all living Chumash avoided it except for periodic pilgrimages to leave offerings at the shrine. Point Humqaq was viewed as a "portal" used by the souls of the Chumash to reach heaven where they awaited their turn at reincarnation. Humqaq Pool, located nearby, is a basin in which fresh water continuously drips and where the Chumash spirit "bathes and paints itself" while waiting to ascend to heaven.[1]

Zaca Lake in the Santa Ynez Valley, also Chumash territory, is still regarded as a sacred location by contemporary Chumash people. A "doorway" to the celestial realm of the Chumash souls is believed to be located at the bottom of this lake.

Sacred springs and rivers were a universal feature among Native Americans. It is unfortunate that scant information has been recorded about these sites and beliefs over the years. The Nomlaki Indians in Northern California often consulted spirits at sacred pools. According to anthropologist Walter Goldschmidt:

> Springs and hallowed places (*sawal*), usually inhabited by a spirit, had powers for good and evil and were of great importance to shamans, warriors, hunters, gamblers, and specific craftsmen. Some springs were said to be good; other were considered bad....Each spring was visited by the person interested in its particular power, and such visits increased his

---

1 Anderson, John. *Kuta Teachings: Reincarnation Theology of the Chumash Indians of California.* Kootenai: American Designs Publishing 1998, 49

luck, purified him, and strengthened him for his endeavor; a person might not visit a *sawal* to which he did not have a specific right.[1]

Likewise, the Wintu who resided just north of the Nomlaki would seek out spirits in sacred pools where they would bathe and then sleep. After awakening, the individual would dive into the pool and seek a charmstone. Over the next few days, the individual would alternate between sleeping and seeking spirit guides through dream, praying and swimming in the same spot in the sacred pool. Through this process, he would accomplish the "seeking of power."[2]

One of the most impressive Native American sites for its water symbolism is located in Roseville, California. In the center of the growing urban sprawl of this Northern California city in the Sacramento Valley is the Maidu Interpretive Center. Situated on the site of an ancient Maidu village (perhaps the village of Pichiku) with history dating back to 5,000 BCE, this village/ceremony site has an astounding mixture of megaliths and petroglyphs with important water associations. Maidu healer Rick Adams guided me among the sacred sites of this village in June 2001.

Photo 22.
"Bear footprint,"
Maidu Indian.

Many of the features at this site are similar to those in Europe that were constructed and utilized around the same time on history's timeline. One megalith known as the "Northstar stone" is a large rectangular stone with several mortars on one side, two on the top, and with several incised lines that run from the top down one side. It is believed that this stone was a central piece used

---

1 Goldschmidt, Walter. "Nomlaki," in *Handbook of North America n Indians: Volume 8-California.* Washington: Smithsonian Institution 1978, 345

2 Lapena, Frank R. "Wintu," in *Handbook of North America n Indians: Volume 8-California.* Washington: Smithsonian Institution 1978, 331

during bear ceremonies thanking the Grizzly Bear and to welcome the change of season from winter to spring. The mortars were used to grind berries and other food items with the juices running down the incised lines into a cachement at the bottom. It is assumed that the Grizzly lured into the area, as part of the ceremony would eat from the cachment. A bear "footprint" was carved into one portion of the Northstar stone representative of a bear walking in a docile manner, the back print overlapping with the print of the forepaw.

The footprint and incised grooves on Northstar are similar to other "rain rocks" found in Northern California. Robert Heizer wrote in his paper "Sacred Rain-Rocks of Northern California"[1] that a rain-rock was discovered along the Klamath River with carvings resembling bear's feet engraved into the rock's surface. Surface engraving was important on rain-rocks with long parallel grooves made to create snow with a groove scratched across the parallel lines to stop the snow. In addition, Heizer noted that shallow conical pits were made to produce rain wind. There are several identical engravings and conical pits on the Northstar stone so it is possible that this stone was important not only in the Bear Dance but also in the creation of weather patterns and in the solstice observations.

The second mortar at the top is called a "shaman's well." During the ceremony, the shaman or healer would go into a trance. By flowing through the sacred spring his spirit would journey through the shaman's well to the spirit world. This concept is a universal one around the world with wells considered entranceways into the spirit or underworld.

Approximately 100 feet south of the Northstar stone is a flat oval stone approximately three feet across with three holes approximately 1-½ inches in diameter and 1 inch deep. These holes are in a triangular arrangement and line up perfectly with the winter and summer solstices as well as the Northstar rock. Looking along the face of the rock to the east it lines up perfectly with the sacred stream. At one time, this stream was always full and wild with salmon. The recent addition of concrete drainage systems and residential construction has permanently altered the stream to its present size and it is now devoid of its traditional fish life.

Another rock grouping nearby has some very interesting carvings that are reminiscent of those found at New Grange in Ireland. Some 30–40 feet from this complex is a standing stone thought to have been used as a fertility shrine. An incised carving of two breasts with pecked holes representative of nipples can be seen at the top of the stone. Below this an incised carving of the vulva appears in the middle of the stone. Young women would rub both during seasonal ceremonies to ensure their fertility. This carving is very similar to that at St. Anne's Well in Llanmihamgel, South Wales, however, at St. Anne's water pours from the

---

1 *Reports of the University of California Archaeological Survey No. 20, March 16, 1953,* 33-37.

nipples and vagina that have been carved into the fountain.[1] Another large standing stone nearby has a carving of several "ripples" symbolic of flowing water. While the exact use and meaning of these pre-historic monuments is unknown, the sacred spring and associated water symbolism, the related fertility stone and the nearby directional stone used during the solstice indicates a complex and well thought out series of related sacred areas. The use of symbolic "wells" for the entryway to the underworld by the shaman is a universal association with water and wells. The ceremonial use of these large standing stones associated with these beliefs, dating to approximately the same age as those in Britain, indicates a collective ritual process among peoples of that age.

Photo 23: Maidu fertility stone.

During July 2001, my wife and I traveled over 1200 miles in Northern California seeking out sacred springs and waterways. What we found was just as magickal and meaningful as those that we found in England. The natural holiness of these sites, no matter where they are located, is the same — they are just as powerful, just as meaningful and with just as much history. Many of the very special sites we found were near Mt. Shasta — one of the seven sacred mountains of the world. Although the sacredness of the mountain is somewhat tarnished by many of the "New Age" groups located near the mountain's base advocating the teachings of the Ascended Masters, the Lemurians, the Pleiadians and others — at a cost of

---

1 Straffon, Cheryl. *The Earth Goddess: Celtic and Pagan Legacy of the Landscape.* London: Blandford 1997, 71

course — the mountain and its special ancient holy sites remain as powerful today as they were in the past. A select few of these sites are discussed below:

HEADWATERS OF THE SACRAMENTO RIVER

Located in the city park of Mt. Shasta is the headwater of the Sacramento River. While it would seem strange that the source of this large river can be found in a city park, the water gushing out of the ground creates a magickal place. Coming out of a small grotto in a fern and vine-covered area, the water spills over into a shallow and calm pool approximately 10 feet in diameter. Immediately it cascades down a small waterfall on its way through the Sacramento Valley.

Not much is known about the original inhabitants' observations at this spot but the tranquil atmosphere here is a welcome relief and, undoubtedly, the earlier residents of the area valued it as much or more than we did. Local legend is that this source pool is restorative to one's health and, in fact, while I was there I saw several people stop to fill up plastic bottles and to sit and meditate. One middle-aged woman, obviously suffering from a serious disease, had also stopped to drink the water and to enjoy the quietness. Reports of healings have been made over the years as well as sightings of "angelic beings."

Photo 24: Headwaters of the Sacramento River

Even during times of drought, the headwater source produces an energetic flow that gushes from its mossy covered rocks.

PANTHER MEADOWS

Approximately 14 miles east of the city of Mt. Shasta and half way up Mt. Shasta's 14,200-foot height is Panther Meadows. This site is still regarded as sacred among the Wintu, Shasta, Karuk and Pit River Tribes and is known as *luligawa*, or "sacred flower" among the Wintu. This was one of the holiest-feeling sites we encountered in our travels. Panther Meadow is a sub-Alpine pristine area approximately 2 miles in length, with a wide variety of delicate and beautiful wild flowers, such as alpine laurel, mountain heather, arnica and paintbrush growing among the volcanic rock. The Meadow is nestled in a valley on the mountain's southern slope at the 7500-foot elevation, almost at the tree line. A few eagles, chipmunks and smaller birds are the only wildlife in evidence although the name implies that larger and more fearsome animals also frequent the area. Some pilgrims have also reported seeing faeries and the god Pan as well.

Photo 25: Panther Meadows, Mt. Shasta

Evidence of ancient and contemporary offerings can be seen along the one-mile trail that stretches from the road to the sacred spring. Situated among three large trees, a large boulder is situated with several rocks placed

Photo 26: Rock cairn, Panther Meadows

on top attesting to the continuing use of rock cairns to give offerings of thanks and appeasement to the spirits that inhabit the sacred area. Several smaller cairns were also seen located along the many small streams that form from the source spring.

"Heaps" of small stones like these are commonly found at many sacred wells around the world. Patrick Logan made the following observation in his book, *The Holy Wells of Ireland:*

> Many writers mention the heaps of small stones seen near holy wells. Such a cairn was described at St. Patrick's Well in Kilcorkey parish... and another at Tullaghan Well, Co. Sligo....O'Donnovan wrote that each pilgrim added a further stone to the heap as part of the ritual of the pilgrimage.[1]

Logan believes that those who leave the stones are leaving a substitute offering to a saint due to their inability to leave something of economic value. This would not appear to be the case, however since the practice appears to be universal among many different cultures with many different perspectives on wealth. An 18th century account by a parish minister at St. Fillan's Well stated "all the invalids throw a white stone on the saint's cairn, and leave behind, as tokens of their confidence and gratitude, some rags or linen or woolen cloth."[2] It would seem that the actual origin of such practices has been lost in the distant past but the contribution of individual stones and rags must have a more complex meaning than simply as tokens of confidence.

Photo 27: Headwaters of the McCloud River

At the northern end of the meadow is the sacred spring, the source water of the many streams that eventually become the McCloud River. The headwater is another small rock grotto from which the water flows out of the earth into a shallow and placid pool before becoming a series of small waterfalls. Visitors are advised not to collect water from the source pool itself but from waters flowing further down. Believers say the energy at this place is almost palpable and many regard Panther Meadows as being an "energy vortex" in itself. The Winnemem Wintu still regard Panther Meadows as their church.

McCloud Falls

McCloud Falls is in reality three falls along the McCloud River. I was able to observe the Lower and Upper Falls although the Middle Falls are regarded as the most beautiful. Located approximately 6 miles east of the small former lumber town of McCloud, these falls were sacred to the Shasta Peoples who lived along

---

1 Logan, Patrick. *The Holy Wells of Ireland.* Buckinghamshire: Colin Smythe 1980, 99
2 Anon. "Our Hagiology," in *Blackwood's Edinburgh Magazine*, Vol. 82, October 1857, 454

the banks at one time. Today the falls are reputed to clear emotional disturbances and to renew one's spirit.

Photo 28: Lower Falls

The Upper Falls is a powerful cascade of water, which flows into a dark blue pool at the bottom. Situated in a dense forest of redwoods, pine, cedar and lush water plants and ferns, these falls are very special places and well worth visiting. The Lower Falls are much more serene but just as mystical as they tumble over the volcanic rocks into a series of small falls through a beautiful gorge. Other than a few small lizards and chipmunks, and the calls of birds, these areas were devoid of visitors except for a few boys swimming in the Lower Falls.

BURNEY FALLS

Another 40 miles past the McCloud Falls is Burney Falls. This waterfall is majestic in its size — 129 feet. Roaring water flows over the lip of the cliffs above and falls into a large green pool that is approximately 24 feet in depth. The cool spray blows over the rock-strewn beaches around the pool but the day I was

there some unusual wind also played. At Burney Falls, there was no lack of visitors with a couple dozen children playing on the volcanic rocks and shouting to be heard over the water. Suddenly, a hot wind blew through the area, pushing the water spray away — almost as if the Spirits of the falls were angry at the intrusion and trying to wipe it away with a blast of hot wind. Among the Jivaro Indians of Ecuador it is thought that waterfalls are gathering places for the souls of ancestors. The Jivaro believe that the souls wander around as breezes, blowing the water spray as they travel through the falls.

Photo 29: Burney Falls

The local tribes considered Burney Falls sacred for hundreds of years and journeyed to the falls in vision quests and meditation. Local stories tell of water spirits and elves frequenting this spot.

The last healing water site within the Mt. Shasta influence is found at Castle Crags State Park.[1]

Castle Crags Mineral Spring

Castle Crags is a series of granite towers reaching 6500 feet in elevation within view of Mt. Shasta. At 225 million years in age, they emit a feeling of antiquity and mystery. Over the years, occultists have advanced theories that Castle Crags are the remains of the lost continent of Lemuria and a landing port for UFOs. What *is* known is that the Indians left rock art here and utilized a small mineral spring.

The spring is located on the edge of the Sacramento River on the outskirts of a State Park picnic area — one not frequented when I was there. The spring is nestled in a rock enclosure, forming a well structure, built around 1880 when white men first attempted to commercialize it. Today it still offers a sulfuric smell as it bubbles up out of the ground. Known for its restorative powers the well nevertheless has failed the California water quality test and people are advised not to drink from it. However, these mineral springs were not intended for ingestion but for bathing for the waters therapeutic properties. Sulfurated water has been found to be an excellent treatment for skin diseases, wounds and the creation of blood lymphocytes. In addition, sulfuric waters have been found to be useful in the treatment of liver and gastrointestinal conditions, gynecological problems and arthritis.[2] It is more than likely that the Native Americans used this spring for these healing qualities also.

Photo 30: Castle Rock Mineral Well

The Castle Rock area was Wintu land when, in 1855, miners swarmed into the area and intentionally polluted the streams that were holy to the Wintu people, attacking any of the Wintu who attempted to protect their holy land. This

---

1 It must be acknowledged that these special places would no longer exist in their present form, if at all, except for the protection of the California State Parks system and the City of Mt. Shasta. Without their diligence and care, the characteristics that make these sacred water places sacred would have been altered beyond recognition. Burney Falls, McCloud Falls, Panther Meadows and Castle Crags are all under the jurisdiction of the State Parks, which continues to work with the Indian Tribes who once occupied this whole area to keep these sites healthy and as pure as possible.
2 Altman, Nathaniel. *Healing Springs: The Ultimate Guide to Taking the Waters.* Rochester: Healing Arts Press 2000, 60

was not only an assault upon the Wintu fishing and drinking sources but also an assault upon the basic spirituality of the Wintu.[1]

During the 1890s, the Castle Rock Mineral Water Company was formed and cases of the water were sold and shipped all over the world. The Peruvian consul had a standing order of 50 cases a month. This lasted until shortly after the 1906 San Francisco earthquake when the company could no longer operate — it finally closed down for good after the 1929 stock market crash ruined the company's plans to divide and "develop" the land. It was at that time that the California State Parks purchased the land, preserving it as it is today. The rock enclosed-well next to the flowing Sacramento River nestled amongst the ferns, water plants, and large trees all add to the feelings of being at one with nature.

When I next visited the mineral well a few years later, I found it had been visited by others who placed flowers on the water's surface in an offering to the water's spiritual and healing presence.

Photo 31: Castle Rock Mineral Well

OTHER SACRED SPRINGS IN CALIFORNIA

Harbin Hot Springs

Continuing our journey, we found dozens of hot springs and sacred sites in Sonoma and Lake Counties two hundred miles to the southwest of Mt. Shasta. One of the most famous is Harbin Hot Springs, located four miles outside the town of Middletown. Due to the facility's clothing optional policies, I was not allowed inside the facility to take photographs or to see the source spring, which has been capped over with cement anyway. Unfortunately, many of the most sacred and healing of springs have come under private ownership, invariably resulting in commercialism and the alteration of the spring's natural appearance. However, the natural healing properties of the water are still very potent. Situated above a large magma chamber 4 miles underground and 13 miles in diameter, the water is heated and rises toward the surface as steam where it cools and returns to its liquid state.

According to Nathaniel Altman, the Coast and Lake Miwok used the present Harbin site "as a seasonal camp and sacred ground, with the hot springs both a place of healing and a path to the spiritual realms."[2] During the Miwok settlement of the area, Harbin was called *eetawyomi*, or "the hot place." The hot springs have been active at Harbin for over a million years[3] and its waters are composed

1 Lapena, op. cit 325

2 Altman, op. cit., 41

3 Klages, Ellen. *Harbin Hot Springs: Healing Waters Sacred Land.* Middletown: Harbin Springs Publishers 1991, 7

primarily of sulfur, iron and arsenic with sodium, potassium, magnesium, carbonates and other elements evident.

By the time Spanish explorers reached the land of the Lake Miwok, pools had been dug into the ground at Harbin where the Miwok would bathe in the hot spring water. Ellen Klages, in her history of Harbin, wrote that the springs were "owned" by the Lake Miwok but were accessible to all tribes:

> Men and women who were sick were brought to the springs for its curative powers; Pomos, Wappos and Wintuns camped there routinely; and any tribes traveling through from the coast to the inland valleys were also welcome.[1]

The hot springs were also regarded as an entryway into the underworld — as are many other sacred wells and springs around the world. Shamans would enter a trance state and then their spirits would travel from the physical realm to the spiritual where they would talk with the spirits to learn. The shaman would then return to the physical world to heal with the newly learned knowledge.

After the Mexican and then American settlement of California, the hot springs became a popular resort and remains so today.

Vichy Springs

Located in Ukiah, north of Middletown, Vichy Springs is also a contemporary resort on an ancient spring. A beautiful natural grotto encloses the bubbling mineral spring source. This water is not hot but is warm bicarbonate water. Bicarbonate water is very effective in the treatment of gastric disorders, ulcers, colitis, irritable colon, pancreatitis and diabetes, rheumatism, arthritis and skin ailments including sunburn and poison oak. Bathing in this water is also beneficial to the vascular system. This is another spring was used by the Native Americans long before it's "discovery" by the white man in 1848 and its development into a resort in 1854. Due to its sulfurous smell, the Pomo Indians knew the spring as *katuct* ("rotten eggs water"). The spring water comes from 30,000 feet below the earth and its water is over 6,000 years old. The office of Vichy Springs has an old photograph of Mark Twain "taking the waters" at the grotto. Vichy Springs is the oldest continuously operated mineral spring resorts in California. Its waters are the closest in nature to those of the famous Vichy springs in France at Grand Grille Springs.

Photo 32: Vichy Springs, Calistoga

Finally, my explorations around Northern California brought me to the town of Calistoga — long famous for its hot springs and spas. The whole area is

---

1 Ibid. 55

ripe with bubbling and steaming water sources as well as geysers. "Old Faithful," one of only three "old faithful" geysers in the world, still shoots a stream of water 60 feet into the air at 350 degrees in temperature every 13 minutes, day and night.[1] Approximately 30 feet away from the geyser an old "wishing well" stands. Constructed near the beginning of the 20th century, this well used to be filled with the hot mineral water and people would toss coins into it and, it is reported, even be baptized in it. The present owners of the site have drained the water "for safety concerns" but the steam still curls up from the coin covered bottom. The Miwok used these mineral and hot springs for hundreds of years prior to Samuel Brannan's "discovery" and development in the 1870s. These waters, also rich in sulfur, are known for their effective treatments of arthritis, rheumatism and stress related problems.[2] Calistoga water is sold throughout the world in plastic bottles and is still obtained from a protected geyser nearby.

Photo 33: Calistoga's "Old Faithful"

MONO LAKE

Situated on the California-Nevada border, Mono Lake is today an eerie but wonderful place. Located on the California -Nevada border it is the birthplace of 90% of all California Gulls (50,000 a year nest at Mono Lake) and home to over one million Eared Grebes and 80 other species. Mono Lake is also one of the oldest existing lakes in North America being at least one million years old. Strange tufa formations rise out of the water resulting from a chemical reaction between the freshwater springs that flow underground into the salty lake water. The tufa towers range in age from 200 to 13,000 years old.

The active volcanoes in the area have created a number of hot and warm springs as well as the islands that exist in the lake — one of which, Paoha Island, is only 300 years old.

The water contains sodium chloride, sodium carbonate and sodium sulfate and the lake is known as a chloro-carbonate-sulfate "triple water" lake. I visited Mono Lake in January 2003, wanting to experience the hot springs and the strange formations in and around the lake. The heavy snow cover and cold temperatures of this time of year kept me from seeing many of the places I had desired to see but my four-wheel drive vehicle traversed the two-mile snow covered dirt

---

1 On my visit to Old Faithful, over an hour in duration, I observed this geyser erupting every 13 minutes but the duration and periods between eruptions depend upon the moon, barometric pressure and earthquake activity. The average time is 40 minutes between eruptions on a yearly basis.

2 Altman, op. cit., 177

road to the South Tufa Area. Utterly silent and cloaked in snow and fog the lake looked surreal.

Photo 34: Mono Lake and its Tufa towers

There are few legends about Mono Lake but it is known that the Indians frequented it often to collect the pupae of the alkali fly, which was harvested as a favorite food. The pupae, being rich in fat, protein, and flavor, were an important trade item between the Kuzedika'a and the Yokut and Yosemite Miwok peoples. The Mono Paiute called themselves "Kuzedika'a" meaning "fly eaters." The Yokut called them "Mono" which also means, "fly eaters."

One of the stranger legends has to do with a water serpent. The Walker Lake Paiute have believed that a large water monster, similar to the Loch Ness Monster, resides in Walker Lake. An early newspaper account in the *San Francisco Cable* told of a sighting near Goldfield, Nevada:

> ...a man named Peters is said to have discovered the serpent some time ago in shallow water near the shore, and on being aroused it disappeared in deep water. There is also said to be legend among the Paiute Indians near Shurz concerning the existence of a great serpent in Walker Lake.[1]

Legend says that two serpents, a male and female, live in Walker Lake and arrows fired by the Paiute warriors simply bounced off their thick hide. Indian children were cautioned not to make fun of the legends out of fear of the serpent's

---

1 *San Francisco Cable*, July 1907

anger. Legend also says that these two serpents originated in Mono Lake. An article in the *Review Journal*, on June 4, 2000 remarked that when the Northern Paiute were forcibly removed from their ancestral lands "moving the tribe also took them away from the serpent that members of the tribe believe dwells there. The tribal offices have a photo purportedly showing the serpent, which bears a striking resemblance to the Loch Ness monster."[1]

Another story accounts for the creation of Paoha Island. It seems, the legends say, that Bear and Rabbit decided to race and as Rabbit pulled ahead of Bear, Bear decided that he wanted to kill and eat Rabbit — not just beat him in the race. As Rabbit raced along the Controller of Water, a gigantic creature who sat in Mono Lake and controlled the water levels, stretched his legs out so that Rabbit could race across the lake to safety. As Bear started to also cross the giant's legs the Controller of Water pulled them back allowing the water to cover Bear, drowning him. Bear floated to the surface, becoming Paoha Island. There are many hot springs around Mono Lake and Kawaiisu legends say that the springs become hot because the sun sinks into the waters each evening.[2]

Due to the need for water in the Los Angeles basin, Mono Lake was almost completely drained by the Los Angeles Department of Water and Power (DWP). In 1998, the California Water Resources Control Board approved the plans of the DWP to restore Mono Lake to its pre-dewatering 1941 period when the water level was 45 feet higher than it is today. While the plan will only allow half of the water loss to be regained it will provide for much of the loss in bird and riparian habitat. The importance of the restoration of Mono Lake is such that the International Lake Environmental Committee is monitoring its progress along with 24 other lakes around the world.

These few examples of sacred and healing waters in North America — California in particular — demonstrate that the United Stated also has a rich and expansive tradition of these sites. There are an estimated 1800 hot springs in the United States with the majority situated in the West. Only 100 or so have been commercially developed over the years, the rest remaining as they have for untold centuries. There are many more such sacred places in North America and many of these remain in isolated and pristine condition. The Old Ways may still be experienced at these locations.

---

1 Rinella, Heidi Knapp. "Northern Paiutes changed with move." *Review Journal*, June 4, 2000. *http://www.reviewjournal.com/lvrj.home/2000/Jun-04-Sun-2000/news/13509450. html*

2 Phillips, Santos. "The Race Between Frog, Coyote and the Sun," in *Kawaiisu Mthology: An Oral Tradition of South-Central California* by Maurice L. Zigmond. Menlo Park: Ballena Press Publications 1980, 147

Chapter 3. Sacred Wells — Holy Trees

Certain kinds of trees have been associated with sacred wells since ancient times. Like the standing megaliths, trees represent the male, phallic powers of the universe and the well represents the feminine, life giving powers. Being symbols of the cosmic energy and power within the universe, trees and wells obviously have deep roots in humankind's sub-consciousness. Trees are both male and female. They jut out from the mother earth and reach for the sky in all of their maleness and at the same time they provide food, shelter and nests for animals. While the phallus symbolism is obvious, Janet and Colin Bord note that not all trees associated with wells have the phallic shape. "The contrast," they write, "lies rather in the receptive, inward-looking nature of the well and the vital, outward-growing nature of the tree."[1]

They are protective; they are nurturing. Trees have been viewed as the World Center (the "World Tree") in many cultures, joining the underworld, the world where humans reside, and the heavens. Wells provide the life-blood needed by all living things — water. Water itself is symbolic of the Great Mother, of birth and of the womb. Water purifies. This ancient association is recognized in the Old Testament where the Waters of the Fountain of Life rise from the roots of the Tree of Life in the Garden of Paradise. The sacred well is the womb of the Great Mother, containing healing waters, wisdom and wish fulfillment.

Paul Bauschatz noted, "the figure of well and tree is sustaining not simply of its own structure, but in the process of growing into itself; it is in constant state

---

1 Bord, Janet and Colin. *Earth Rites: Fertility Practices in Pre-Industrial Britain.* London: Granada Publishing Limited, 1982, 103

of self-enlarging transformation." It is then a symbol of the growth and "sustaining of the cosmic structure."[1]

Sacred trees associated with holy wells are hawthorn (also called quickthorn or may), elder, ash, oak, hazel, holly, yew, and rowan. On the Isle of Man, the well of Chibby Drine ("Well of the Thorn Tree") is indicative of the intentional planting of a sacred tree over a holy well. Hawthorns are also found in West Yorkshire at Lady Well, Margaret Well, Hesp Hills Well, and Fairy Well at Harmby and at Ffynnon Cae Moch at Glamorgan in Wales. Sir James Frazer noted in *The Golden Bough* that one ancient custom still present in his day was the decoration in Cornwall of front doors with hawthorn boughs on May Day.[2] **The Hawthorn**, in folklore, was considered a protection against sorcery and was regarded as a magic "fairy tree." The Hawthorn was sacred to the Tuatha de' Danaan and the Graeco-Roman goddess Maia (thus "May Day") and the "White Goddess" also associated with Spring and rebirth. Maia, "Great Goddess of Maytime festivals,"[3] was also the mother of the God Hermes who was the conductor of souls to the underworld. Again, the linkage of the sacred tree, the sacred well and the passage to the underworld is reflected in this sacred tree.

The Hawthorn was also thought to be purifying and a tree of chastity to the Irish (and in fact symbolizes virgin conception) and a tree of eroticism by the Turks.[4] It is known as a "fairy tree" because faeries and spirits are said to meet under the Hawthorn tree. Solitary Hawthorn's standing near sacred wells act as markers for the faery realm.

One of the legends of Joseph of Arimathea is that when he and his followers reached Glastonbury (the Isle of Avalon), they were so exhausted from their travels that he called the spot where they stopped "Wearyall Hill" — as it is still known. On Wearyall Hill Joseph struck his staff on the ground where it instantly blossomed into a Hawthorn tree. During the Reformation, Puritan fanatics attempted to cut down the original Glastonbury thorn with axes. The tree lived only another 30 years but numerous cuttings were taken from which the surviving trees descend. That tree, through its descendants, is still on Wearyall Hill and other places around Glastonbury. Two rather remarkable things about this tree is that it is only found in one other location in the world — the Middle East, and that it blooms in May and December each year.[5]

The Ash is sacred not only in the British Isles but also throughout Scandinavia. The Ash is the World Tree, the Cosmic Tree, and *Yggdrasil.* Yggdrasil is the

1 Bauscharz, Paul C. *The Well and the Tree: World and Time in Early Germanic Culture.* Amherst: University of Massachusetts Press, 1982, 27

2 Frazer, Sir James. *The Golden Bough: A Study in Magic and Religion.* Hertfordshire: Wordsworth Editions, 1993, 121

3 Walker, Barbara G. *The Women's Encyclopedia of Myths and Secrets.* Edison: Castle Books, 1983, 572

4 Pepper, Elizabeth. *Celtic Tree Magic.* Middletown: The Witches' Almanac, Ltd., 1996

5 Capt, E. Raymond. *The Traditions of Glastonbury.* Muskogee: Artisan Sales 1983, 86

Sacred Tree of Odin, Zeus and Jupiter. At the foot of the Cosmic Tree was the Fountain of the Fates. The Fates, or Norns, were also referred to as the "Wyrd Sisters " — three sisters who revealed the secrets of the universe and wrote each souls fate in the Book of Destiny. These sisters represented the goddess Triad — Urth (or Mother Earth) who represented creation and Fate; Skuld represents "necessary or obligatory action;"[1] and Verthandi the goddess of "Being." These three goddesses predated all patriarchal gods and ruled over the other deities. Urth's Well was said to exist at the foot of Yggdrasil and was the "Well of the Past." Two other wells also existed at the foot of the Cosmic Tree — Mimir's Well (the "Well of Wisdom"), and Hvergelmir, the "spirit infested" well.

The Ash is also associated with the goddess. West of Glastonbury in an area referred to as the "Bell Tracks," a block of ashwood approximately 6.5 inches high, dated to approximately 2890 BCE, was found carved in the form of a woman. It is assumed the carving was that of a goddess and was deposited in this wetland area as an offering.[2]

Wells with ash trees associated with them occur in Yorkshire at the Holy Ash Well and two others nearby in Bradford and Helliwell; Syke Well, Peggy Well, True Well and White Well located in Priestly Green, Riddlesden and Harden. St. Nun's Piskie Well in Pelynt has not only an ash tree growing over it, but also an oak and a thorn — all three sacred trees. The sacred ash called the Crann a'hulla, located two miles southeast of Doneraile, County Cork is said to have sprung from the site where a beautiful girl called Craebhnat plucked out an eye and threw it to the ground in response to a marriage proposal by the prince of Munster.

On the Isle of Man, there is a Well of the Ash-tree where votive offerings are hung on the nearby Ash-tree. According to folklore, the Ash symbolizes adaptability, prudence and modesty.[3]

The elder tree is also called a "witches tree" and a "fairy tree." The Elder Mother is a Scandinavian goddess who watched over the Elder tree to ensure that no harm was done to it. Elder trees are known to exist or to have existed near Fairy Well in Roberttown, England, at Abbey Well near Norr, and near several wells in Wales. The power of the Elder tree and its association with paganism resulted in the Archbishop of York, Wulfstan, issuing a series of edicts between 1000 and 1002, which outlawed the singing of pagan songs and games during Christian feast days. The worship of any pagan deity or the "veneration of the sun, moon,

---

1 Bauscharz, op. cit., 15

2 Straffon, Cheryl. *The Earth Goddess: Celtic and Pagan Legacy of the Landscape.* London: Blanford, 1997, 92

3 Cooper, J.C. *An Illustrated Encyclopaedia of Traditional Symbols.* London: Thames and Hudson Ltd., 1978, 16

fire and water" was forbidden[1] and any such sanctuaries that were around wells, rocks, or trees, "especially the elder" were condemned.[2]

The Oak, recognized since ancient times for its strength, its power and its beauty, is held sacred to Zeus, to the Judeo-Christian Yahweh, Hercules, The Daghda, and Thor and to the Great Goddess. The Oak has been called the "Mother Tree" and the "Great World Tree." Many sacred oaks also had a sacred spring at its foot. The oak was so important and meaningful for the intellectual class of the Celts that the Indo-European word *dru-wid*, meaning "oak-wise," became the name of this class (*"Druids"*). Another word for oak is *duir*, which also means "door" in many European languages and, in fact, is the origin of the English word *door*. For the oak is an oracular tree providing a doorway to the future as well as to the otherworld. Holy wells with the sacred oak nearby occur at Healy Well Oak in Drighlington, England, Llancarfan Well in Glamorgan, Priests Well at Monmouth and Ffynnon Dderw at Carmarthen, Wales.

The Hazel tree is another sacred tree of the Celts. It was also Sacred to the Greek god Hermes (and thus represents reconciliation and communication), as well as Thor. Robert Graves speaks of Connla's Well near Tipperary "over which hung the nine hazels of poetic art which produced flowers and fruit (i.e., beauty and wisdom) simultaneously.... All the knowledge of the arts and sciences was bound up with the eating of these nuts..."[3] The Hazel is the tree of wisdom in Celtic mythology. Wands made from hazel are used to make rain and to locate water, in Ireland the hazel is believed to counter witch craft. Hazel trees are found in Glastonbury at the Chalice Well, at Ffynnon Cyll and Ffynnon Collen in Carmarthenshire, Wales as well as at Diana's Well in Yorkshire.

One of the ancient ritual shafts found at Ashill contained not only votive offerings such as bones, potsherds and a skeleton of a frog, but the remains of a bucket and hazelnuts.

The Holly, regarded as one of the Two Divine Kings along with the oak, was viewed as having magickal powers for divination and to protect the home from fire and lightning. Holly, mistletoe and the oak were all sacred to the Druids. The Druids held the holly as representative of death as well as regeneration. Holly was also sacred to the Romans as symbol of health and happiness. Holly was associated with the sun god. In 563 CE, the Council of Bracara, an early Church council, ruled that holly was forbidden in any Christian household due to its association with "heathen people."[4] Holy Wells with holly nearby are found at Tombling Well and Calverly Wood near Leeds, England as well as several in Wales.

1 Hutton, Ronald. *The Pagan Religions of the Ancient British Isles.* Oxford: Blackwell Publishers, Ltd., 1993, 298

2 Ibid.

3 Graves, Robert. *The White Goddess: A Historical Grammar of Poetic Myth.* New York: The Noon Day Press, 1948, 182

4 Walker, op. cit 407

The Yew, called the "death tree," has deep roots in paganism. The Yew is one of the five magickal trees of Ireland. Irish "magicians" used to throw Yew sticks to foretell the future.[1] Ogham tablets were commonly made of Yew.[2] Although regarded as a tree of death, it is also symbolic of immortality among both the Celts and the Christians. After the destruction of Druid influence, the Yew groves of the Druids became sites for Christian churches and cemeteries. There are six holy wells in Wales that have the Yew associated with them. Jacob's Well in Hensting, Hampshire was surrounded with Yew trees at least through the 19th century. At Ffynnon Beuno it was formerly the practice to sprinkle cattle with Yew boughs dipped in the well. As previously noted, the Yew was an important sacred tree at Glastonbury and a peculiar yew found at the Abbey has grown into a vulva form indicative of goddess Trees.

The Rowan has a reputation for divining the future and protection against black magic. In Scotland through the last half of the eighteenth century, herdsmen, during Beltaine, would place Rowan sticks over the barn doors where their cattle were housed to protect them from witches who would fly over "casting spells on cattle and stealing...milk."[3] Graves notes that the Rowan was "used by the Druids as a last extremity for compelling demons to answer difficult questions."[4] But the Rowan was also valued for its oracular powers; groves of Rowan were reported to be growing around many of the stone circles in the 1700s. There is no evidence that the Rowan was deliberately planted near sacred wells, although it would likely be seeing that it was valued as an oracular tree as well as providing some protection against black magic. Children used to decorate Priest's Well near Narberth during May Day to keep witches away.

---

1 Kennedy, Conan. *Ancient Ireland: The User's Guide.* Killala: Morrigan Books, 1997, 105
2 Bonwick, James. *Irish Druids and Old Irish Religions.* New York: Barnes & Nobles, Inc. 1986, 237 (a reprint of the 1894 edition)
3 Frazier, op. cit 620
4 Graves, op. Cit. 167

Chapter 4. Wells and Votive Offerings

Throughout the history of humankind, the people of every continent and isle have left offerings to the many spirits, ancestors and gods that inhabited places of power and mystery. These offerings are made in thanks, as wishes, as an insurance policy against disaster and even as bribes. Rivers, lakes and springs are universally recognized by all cultures as places of sanctity. Anthropologist Clyde Kluckhohn wrote, "when Navahos go near sacred places they will visit the shrines and leave offerings. Some shrines lie on the summits of mountain peaks; others are found... by streams or springs. They are located wherever events of great mythological significance are thought to have occurred."[1]

Offerings take many different forms from strips of cloth, to bent pins, to coins and food and to rock cairns. As previously indicated, many of the sacred wells I visited in England had strips of cloth hanging from nearby trees. This form of votive offering has been common for hundreds, if not thousands, of years. Donald A. MacKenzie wrote in his 1917 work, *Crete & Pre-Hellenic Europe* that in Crete "rags of clothing are attached also to trees or bushes overhanging wells anciently sacred. This practice obtains in Crete as well as in the British Isles and throughout Western Europe."[2] It was MacKenzie's understanding that people hung these strips of cloth near holy wells to affect "a ceremonial connection with a sacred place to 'switch on' the good influence and 'switch off' the evil influence, which was negatived by being bound."[3] Likewise, Bonwick noted, "Irish wells are not the only

---

1 Kluckhohn, Clyde and Dorothea Leighton. *The Navaho.* New York: Anchor Books 1962, 204
2 MacKenzie, Donald A. *Crete & Pre-Hellenic: Myths and Legends.* London: Senate Publishers, 1995, 301 (A reprint of the 1917 edition originally titled Crete & Pre-Hellenic Europe published by The Gresham Publishing Company, London)
3 Ibid.

ones favoured with presents of pins and rags, for Scotland, as well as Cornwall and other parts of England, retain the custom."[1]

Votive offerings however, were not and are not restricted to strips of cloth or pins. Some ancient wells have thousands of Roman coins, pebbles, bent pins, stone carvings, human heads, sacrificed animals as well as a treasure-trove of beautifully made weapons, cauldrons and jewelry. The reasons for such offerings were probably many, from thanking saints and gods and goddesses for wishes granted or ills cured to "paying" for curses to be enacted. Macaulay wrote in his *History of St. Kilda* that the sacred spring on the island of Tobirnimbuadh could not be approached with empty hands:

> Near the fountain stood an altar, on which the distressed votaries laid down their oblations. Before they could touch sacred water with any prospect of success, it was their constant practice to address the Genius of the place with supplication and prayers....The offerings presented by them were the poorest acknowledgments that could be made to a supe-rior being, from whom they had either hopes or fears. Shells and pebbles, *rags of linen or stuffs wore out*, pins, needles, or rusty nails, were generally all the tribute that was paid....

One of the richest deposits of offerings was discovered in 1876 at Carraw-brough, Northumberland, England. Coventina's Well, dedicated to the goddess Coventina ("she of the covens") by Roman soldiers, contained thousands of coins, twenty-four Roman altars, a votive tablet, vases, rings, beads, brooches, skulls and other items. It is likely that some of the items were not placed in the well as offerings but were deposited there by well-priests after Emperor Theodosius enacted laws to exterminate pagan practices in 386 BCE.

One individual in the 19th century wrote, in a rather irritated fashion, "offer-ings generally consisting of rags, and pins so multitudinous that future geologists are not unlikely, in some instances, to think they have found a vein of copper."[2] Let us examine each form of offering:

Cloth or "Rag" Offerings

The leaving of bits and pieces of cloth at holy wells has been a custom in Eu-rope for ages. Kemmis Buckley, in a talk given to the Llanelli Art Society in Wales, stated "the origin of leaving rags, either at the well or on trees near the well, is likewise unknown. It is suggested variously that the custom may represent the idea that the disease will be left in the discarded rag; or it may be that it is a relic of the habit of leaving the whole of the garment as an offering. It may equally be a

---

1 Bonwick, James. *Irish Druids and Old Irish Religions*. New York: Barnes & Noble, 1986, 243 (A reprint of the 1894 edition)
2 Anon. "Our Hagiology," in *Blackwood's Edinburgh Magazine*, Vol. 82, October 1857, 453

sign of penance, or a sign of thanksgiving — a forerunner perhaps of the crutches and other indications of debility cured by faith which one sees today...."[1]

Another theory is that as the cloth rotted away, so did the disease in the individual who placed the cloth at the well. This "transference of evil," as Sir George Frazer refers to it in *The Golden Bough*, is most commonly used in Europe and is usually in association with trees or bushes. Sacred wells apparently only added to the sureness of the transfer. Others believe that those who have been cured leave behind pieces of cloth as offerings of thanks.

In the United States, it was more of a mundane practice rather than one of spirituality. Folklorist Wayland D. Hand noted that in Illinois it was common for someone suffering from warts to rub the wart with a string and then tie a knot for each wart. The individual would then "throw (the string) over the shoulder into a well, against which the sufferer had already backed up to position himself."[2]

That rag offerings are universal is evident in this account of a shrine at a sacred stone visited by pilgrims in the Turkish village of Telekioi:

> The worshipper who would conform to the full ritual, now fills a keg of water from a spring that rises near the shrine — another primitive touch — and makes his way through a thorny grove up a neighbouring knoll, on which is a wooden enclosure surrounding a Mohammedan Saint's Grave or Tekke. Over the headstone of this grows a thorn-tree hung with rags of diverse colours, attached to it — according to a widespread primitive rite — by sick persons who had made a pilgrimage to the tomb.[3]

It is interesting that this account has several pre-scripted forms identical to those associated with well worship; 1) a saint's tomb situated near a spring, 2) a thorn-tree growing over the headstone and, 3) individuals who make pilgrimages to the shrine and leave offerings of rags on the thorn-tree.

Another account of the Clootie Well ("Clootie" being a Scottish term for "cloth") is that the rag, or "clootie," is tied to a tree near the well and left to rot. It is believed "bad luck will result if they are removed." [4] A far more sinister origin proposed is that the strips of cloth mimic the strips of cloth torn from the clothing of human sacrifices in ancient times. During that time strips of clothing were hung from the sacred trees in many sacred groves.[5] Anecdotal accounts of sacrifice in sacred groves where "every tree was sprinkled with blood" and, where parts of victims were hung on tree limbs, may be the originating source for this

1 Buckley, Kemmis. "Some Holy Wells of South Carmarthenshire." A talk given on February 3, 1971 before the Llanelli Art Society.

2 Hand, Wayland D. Magical Medicine: The Folkloric Component of Medicine in the Folk Belief, Custom, and Ritual of the Peoples of Europe and America. Berkeley: University of California Press 1980, 124

3 Willetts, R. F. *Cretan Cults and Festivals*. Westport: Greenwood Press, Publishers 1980, 68 (A reprint of the 1962 edition published by Routledge & Keegan Paul Ltd.)

4 Bord, Janet and Colin. *Mysterious Britain*: Ancient Secrets of Britain and Ireland. London: Thorsons, 1972, 157

5 Ibid., 158

practice although the accounts of the Romans may be attributed more to public relations efforts rather than accuracy. Others have suggested that the hanging of cloth strips to trees dates back to the ancient worship of the trees themselves.[1]

In County Mayo, at Croagh Patrick, according to Philip Dixon Hardy's account of 1840, people "cut up their clothes, be they ever so new, and tie them to these trees (near the holy well), lest on the judgment day the Almighty should forget that they came there, and in order that the tokens should be known, when St. Patrick would lay them before the tribunal."[2] Hardy goes on to note, "the trees that over-shadowed the well (at Castle Connel near Limerick) were entirely covered with shreds of all colours — bits and clippings of gowns, and handkerchiefs... These, I believe, are the title-deeds to certain exemptions, or benefits, claimed by those who thus deposit them in the keeping of the patron saint, who is supposed to be thus reminded of the individuals whose penances might otherwise have been overlooked."[3]

Not all "holy wells" are recipients of this type of offering, however. I saw cloth offerings at St. Nectan 's, Sancreed, and St. Madron's but not at St. Piran's which is near St. Nectan's and much easier to get to, or at Arthur's Well at Cadbury. The nature of each specific well seems to draw a specific action/reaction. Those ancient wells with a probable pagan origin receive offerings while those originating in the Christian era do not. Obviously, the name does not make the well!

Clootie wells are common in Scotland, Ireland and particularly in Cornwall. However, wells called "Rag Well" are found in Dublin Ireland, Newcastle and Benton, both in Northumberland showing a wide distribution in Great Britain outside of Cornwall. In fact, this particular form of offering appears to be wide spread throughout the world from Britain to Turkey to Mongolia. While some Clootie Wells are believed to function only as "wishing wells," most Clootie wells are in reality healing wells. A common practice at the Clootie Wells in Scotland is that an individual wishing a cure must approach the well from the southeast, and drink three handfuls of water while wishing for the desired cure. At this time, a piece of cloth is attached to the tree. Should anyone remove the cloth, the troubles and illnesses of the pilgrim would be transferred to the person removing the cloth. I did not see any evidence that offerings had been removed. Native American people, such as the Kitanemuk living in the Tehachapi Mountains, were also prone to leave offerings at sacred sites. They too believed that death would be the result for anyone stealing from the shrines.[4]

1 Hope, Robert Charles. *The Legendary Lore of the Holy Wells of England.* London: Elliot Stock, 1893, xxii (A facsimile reprint by Llanerch Publishers, Felinfach Wales, 2000)

2 Hardy, Philip Dixon. *The Holy Wells of Ireland.* Dublin: Hardy & Walker, 1840, 29

3 Ibid., 51

4 Blackburn, Thomas C. and Lowell John Bean. "Kitanemuk," in *Handbook of the Indians of California: Volume 8-California.* Washington: Smithsonian Institution 1978, 568

Many of the cloth strips that I saw as votive offerings at holy wells were red or weathered pink in color. Logan wrote that red cloth was left for a wide variety of magickal purposes, stating, "It is the color which is believed to resist the power of evil spirits..."[1]

When I first wrote this book, however, the red color also symbolized the resistance to the modern scourge of humankind in the form of AIDS.

Other accounts note that the individual would dip the rag into the well water and wipe the area of affliction prior to hanging the clootie to the tree.

MacKenzie gives an account of the clootie wells in Crete at the turn of the last century:

> I passed a curious tree covered with fetishes...Near a ruined church stands an olive-tree hung with bits of rag which the peasants tie on the branches, hundreds of shreds of every color, worn by rain and wind...I asked what the curious decoration of the tree was, and was told that anyone who suffered from malarial fever binds it to the tree with a shred of his clothing, a handkerchief, or a ribbon, and says a prayer, hoping to be cured thereby...Rags and dirty bits of stuff, into which the witches profess to have banished diseases, are constantly found in the walls of churches.[2]

Additional rag wells were at Vinnitsa, Ukraine where the ill hung shirts and handkerchiefs after bathing in the holy well there, as well as Ardclines at Antrim, Erregall-Keroge in Tyrone, St. Bartholomew in Waterford and St. Bridgid at Sligo. Another clootie well has been documented at Tuva in a former Russian possession in northwest Mongolia. Ralph Leighton in his book *Tuva or Bust* wrote, "walking in the nearby woods, we descended from the main trail to a mineral spring. Handkerchiefs and strips of cloth...adorned the bushes and trees nearby."[3] The spring here was also a healing spring. In the 1960s, it was still a tradition in Estonia to offer scarves to the "lake mother." As in Great Britain, it was also a common tradition in Estonia to wash the afflicted body part with spring water. In addition, it was common "to cast into the water a clean piece of cloth, towel or handkerchief, some salt, a coin or a piece of silver that had been held at the sick place and wrapped in the cloth."[4] In Wales only a few rag wells are known (approximately 10) and they occur mostly in Glamorgan, one being Ffynnon Cae Moch. The most common form of offering in Wales is the bent pin.

BENT PIN OFFERINGS

How offering pins to the water spirits began as a tradition is unknown. It apparently is more widespread than clootie wells. Kemmis Buckley noted that

---

1 Logan, Patrick. *The Holy Wells of Ireland.* Buckinghamshire: Colin Smythe 1980, 116
2 MacKenzie op. cit., citing writer Angelo Mosso
3 Leighton, Ralph. *Tuva or Bust: Richard Feynman's Last Journey.* New York: W.W. Norton & Company 1991, 223
4 Västrik, Ergo-Hart. "The Water and Water Spirits in Votian Folk Belief," in *Folklore,* Vol. 12, December 1999, 30. Institute of the Estonian Language.

pin offerings are of "considerable antiquity and was widely practiced both in this (Wales) country and on the continent. The latest example of this practice...is at Saint Clare's Well in the parish of Llanarthney...where, even into the 1930s, children used to throw a bent pin into the well and 'wish.'"[1] For good luck, it was best to drop a pin into a holy well on a Saint's day. In Wales, it was customary for newly married women to drop pins into the house-well as soon as she entered her new home to ensure good luck. One account of pin offerings is that of Ffynnnon Enddwyn in Merioneth, Wales. Here, it is said, "pilgrims threw pins into the water to ward off evil spirits.... At some wells also it was the practice to prick one's finger with a pin to draw blood and then throw the pin into the water as an offering..."[2] Obviously, this is a variation of blood offerings that must have pre-Christian origins. While it would seem that pins would be of little value as an offering, Nigel Pennick noted, "in pagan times there was no relic considered unfit to be deposited at a shrine."[3] In fact, it is probable that the pin is a "survivor" offering from the ancient past. Huge amounts of goods, including coins, jewelry, bronze figurines, pottery, weapons, animal and human remains were deposited into rivers, streams and sacred wells. The "Pin Well" located in a County Tyrone Celtic monastery graveyard, has a beech tree, which has been stuck with thousands of pins and nails. Jordan remarks that the practice of sticking pins into trees "is an interesting motif: perhaps it is used to fix and bind the spell, or to control the ghost (if one was thought to frequent the site) and prevent it from doing mischief."[4] In addition, it is believed that individuals would "pin" or "bind" their ailments to the tree and thus transfer the illness.

The Bord's link the offering of pins to a symbolic reference to fertility — specifically to childbirth.[5] It was a traditional practice at St. Piran's Well in Cornwall to drop two pins into the well whenever a child was baptized there. Anecdotal evidence, however, suggests that such offerings are left to ensure good health, to combat blindness, for good luck, etc., and as such are not specific to fertility. Bonwick noted that St. Breward's Well in Wales "cured bad eyes, and received offerings in cash and pins."[6] Pins were used to divine the future at many wells. At St. Gundred's Well near Roche, it was said "maidens would repair on Holy Thursday, to throw in pins and pebbles, and predict coming events by the sparkling of the bubbles which rise up."[7] Alsia Well in Cornwall was also used

---

1 Buckley, op. cit.
2 Rowan. "Buttons, Bras and Pins: The Folklore of British Holy Wells," in *White Dragon*, Lughnasa 1996
3 Pennick, Nigel. *Celtic Sacred Landscapes*. London: Thames & Hudson, 1996, 158
4 Jordan, Katy. *The Haunted Landscape: Folklore, ghosts & legends of Wiltshire*. Bradford on Avon: Ex Libris Press 2000, 47
5 Bord, Janet and Colin. *Earth Rites: Fertility Practices in Pre-Industrial Britain*. London: Granada Publishing Ltd., 1982, 98
6 Bonwick, op. cit., 240
7 Hope, op. cit., 25

by young girls to divine the number of years before their lover would be found. They would drop a pin into the water and count the number of bubbles that rose to the surface — each bubble representing a year. Pins were also used to "get the goodwill of the Piskies" who appear to have been appeased with such an offering at St. Nun's Well in Pelynt, Cornwall.

Perhaps the most reasonable explanation for pin offerings is that given by Walter and Mary Brenneman in their book *Crossing the Circle at the Holy Wells of Ireland:*

> Water and pin both participate in enclosing and securing yet when loosened, bring forth the means of regeneration, a symbolic 'giving'. A pin or brooch given to the water in the well facilitates the freeing of power at that place. The putting together of pins and waters symbolically encourages the releasing of regenerative forces today...[1]

Other wells with pin offerings are found at St. Helen's Well in Sefton, Lancashire where pins were dropped into the well for "good luck" as well as to divine the fidelity of lovers. Pins were also left at Coventina's Well at Carrawburgh, which is associated with the Roman fort of Brocolitia; Pin Well at Chepstow, Monmouthshire where supposedly the healing powers of the water could be tested by dropping a pin into it, and at St. Ninian's or Pin Well in Alnwick, Northumberland where it was believed a faery maintained the well and had to be propitiated by an offering of a bent pin. Pins stuck in cork were floated in the wells of Ffynnon Elian and Llanylian yn Rhos in Wales. Jones and Pennick report that "on the island of Maelrubha in Loch Maree, the sacred oak tree of Mhot-Ri was studded with nails to which ribbons were tied. The sacred oak was associated with a healing well reportedly capable of curing insanity.[2]

Pin wells in Ireland are St. Boey's in County Leitrim, St. Finan's at Killemlagh, County Kerry, Sunday Well, and St. John's Well at Drumcullen Abbey in County Offaly, Pin Well in County Armagh and at Magherinagaw in County Antrim. Another site in Ireland is called the Bay of the Pin where, in Celtic myth, a baby god was pinned in a cloth to be drowned by the king. The baby slipped out of his binding, through the release of the pin, and grew to fulfill his destiny in slaying his grandfather and becoming the new ruler.

Offerings such as these at the various Holy Wells resulted in several attempts by the Church, both in Early and Medieval times as well as the Protestant clergy, to suppress it. The Council of Rouen in the seventh century declared such offerings as "sacrifices to the devil."[3]

---

1 Brenneman, Walter L. & Mary G. *Crossing the Circle at the Holy Wells of Ireland.* Charlottesville: University Press of Virginia 1995, 17-18

2 Jones, Prudence and Nigel Pennick. *A History of Pagan Europe.* New York: Barnes & Noble, Inc. 1995, 107

3 Bonwick, op. cit., 239

Other sacrifices to wells, involving both animal and human were, however, common in the past.

OFFERINGS OF FOOD

Many of the wells I visited in Cornwall, which had votive offerings of rags, figurines, coins, crystals and other items, also had small food offerings. I, my-self, participated in the tradition and left small cakes for the Faery Folk at St. Nectan's Glenn. Sometimes pieces of bread were used to divine future events. If the bread floated it was a favorable sign, if it sank bad news was in waiting. It was a practice of sailors to toss pieces of bread into the water at the fountain of Recourrance (also known as St. Laurence) near Morbihan to determine favour-able sailing conditions. If the bread floated, the weather would be fair but if it sank no fishing boat should put to sea. The act of throwing pieces of bread into springs was so common during the 5th century that St. Martin of Braga called it an act of Devil worship.[1] A lake near Gëvaudan, France received pieces of cheese, bread and beeswax among other things as offerings. Until the 1950s, lumps of butter were cast into rivers and streams in Ireland on certain dates when farmers would swim their cattle and horses across to protect them from diseases. It was believed that the butter would activate the healing powers of the water, which would restore the livestock to health.

Bread and rags were left at Doo Loch in Scotland after patients were sprin-kled or immersed in the healing waters for treatment of palsy.

Near Inverness, Scotland a "cheese well" exists and it was thought that such an offering of cheese would enable pilgrims to see in foggy mists so that they would not become lost.

ANIMAL AND HUMAN SACRIFICIAL OFFERINGS

Animal and human sacrifices have occurred over thousands of years in almost every location where large groups of people have resided. These events, although obviously distasteful and against modern mores, were only observed when a great need dictated them. Droughts, famine, war — times of cultural calamity were often met with a sacrifice to offer a sacred life in exchange for a resolution to the disaster. As we will see, some of these rituals continue in modern ages in the form of folk festivals.

One of the oldest possible examples of human offering was discovered in the Kissonerga region north of Paphos, Cyprus.[2] The ancient well was unearthed by researchers from the University of Edinburgh in 1994 and was found to contain the entire skeletal remains of a child along with bones of sheep, pig and deer and

1 Hillgarth, J.N. *The Conversion of Western Europe, 370-750.* Englewood Cliffs: Prentice-Hall, Inc. 1969, 61
2 Freeman, Mara. "Sacred Waters, Holy Wells," in *Parabola*, Volume XX, Number 1, Spring 1995, 55

seeds of domesticated plants. There is no evidence that the child was sacrificed and it is quite probable that it was simply buried in the well with the other items after death.

The bones have been dated to 8300 BCE and may represent the earliest settlement of Crete. It may also represent one of the earliest human offerings to a sacred well. Nearby another well, somewhat younger in age, was found to contain the skulls of more humans as well as animal bones. This theme, as we will see below, was common throughout Europe and over vast stretches of time.

Many holy wells in Britain have contained the severed head of one or more individuals. The Celtic head cult was very much associated with the reverence of water. This ancient ritual has been carried over in many of the Christian legends concerning the founding of many wells dedicated to specific saints. Mara Freeman noted in her essay *Sacred Waters, Holy Wells* that Celtic well-pilgrims would drink water from sacred wells and pools only from a cup made from a human skull, believing that by doing so they created a direct link between the living and the residents of the Underworld.[1] This practice continued at a well in Pembrokeshire into the twentieth century.

Human skulls have been found in Coventina's Well at Carrawburgh and the River Trent in Nottinghamshire dating back to the late Neolithic, as well as at Caves Inn and a first century well in London. The placing of human heads in wells and other sacred water sites may have a dual meaning, healing and regeneration as well as resurrection from death. It is probably this last meaning that gave rise to the many Christian myths associated with wells. Ralph Merrifield noted that the placing of skulls in wells can only occasionally be attributed to a well that "is itself demonstrably a holy place and the home of a water deity...more usually they occur in wells that have previously been used to supply water for domestic or industrial purposes, and are reminders of the pervasive character of ancient religion in everyday life."[2]

Many holy wells, according to Christian mythology, originated instantly when the head of a decapitated saint landed on the ground. One of these wells is at Holywell, Wales. St. Winifred's Well is probably the most continuously used sacred well in Britain. In use since pre-Christian times, it is the primary holy well of Britain and continues to attract pilgrims from around the world. According to legend, St. Winifred (whose real name was Gwenfrewi) was a seventh century nun living in Wales. One day Prince Caradog came upon her while she was alone and attempted to rape young Gwenfrewi. She fought him off and ran toward a nearby church where the Prince caught her and cut off her head. Brother Beuno who resided at the church cursed the Prince who (depending on the version of the story) immediately melted. The brother then put Gwenfrewi's head back on

1 "8300 B.C. Child's Remains in Cyprus" in *The Globe and Mail*, December 30, 1999
2 Merrifield, Ralph. *The Archaeology of Ritual and Magic*. New York: New Amsterdam Books 1987, 45

her severed neck, prayed over her and restored her to life. The place where her head fell immediately burst open in a spring of healing water. As the monk and Gwenfrewi sat and discussed the event, he told her that anyone who came to that spot and prayed for assistance would receive it. From that time on the well became a place for pilgrims to visit. There is evidence that Gwenfrewi actually lived and was a member of the royal Powysian family, which included St. Tenoi, her aunt and St. Beuno, the same monk who restored her to life who was also her uncle. St. Winifred's well is the most visited and best known holy well in Wales today. There is also another St. Winifred's Well located in Shropshire, England with the same legend attached to it.

A very similar legend is that of St. Eluned. Eluned, one of twenty-four daughters of a fifth century Welsh king by the name of Brychan Brycheiniog, became a Christian at a very young age. One day a pagan prince tried to force himself upon her and after tracking her down across Wales, he caught her and beheaded her. Her head rolled down a hill until it came to rest against a stone where a spring miraculously burst forth. While Eluned's head did not rejoin her body as St. Winifred's did, the spring (located at Slwch) became known for its healing properties. St. Eluned's feast day is August 1st — the same date for the pagan celebration of Lammas (also known as Lugnasadh, a harvest festival).

Another, almost identical tale, is that of Saint Noyale in Brittany. A pagan prince, once more enamored by the young maiden who refused his advances, chased Noyale and her nurse from England to Brittany where they had sailed on a leaf. Still refusing the prince, he struck her head off with his sword. Noyale picked her head up and, with the assistance of her nurse walked back to her home. On her way, drops of blood from the head fell to the ground creating instant fountains. Where the saint finally died is now the village of Ste-Noyale.

Other holy wells, which sprang from the spots where heads fell, are at St. Juthware's at Clent and St. Osyth's in Essex. The legend surrounding St. Fremund tells of the saint washing his severed head in a well in Warwickshire. St. Thomas's well at Windleshaw was created when the saint was beheaded during a time of Roman Catholic persecution.

Many more stories of the early saints (almost all reported to have lived during the sixth century) abound with their decapitations resulting in living, healing springs. In France St. Julian of Brioude was beheaded with his head falling near a spring that was later said to cure headaches! The sacred springs of Alesia in Burgundy, even though in use long before Christianity, are said to have resulted from the decapitation of St. Reine. The Fountain of St. Osyth in Essex, England is another. The well, named after a saint who was decapitated by the Danes in the 7th century, sprang forth where the saint's head fell. Hope wrote that "her head was cut off; the body rose, and taking the head in her hand walked — guided by angels — to the church. Here it knocked at the door, and then fell to the ground."[1] The Fountain of St. Osyth became known as a healing well, "a remedy for many diseases." It is said that the ghost of St. Osyth still walks with head in hand through Nun's Wood and visits the well and church on a regular basis.

A similar story is that of St. Decuman who, it is said, was murdered by "pagan robbers" and, of course, beheaded. Where the head fell, "a great spring of water appeared" which is now known as St. Decuman's Well, located in Watchett, Somerset. The legend says that after the saint lost his head he picked it up and carried it to the well.[2] As previously mentioned some wells have a tradition that by only drinking the water from a certain skull will healing be obtained. This is true of St. Teilo's skull used at the well named after him located at Llandeilo Llwydiarth in Pembrokeshire. Evidently the water from the well "was said to be particularly effective in the treatment of chest complaints and it was doubly so if it was drunk out of the skull."[3] Epilepsy was effectively treated in Scotland by drinking well water from the skull of one's own ancestor and it is said that skulls were often kept at wells for the use of pilgrims.

Sheila Livingston noted in her book *Scottish Customs* "the skull of a suicide was eagerly sought after and treasured. It was supposed to be dug up after sunset and before sunrise to be used as a vessel for water from a holy well. If it was given to an epileptic to drink and the operation was conducted in silence a cure would result."[4]

Contemporary survivals of the "head cult" are found at St. Ciaran's Well, St. Patrick's Well and the Well of the Wether's in Ireland where carvings of heads have been worn down from being kissed and rubbed by pilgrims for hundreds of years. Diana's Well in East Witton has a large stone carving of a head in which the well water spews forth. In addition, St. Helen's Well in Wharfedale, Yorkshire, has three skulls slightly submerged in the semi-circular curbstones, which retains the well water.

Other peculiar forms of human sacrificial offerings at wells included that of the Roman site of Goadby in Leicestershire. The well there contained the skeletons of two humans who had been buried headfirst and then covered with stones. An obvious survival of this ritual death is mentioned in the 1911 essay of Charles J. Billson called *Vestiges of Paganism in Leicestershire*:

> Among other customs of pagan origin may be mentioned the time-honoured practice of "Beating the Bounds," which is still maintained in some parishes....[W]hen the procession of boundary-beaters reached Redhill, near the Narborough Road, "a homily was read by the vicar in a part of the field surrounded by a bank of earth, after which a hole was dug, and any

1 Hope, op. cit., 73
2 Harte, J.M. "The Holy Wells of Somerset," in *The Source*, Issue #2, July 1985
3 Buckley, Kemmis. "Llandeilo Llwydiarth-The Well and the Skull," in *The Source*, Issue 2, Winter 1994
4 Livingstone, Sheila. *Scottish Customs*. New York: Barnes & Noble 1996, 87

newly appointed parish officer was seized, turned topsy-turvey, and his head placed in the hole, whilst his "latter end" was saluted with the shovel. It was also usual to flog a boy at certain points of the parish boundary, ostensibly to make him remember them. But both these proceedings suggest a very attenuated form of survivals from the days of human sacrifice.[1]

Similar upside-down "burials" have been found at Cadbury in the foundation of the hill-fort said to be Arthur's Camelot,[2] as well as at Maiden Castle and Nod Hill, all Iron Age forts. The famous Celtic cauldron known as the Gundestrup Cauldron depicts a god or priest holding a man upside down over a cauldron — presumably in the act of drowning the victim. Mallory noted in his book, *In Search of the Indo-Europeans* that drowning was one means to satisfy fertility deities.[3] However, it is also possible that the scene depicted is that of The Daghda holding an individual over the Cauldron of Regeneration to bring life back to the individual's body rather than to take it away.

Some of these sacrifices were undoubtedly representative of the "Threefold Death" which was common among the Germanic and Celtic cultures. The most famous of these is the Lindow Man who was, if not a Druid (mistletoe was found in his stomach which is a strong indication that this man was a Druid), a young man of some royal bearing who was bludgeoned, garroted and had his throat slashed prior to being placed in a shallow bog pool.[4] While some researchers do not believe that the archaeological evidence indicates that the ancient British practiced human sacrifice,[5] it would appear from the evidence thus far illustrated in this text that sacrifice was an important part of ancient British society.

Animal sacrifices were much more common in wells, springs and rivers. Dogs apparently were the most favored of sacrificial animals; recall that the hound is associated with the Wild Huntsman and the journey to the Underworld. In addition, dogs are associated with the goddess Hecate and were often sacrificed to her. To the Celts, the dog was especially esteemed and was used many times in mythology and incorporated into the names of Celtic gods. The 200-foot well at Muntham Court, in Sussex had numerous dog skeletons as well as a "votive" leg, made from clay, indicating that the well was valued for its healing properties. In other wells, such as Coventina's, dog figurines were given to the well instead of

---

1 Bilson, Charles. *Vestiges of Paganism in Leicestershire.* Loughborough: Heart of Albion Press, 1994, 17 (a reprint of the 1911 edition published by George Allen)

2 Alcock, Leslie. Was This Camelot? Excavations at Cadbury Castle 1966-70. New York: Stein and Day 1972, 103

3 Mallory, J.P. *In Search of the Indo-Europeans: Language, Archaeology and Myth.* London: Thames and Hudson, 1989, 139

4 Green, Miranda J. *The World of the Druids.* London: Thames and Hudson, 1997, 81. See also Dr. Green's article, "The Religious Symbolism of Llyn Cerrig Bach and Other Early Sacred Water Sites" in *The Source,* Issue 1, Autumn 1994

5 NicBhride, Feorag. "The application of archaeological theory to the study of 'Celtic' water cults, with particular reference to holy wells studies." A talk given to the Perth Source Moot, 1998

actual animals. Dogs in early Celtic society were symbolic of both healing and death. These two symbolic aspects are reflective moreover, of the dogs' representation of rebirth and their sacrifice to wells, pits and ritual shafts is fitting.

It is interesting that the use of dog skulls to rub ointment on the swollen legs of horses and cattle continued into the 17th century and this method of healing was thought to be even more effective of the local priest had blessed the skull beforehand.[1]

Hutton and Merrifield note that dogs were frequently sacrificed to wells at the time of the termination of the well's use — especially during the Roman occupation of Britain. A pair of dogs was sacrificed at Farnworth in Gloucestershire during the 4th century CE, two in Southwark dated to the 3rd century and eight pairs in a well in Surrey (along with red-deer antler, two complete dishes and a broken flagon).[2] A recent excavation at an ancient well at Shiptonthorpe in Yorkshire uncovered a number of dog skulls as well as the remains of bundles of mistletoe. Because mistletoe was so important in Druidic rites, this well may have been an important ritual site.

Other animals found sacrificed in wells include birds, cows and horses. Again, these animals were also represented in figurines as well as skeletal remains. Horses, like dogs, were especially valued as sacrifices due to their close relationships to, and value by, humans. Squire wrote "in olden times the rich would sacrifice one of their horses at a well near Abergeleu, to secure a blessing upon the rest." The Scandinavians and Celts often sacrificed horses to rivers and the seas among many other people in the Indo-European regions, as did the Japanese. Andrews wrote, "they sacrificed horses to the sea gods because horses symbolized the power of the mighty waves. People sacrificed bulls to waterfalls because they likened the roar of the bull to the sound of falling water, and they sacrificed black sheep to the rain gods because they likened their dark fleecy bodies to the dark fluffy clouds."[3] Fowls were offered at St. Tegla's Well, near Wrexham, by "epileptic patients."[4] While figurines are commonly found deposited in wells and other sacred water sites, at times whole animals or parts of animals were also used. At Bekesbourne in Kent, a circle of horse teeth had been deposited as well as whole pots.

In Estonia, the head of a black cat was thrown into the waters of the sea, lake or river to ensure a good catch of fish. Also in Estonia, it was traditional to sacrifice a ram and offer the head and feet to the River Lauga on St. Elijah's Day

1 Briggs, Robin. *Witches & Neighbors: The Social and Cultural Context of European Witchcraft.* New York: Viking Press 1996, 121

2 Hutton, Ronald. *The Pagan Religions of the Ancient British Isles: Their Nature and Legacy.* Oxford: Blackwell Publishers Ltd., 1991, 231 and Merrifield, op. cit., 47

3 Andrews, Tamra. *A Dictionary of Nature Myths: Legends of the earth, Sea, and Sky.* Oxford: Oxford University Press 1998, 166

4 Squire, Charles. *Celtic Myths & Legends.* New York: Portland House, 1997, 415

(July 20th or August 2nd) to avoid human drowning caused by water spirits.[1] Tradition in Kingsteignton, Devon required that a lamb be sacrificed each Whit Monday. According to the Radfords:

> ...way back in history, the village suffered a dearth of water, and the inhabitants prayed to their pagan gods for the liquid. A spring welled up in reply and ever afterwards supplied all the needs of the villagers. So the lamb was annually sacrificed.[2]

Pots, Pans, Coins and Weapons

The most common offering in sacred wells and waterways is that of metal. The Celts used to give back to the gods what they took in battle. After ritually breaking them, thousands of weapons were periodically tossed into the Thames and other rivers, wells and springs. One such offering occurred at Illerup, Denmark. "Here the equipment of about seventy warriors had been burned on a pyre, and the swords and shields collected from the ashes, deliberately bent and dented, and carried into the middle of the bog...Some of the weapons were flung into a deep pool, and others left lying on the earth nearby, in a spot still reputed to be haunted."[3] This offering was made somewhere around 400 CE. That metal offerings became so common as far back as the Bronze Age signifies, according to Merrifield, "a fundamental religious change in the Middle Bronze Age, when the old gods of sky and earth...were displaced in favour of water deities."[4] Merrifield speculates that such a displacement may have been the result of climatic changes.

At the "Giant's Spring" at Duchov, Czech Republic, a huge bronze cauldron filled with 2,000 bronze bracelets, brooches and other items had been deposited in dedication to local deities around the third or second century BCE. It is possible that at Duchov the natural spring was particularly sacred to women.

At Toulouse, gold and silver ingots had been offered to a lake, and at Lake Neuchatel, Iron Age offerings of 400 brooches, 270 spears, 170 swords and 27 shields were cast into the waters. In many Northern European lakes large cauldrons have been found, including the famous Gundestrup Cauldron, the Bra Cauldron from Jutland (which could hold 600 litres) and the Orastie Cauldron from the Czech Republic. The Orastie Cauldron, dating from the 6th or 7th century BCE, was so large it had to be mounted on wheels.[5]

Coins were also popular votive offerings. At Coventina Well in Carrawburgh dedicated to the British water goddess, more than 16,000 coins have been recov-

---

1 Västrik, op. cit 19 & 25

2 Radford, E. and M.A. *Encyclopaedia of Superstitions.* New York: The Philosophical Library 1949, 207

3 Davidson, H.R. Ellis. *The Gods and Myths of the Viking Age.* New York: Bell Publishing Company 1964, 56

4 Merrifield, op. cit 24

5 Green, Miranda. *The Gods of the Celts.* Phoenix Mill: Sutton Publishing, 1986, 147

ered from a sacred well used not only by the Britains but also by the Romans soldiers.[1] In a spring at Horton in Dorsetshire, a small cache of 140 Roman coins dating back to Augustus along with seven vases was found in 1875 and a "heap" of coins dating from the Roman Republic was found by London Bridge. Coins, curse tablets and small "sun wheels" were tossed into the pools at Bath as offerings to Sulis, an important water goddess believed to have given healing properties to the hot springs known as Aquae Sulis.

Photo 35: The Sacred Waters at Bath

A common practice during the Middle Ages was for pilgrims to toss their "pilgrims' badges," small pewter and lead souvenirs purchased at individual shrines, into rivers. Nowadays these are sometimes found at river crossings and, in fact, 250 were discovered in 1977 on the south bank of the Thames River. Merrifield speculates that these badges were believed to be protective amulets and were thrown into the water to invoke a saint's protection or to give an offering in thanks for safe passage received.[2]

Perhaps the original story of El Dorado, which caused the eventual downfall of the Aztec tribes, can be attributed to a man and not a place. El Indio Dorado, the Golden Indian, was said to be a chief who, once a year, would cover himself

---

1 Scullard, H.H. *Roman Britain: Outpost of the Empire*. London: Thames and Hudson, 1986, 161
2 Merrifield, op. Cit., 109

in gold dust, float out on Lake Guatavita, 31 miles northeast of Bogotá, and throw jewels and other golden items into the lake in sacrifice.[1]

WISHING WELLS

The tradition of tossing coins into fountains and wells is an ancient one and still obviously continued today. It is doubtful that many of us realize just how far back in history it is that the offerings to sacred waterways (now referred to as "wishing wells ") still prompts us to toss coins into them.

Pliny the Younger wrote of the many coins glittering in the shallow waters of one of the Italian rivers. The obvious intent is to give up a possession of some value in exchange for something desired — be it health, wealth, love or some other item of value. Originally, it was an act of sacrifice. The coins we toss in a fountain today may not have the same value they did in far earlier times but the act is the same — even if the act of tossing the coins has become automatic rather than thought out. Examples of ancient wishing wells are those of Menacuddle ("the hawk's stone") Well near St. Austell in Cornwall and St. Gundred's which is north of St. Austell, which was also used for divination purposes. In Dorset-shire at Upwey, there is a wishing well where one used to take a glass full of water, drink from it, make a wish and then toss the rest over the shoulder.

Another wishing well is located at Ashwell, England (the town was named after a sacred ash tree that grew near the holy well). An inscription above the well reads:

> All ye who hither come to drink,
> Rest not your thoughts below,
> Look at that sacred sign and think,
> Whence living waters flow.

St. Boniface's Well in Hampshire was also viewed as a wishing well and if one were to walk backward to the well while drinking its water and making a wish at the same time the wish would be granted. Also in Dorsetshire at Abbotsbury, near St. Catherine's chapel, is a wishing well where, again, wishes were made after drinking from the well. Hope noted that single women visiting this well would use the following invocation:

> A husband, St. Catherine
> A handsome one, St. Catherine
> A rich one, St. Catherine
> A nice one, St. Catherine
> And soon, St. Catherine [2]

The wishing-wells at Walsingham were once renowned for their healing of head and stomach disorders but by the late 19th century had taken on the pow-

1 Fish, Brenda. "The Legend of El Dorado," in *Legends of the World*. Richard Cavendish, editor. New York: Barnes and Noble 1994, 259
2 Hope, op. cit 67

ers of granting wishes instead. Only silent wishes made while drinking of the well's waters had the possibility of realization although it could take as long as twelve months. A similar silent wish requirement with a twelve-month period of realization was at the Bore-Well in Bingfield, Northumberland. However, the Bore-Well's power to grant wishes appears to have been most effective for the cure of barrenness.

TWENTIETH CENTURY OFFERINGS

Doon Well in County Donegal has the most varied of offerings. An old photograph dating to the first half of the 20th century shows a field of crutches swathed in rags standing upright in front of the well. Crutches left presumably as offerings of thanks by those cured or as a symbol of the ailment that the individual desired to be rid of. The offerings have changed over the years and in the 1980s it was common to see not only rags tied to bushes but eyeglasses, asthmatic ventilators and menstrual tampons.[1]

As previously mentioned I saw offerings of cloth strips, or rags, food and figurines at many wells in Cornwall which attest to the continued popularity of pilgrimages to holy wells and the belief that an exchange between the human and the divine is still possible. Rag wells continue to exist and to flourish. The old traditions continue to thrive.

WELL DRESSING

"Well dressing," also known as "well flowering," was originally a pagan propitiation of the water deities and continues as an annual ritual in Britain, France and in many Mediterranean countries. During the well dressing the local holy well is decorated with a wooden framework which is then coated with flowers, leaves, berries, moss, feathers, seeds, cones and other vegetative matter. Many times, the leaves and flowers are fashioned into pictures, normally of a biblical scene. In the past, the decorated boards were placed over the running water so that it appeared that the water was issuing from the arrangements of flowers and leaves. The early Christian Church banned well dressings, referring to the practice as "well worship." Church councils under King Edgar, King Canute and the Archbishop of Canterbury in 1102, prohibited well dressings as reflecting pagan tradition. Today most well dressings are done with the approval, if not participation, of the local church.

The framework, with the vegetative Christian pictures, is usually manufactured the night before the celebration and carried in a procession, either a joyful one with dancing and floats, or paraded soberly, to the well. At this point, the local vicar blesses the well thus ensuring a supply of water for the community into the next year. As noted in *A History of Pagan Europe*, "originally a local saint

---

1 Delaney, Frank. *The Celts.* London: Grafton Books 1989, 86

was associated with the well, the successor of the original Celtic deity, but this feature has sometimes been lost in Protestant times."[1]

For some reason Derbyshire in England has the largest number of villages which dress wells, approximately 14. Well dressing in these towns occurs mostly in May (the pagan festival of Beltaine) or at Midsummer (the equinox). Similar well dressings have occurred at the seven wells of Brisley on Ascension Day since the 19th century. After a short church service, the local vicar, a band and the townsfolk parade to the wells where they are blessed and decorated with flowers.[2]

This form of ritual has remained unchanged since the early 1800s and most likely far longer. R.R. Rawlins, in a letter to a British magazine in 1823, wrote:

> The method of decorating the Wells is this. The flowers are inserted in moist clay, and put upon boards, cut in various forms, surrounded with boughs of laurel and white-thorn, so as to give an appearance of water issuing from small grottoes. The flowers are adjusted and arranged in various patterns, to give the effect of mosaic work, having inscribed upon them texts of Scripture...[3]

Rawlins wrote that he believed the custom of well dressing "originated among Christians, to commemorate the return of the spring." However, evidence indicates that the origin of well-dressing may have originated with the Roman incursion. The Roman festival of Fortinalia involved decorating springs in greenery as a gift to the water nymphs. Fortinalia was named after Fontus, the son of the god Janus. Fontus was a name derived from Fons meaning, "Well." Knowlson noted in 1910 that well dressings "show how an old superstition can be purified of its worst elements, and transformed into a truly Christian celebration." [4] On the Black Isle in Scotland a faery pool existed, which children would visit each summer to dress the well with white stones and flowers "for the little people."

While many wells had an annual well-dressing festival in the past, until very recently only residents in Derbyshire and Staffordshire had continued the tradition. Over the years, many of the sacred wells of Great Britain have become neglected and forgotten. Recently, however, due to the renewed interest in the Old Religions and traditional ways of the past, many of these wells have been renewed, "revenerated" and incorporated into the contemporary well dressing festivals. One man in a Cambridgeshire village recently wrote that:

> ...the village in which I live...has lost over the years many of the old traditions which marked it as a typical rural Fen village. As more and more

1 Jones, Prudence and Nigel Pennick, op. cit., 84
2 Hunt, Laurence. "Some Ancient Wells, Springs and Holy Wells of the Cotswolds," in *The Source*, Issue #4, Winter 1995
3 Rawlins, R.R. "On the Ancient Custom of Decorating Wells with Flowers, etc.," reprinted in *The Source*, Issue #2, July 1985
4 Knowlson, T. Sharper. *The Origins of Popular Superstitions and Customs*. London: T. Werner Laurie Ltd., 1910, 200

modern housing is erected on what was once farmland, I suppose this is sadly inevitable.

I have been aware of the existence of an old disused well in the village for some time now, but it was only about three days ago that the thought struck me of the ancient festival of 'Well Dressing'!

I enquired from a very knowledgeable local man (Old Harry) as to how old it was and how deep, etc. He informed me that it was only discovered in 1979 when a wall was being built, that it was clay lined and 22 feet deep! He knows because he went down it! The owner of the wall was all for filling the well in, but Old Harry stopped him and now the Well is built into the wall as a feature.

Old Harry (who is the leading light in the local History Society) thinks my idea of 'Well Dressing' is a great one, and the pair of us are now pursuing the matter with the owner and the local Parish council. This is something that the entire village can join in.

I dare say that the local church will want a hand in it, but more importantly so will the small but growing band of local Pagans...next Spring the village will have it's own sacred well![1]

In the last year, traditional well dressings have occurred at Frome in Somerset, Malvern Hills, Knutsford in Cheshire and Derby City. Well dressings have come into popularity once again in the British Isles. In fact, well dressing has become so popular that even villages without a holy well invent them just for the festivities. One such village in Derbyshire has recently obtained an old horse trough that has been festooned in the traditional way.

Cursing Wells

While most wells are renowned for their healing power, good luck and connections to such mystical beings as elves, goblins and saints, some were used for a darker purpose — to curse.

Although pins and rags were left at healing and wishing wells, people who believed that they had been wronged left lead tablets inscribed with pleas for revenge to the gods and goddesses at other wells. Placing curses in wells was particularly popular with the Roman's in Britain. In fact, the practice of writing curses as pleas to the gods was widespread throughout the Mediterranean.[2] Some of the curses discovered so far were written to fix horse races, win legal disputes, destroy rival businesses, and to obtain lovers. In addition, curses were commonly used to call down punishments on thieves such as this one recovered from the Little Ouse River in Suffolk:

---

1   Bamford, Ken. Personal Communication. December 8, 2000
2   Green, Miranda. *The World of the Druids*, op. cit., 46

...whether male slave or female slave, whether freedman or freedwoman, whether woman or man...has committed the theft of an iron pan, he is sacrificed to the Lord Neptune with hazel.[1]

This particular tablet dates from the 5th century showing the continuation of pagan traditions long after the supposed destruction of the Druids and the Old Religion.

Lead curse tablets, often rolled in thin layers, found at Bath in the Temple of Sulis and at Uley were of a highly formulaic magical invocation. Priests or professional scribes carefully wrote these tablets, mostly in Greek and Latin. Of the more than 1600 lead tablets known, two thirds were written in Greek, the rest in Latin. Fifty tablets were found in 1994 in a well at Caesarea Maritima in Israel. In 1977 162 rolled curses were found at Uley in Gloucestershire were they were probably nailed to the temple walls. These tablets date from the 4th century CE. The intent of these curses was simply to inscribe the name, if known, of the individual who was thought to be the evildoer with a related curse. It was believed that the name and the person were one of spirit and easily punished through this method. The most common curse was to address a theft. Another tablet read, "I fix Tertia Maria and her life and mind and memory and liver and lungs...fate, thoughts, memory..."[2] — a very all-encompassing curse affecting this person's total existence.

More recently, a lead tablet written in Greek was discovered at the old kingdom of Amathus on the island of Cyprus. Part of the text reads: "May your penis hurt when you make love." This tablet has been dated to the 7th century CE, long after Christianity had been established on Cyprus. Archaeologists believe that it signifies a survival of pagan shamanism or witchcraft.[3]

Curses such as these probably originated with the Greeks as katadesmoi, a form of "aggressive magic" which was used to bind individuals to a particular fate, a fate of being turned over to the demons and ghosts of the dead. Katadesmoi were in use from the 5th century BCE throughout the Mediterranean area.

Curse tablets were commonly left in graves to bind the souls of the dead and in wells. Lead was the chief material used, as it was cheap, soft to allow writing, and cold to "chill" the intended victim. Daniel Ogden notes that most of the tablets were addressed to specific gods but one, at least, was used to address the specific spring it was placed in and another a ghost that inhabited a well.[4] It is thought that by placing these tablets in wells and springs the intended curse

---

1   Ibid., 73

2   Scullard, op. cit., 160

3   "Sex Curse found at ancient Cyprus site: report" Agence France-Presse, *http://afp.google. com/article/ALeqM5gs7KYHLwaf0TeF4bnNkYplxS6ZvQ*, 7/12/2008.

4   Ogden, Daniel. "Binding Spells: Curse Tablets and Voodoo Dolls in the Greek and Roman World," in *Witchcraft and Magic in Europe: Ancient Greece and Rome*. Edited by Bengt Ankarloo and Stuart Clark. Philadelphia: University of Pennsylvania Press 1999, 23

would be that much more effective since the water sources would also transmit the message to the Underworld and the "infernal powers" that resided there.[1] Ogden reports the find of a "recipe" for the manufacture of curse tablets which recommends that the tablets, after completion "be deposited in 'river, land, sea, stream, coffin or well'." Early Greek tablets found in wells, according to Ogden, "may have been...thrown down the well as rubbish."[2] This seems unlikely with the prescribed "recipe" noted above unless the power of the well's water to purify was regarded as the perfect way to dispose of negative energy.

Photo 36: 2nd century CE lead curse tablet uncovered at Leicester, England. (Photo courtesy University of Leicester)

The practice of leaving written curses at wells continued long after the Roman's left Britain — in fact well into the 19th century. At St. Aelian's (also spelled "Elian") Well at Llanelian yn Rhos, writing curses flourished into the early 19th century. The names of the victims were scratched on slate tablets or written on parchment and placed inside the well. Pins were also tossed into the well while curses were uttered over them. Reportedly a "keeper" was stationed at St. Elian's and for a price the curse could be retrieved. This keeper also supervised the casting of curses into the beginning of the 19th century. Curses were also written on pieces of paper and placed under a stone at St. Cybi's Well near Holyhead. St. Cybi's was also a healing and a wishing well. It should be noted that not all curs-

1 Ibid.
2 Ibid., 15

es were meant to inflict evil on people. Janet Bord notes that people would also go to the well to curse their particular ailments, hoping for a cure as a result: "a cancer could be cured by cursing it, while the sufferer washed in the well water (at Penrhos), and dropped pins around the well."[1] Other reasons for the use of lead curse tablets were litigation curses, competition curses, trade curses, erotic curses to attract or to repel lovers, and prayers for justice.[2]

The placing of curses was also a practice in rural America through the early 20th century. It was common to place harmful substances and tokens along paths taken by the intended victim so that the individual coming into contact with them would absorb the harmful energy. Public wells were preferred places to leave "conjure bags" as were surrounding trees and bushes.[3]

Votive offerings of pins, discussed earlier, also had another purpose as part of the cursing ritual. Bord wrote, "[P]eople cursing their enemies at the holy well close to Llanllawer churchyard (Pembrokeshire) would throw bent pins into the water, while straight pins were used if the wishes were good ones."[4] Joseph Downes mentioned cursing implements in a story printed in the July 1845 issue of *Blackwood's Edinburgh Magazine*:

> "Curse him to St, Elian!" roared the other; then dropping his voice into a solemn tone, "put him into his well."

Downes supplies a footnote to this exclamation:

> St. Elian. – A Saint of Wales. There is a well bearing him name; one of the many of the holy wells or *Ffynnonan*, in Wales. A man whom Mr Pennant had affronted, threatened him with this terrible vengeance. Pins, or other little offerings, are thrown in, and the curses uttered over them.[5]

Votive offerings are still very much in existence today. As mentioned earlier, one of the most interesting was a small white statue of Merlin left on a niche inside the well at Sancreed. While many leave their offerings under a Christian guise, the purpose remains as it has for time untold, one far more attuned to pagan gods and goddesses, Faery Folk and the other denizens of the Other World.

---

1 Bord, Janet. "Cursing Not Curing: The Darker Side of Holy Wells," in *The Source*, Issue #4, Summer 1995

2 Ogden, op. cit., 31

3 Hand, op. cit., 222

4 Bord, "Cursing Not Curing," op. cit

5 Downes, Joseph. "David the 'Telynwr;' Or, the Daughter's Trial: A Tale of Wales," in *Blackwoods Edinburgh Magazine*, Vol. 58 (357) July 1845, 96

Chapter 5. Myths and Legends

There are as many myths and legends surrounding sacred wells and waters as there are sacred wells and waters! Many wells have a multitude of stories and traditions centered on them while others just have elusive snippets of ancient lore. The importance of water as a sacred element is reflected in the number of myths and legends associated with it throughout time and throughout all cultures. "Living water" represents both physical and spiritual life, it purifies, it renews. Living water also is symbolic of the transmission of knowledge and the transmission of the fertile power of nature. It is a passageway to the Underworld and to Heaven. These elements are all parts of the many myths discussed below.

Many of the Celtic saints were said to create holy springs by striking the ground with their staves. Such miracles have also been attributed to St. Patrick at Tobar Lastra (Well of Light) in Ireland, St. Arthmael of Wales and St. Fingar in Brittany among others. The Norse god Baldar also created a spring after a battle so that his soldiers could satisfy their thirst. Poseidon was said to have created a spring near Athens with his staff and Moses is said to have created a spring from a rock in the same manner. In addition, Moses was said to have purified a well by casting a tree of unknown species into the waters under God's direction.[1] In "modern" times, Thomas Becket is credited with the creation of a spring and subsequent well at Otford in Kent, England by sticking his staff into the ground. Likewise, the rector of North Marston, Sir John, is said to have caused a healing chalybeate spring to burst from the ground when he struck it with his staff in the 1300s.[2] This particular theme is not isolated to Europe or the Middle East for

1 King James version, Holy Bible, Exodus 15:25 and 17:6
2 Westwood, Jennifer. *Albion: A Guide to Legendary Britain*. London: Paladin Grafton Books 1987, 147

the ancient Hawaiians also told of Ka-ne, the "water finder," using his staff to smash lava rocks, producing a large pool of clear, cool water. Springs and pools found throughout the Islands are called Ka-Wai-a-ke-Akua, meaning, "the water provided by a god."[1] Ka-ne was also the guardian of the Water of Life. According to legend, anyone who was able to obtain this water of life would also obtain the powers of the gods. According to Westervelt, "a sick person drinking it would recover health, and a dead person sprinkled with it would be restored to life."

Giraldus Cambrensis, also known as Gerald of Wales, wrote an account of the wonders of Ireland for Henry II in 1185[2] containing some of the mythology of sacred wells. While his accounts may be fanciful, they do illustrate the mystery surrounding these holy sites.

> "There is a well in Munster," the adventurer wrote, "and if anyone wash-es in its waters, he immediately turns grey. I saw a man who had washed there one part of his beard. It had turned grey, while the other part re-tained its natural dark colour. On the other hand, there is a well in Lein-ster and if a man washes in it, he will not get greyer. There is a well of sweet water in Connacht on the top of a high mountain and some distance from the sea, which in any one day ebbs and overflows three times, imitat-ing the ebbing and flowing of the sea....There is a well in the far north of Ulster, which is so cold that if logs of wood are left in it for seven years, they harden so as to become stones.

> "There is a well in Munster, and if one touches or even looks at it, the whole province is deluged with rain. The rain will not cease until a priest, who is a virgin in mind and body and especially chosen for the purpose, celebrates Mass in a chapel not far from the well...and appeases the well with a sprinkling of holy water and the milk of a cow of one colour. This is certainly a barbarous rite, without rime or reason."[3]

Gerald also spoke of a well in Brittany that would create a shower of rain. The rain would only fall on an individual who, while drinking from the well out of the horn of an ox, happened to spill some of the water on a nearby stone, "even though the sky be ever so clear from rain."

In addition, Gerald wrote, "there is in Sicily a well of a wonderful nature. If anyone approaches it clad in a red garment, a column of water immediately shoots up from the well to the height of the person....if the person in red departs, it resumes its ordinary dimensions, and returns to its former channels."[4]

In Jewish mythology the Well of Midian, said to have been "created in the twi-light of the first Sabbath eve," reacted in a similar manner when Moses lowered a bucket to draw up some water. It was said, "the water leaped up and flowed with

---

1 Westervelt, William D. *Hawaiian Legends of Old Honolulu*. Rutland: Charles E. Tuttle Com-pany 1963, 37

2 Gerald of Wales. *The History and Topography of Ireland*. Translated by John O'Meara. Lon-don: Penguin Books, 1982

3 Ibid., 62-63

4 Ibid., 63

such abundance that one bucketful was sufficient to water the herds of Jethro and also of the other shepherds."[1]

Another early travel writer was the 14th century English knight, Sir John Mandeville. His work *Travels*, written around 1356, was translated into every major European language by the year 1400, was one of the books that Leonardo da Vinci took with him to Milan in 1499 and was used by Columbus to plan his voyage to China. Mandeville wrote of a forest near the city of Polumbum, India:

> Beside it is a mountain, from which the city takes its name, for the mountain is called Polumbum. At the foot of this mountain is a noble and beautiful well, whose water has a sweet taste and smell, as if of different kinds of spices. Each hour of the day the water changes its smell and taste. And whoever drinks three times of that well on an empty stomach will be healed of whatever malady he has. And therefore those who live near that well drink of it very often, and so they are never ill, but always seem young. I, John Mandeville, saw this well, and drank of it three times, and so did all my companions. Ever since that time I have felt the better and healthier... Some men call that well the *fons iuventutis*, that is, the Well of Youth; for he who drinks of it seems always young. They say this water comes from the Earthly Paradise, it is so full of goodness.[2]

Wells and eternal youth are common themes, which motivated many adventurers and conquerors to pursue their own quests for immortality. One of the legends of the Islamic world is that of Alexander the Great and his vizier, Khidr. According to the legend, Alexander happened to obtain a copy of Adam's will, which mentioned that god had created a spring behind the mountainous barrier around the world, Mt. Qaf which was located in the Land of Darkness. The water of this spring "was whiter than milk, colder than ice, sweeter than honey, softer than butter and sweeter smelling than musk."[3] It also granted eternal life to those who drank from it. Khidr, taking Alexander's army with him, entered the Land of Darkness and found the spring. He bathed in the water, drank of its sweetness, and became immortal. However, when he attempted to show Alexander his find it had become lost once again. Another version of this legend states that Khidr fell into the Well of Life, gained immortality and became the Green Man.[4] Khidr is regarded among the Sufi followers as the Guide to the Sufi Path and is said to appear before Sufi adepts, in their sleep or in person, to help them on their way.

Gerald's legend from Sicily mentioned above seems to mirror that of a far older one of the Well of Segais, or Conlai's Well. The nine hazel trees of wisdom

---

1 Rappoport, Angelo S. *Myth and Legend of Ancient Israel Vol. 2*. New York: KTAV Publishing House, Inc. 1966, 252

2 Mandeville, Sir John. *The Travels of Sir John Mandeville*. Trans. By C.W.AR.D. Moseley. London: Penguin Books 1983, 123

3 Elwell-Sutton, P. "The Two-Horned One," in *Legends of the World*. Edited by Richard Cavendish. New York: Barnes & Noble 1994, 116

4 Andrews, Tamra. *A Dictionary of Nature Myths: Legends of the Earth, Sea, and Sky*. Oxford: Oxford University Press 1998, 224

grew over the Well Of Segais and the hazel nuts would fall into the well causing bubbles of mystic inspiration. Only the Dagda, the "good god," and his three cup bearers, were allowed to drink from the well. One day Boann, his wife, disobeyed and she drank from it too. At that instant, the waters rose high above the well, chased Boann, and drowned her. The waters formed the river Boann, or Boyne, of today.[1]

E. Estyn Evans wrote of a well in Inishmurray, Ireland, that was regarded as a "wind-well" "which has the power of controlling the wind, the ritual being to empty the well to produce a calm."[2] Another well with the ability to either create a storm or to produce calmness was at Inishkea in county Mayo. This well was buried by order of the Bishop of Tuam in 1640 "for weighty reasons."

Up through the 19th century during times of drought people would visit Gellionen Well in Glamorgan, Wales. They would throw or scatter the well water, dance near the well on a nearby green spot and throw flowers and herbs at each other with the result always being rain.[3]

Another legend tying natural phenomenon to a particular holy well is the well at Sliab Seact in Ireland. In 1938, Clonmany resident James Doherty, then 70 years of age, told of the well which "if anybody goes near it and muddies it, a mist will come and they will go astray and will be lost until the fog clears away."[4]

Holy wells have certain other aspects of their "behavior" which have resulted in other legends of paranormal occurrences. One of these is St. Nunn's or St. Ninnie's Well in Cornwall in the parish of Pelynt:

> An old farmer...once set his eyes upon the granite basin (of St. Nunn's Well) and coveted it, for it was no wrong in his eyes to convert the holy font to the base uses of a Pigsty and accordingly he drove his oxen and wain to the gateway above for the purpose of removing it. Taking his beasts to the entrance of the well, he essayed to drag the trough from its ancient bed. For a long time it resisted the efforts of the oxen, but at length they succeeded in starting it, and dragged it slowly up the hillside to where the wain was standing. Here, however, it burst away from the chains that held it, and, rolling back again to the well, made a sharp turn and regained its old positions, where it has remained ever since. Nor will anyone again attempt its removal, seeing that the farmer, who was previously well to do in the world, never prospered from that day forward. Some people say, indeed, that retribution overtook him on the spot, the oxen falling dead, and the owner being struck lame and speechless."[5]

---

1 Ellis, Peter Berresford. *The Druids.* Grand Rapids: William B. Eerdmans Publishing Company, 1994, 131

2 Evans, E. Estyn. *Irish Folk Ways.* Mineola: Dover Books 2000, 302 (A reprint of the 1957 edition published by Routledge & Keegan Paul, Ltd., London)

3 Trevelyan, Marie. *Folk-Lore and Folk-Stories of Wales.* London: Elliot Stocl 1909

4 Doherty, Mary. "Holy Wells," a Clonmany school manuscript, 1938

5 Hope, Robert Charles. *The Legendary Lore of the Holy Wells of England.* London: Elliot Stock 1893, 17-18 (A facsimile reprint by Llanerch Publishers, Felinfach Wales 2000). This

Stories about other moving stones are also common in Ireland. Patrick Logan, in his book *The Holy Wells of Ireland*, relates the tale of a heavy altar slab located near Tobar na Mult in County Kerry:

> ...the story is that an enemy (Cromwellian) once used an ox cart to take it away from the well. When the cart had got as far as Bullock Hill, it stopped and the oxen refused to move it any further, so it was left on the spot until the next morning. Then, to the surprise of some people, the stone was found to have moved back to its original place near the well.[1]

Other "homing stones" are reported to exist at Gorman, near Malin Head in County Donegal, Kilultagh, County Roscommon, Aghabulloge parish and Loch Hyne, County Cork and Aghinagh parish, also in County Cork. The homing stone at Aghinagh Parish is a large flat stone, probably an ancient food grinding stone due to a worn hollow area in the center, located near the Tobar a'Noonan well. Logan wrote, "the stone, which is very large and heavy, was removed and built into a wall, but was found back at the well in the morning."[2]

Another homing stone is at St. Olan's Well, Dromatimore, County Cork. This mysterious stone is an oval quartzite that rests on an ogham-inscribed monolith, it was said to cure a variety of "feminine aliments" and, if worn on the head and carried around the local church three times cured migraines. According to one authority, "it had the gift of locomotion in that, if removed to any distance, it unfailingly returned to its original position."[3]

Cornish wells in particular appear to have had a history of some inherent protective force, which keeps their structures intact. An item in the *Notes and Queries* noted above reported that the writer learned "from a native of the parish that some of the stones of the well (of St. Nun's) have been, at various times, carted away to serve meaner purposes, but that they have been, by some mysterious agency, brought back again during the night."

Some holy wells are also said to move if they become polluted in some manner. Tobar Lastra, which means "the well of light," located in the parish of Donnaghmoyne, Ireland was said to have moved several yards across a meadow after a local Protestant washed his dog at the well. Another Protestant caused yet another well to move in County Roscommon when he washed a child in the well. This would not appear to be a serious offense considering the physical wounds that are washed in holy wells; however, the well moved to another location leaving only an ugly hole in the ground where no water will collect. In 1936, according to legend, a little girl and boy were playing at St. Columcille's Well in Conmany, Ireland and accidentally "dirtied the well." It is said that the next day the well

---

story was also reported verbatim in the November 18, 1854 issue of *Notes and Queries*, page 397 and it may have been this story which Hope repeats.

1 Logan, Patrick. *The Holy Wells of Ireland.* Buckinghamshire: Colin Smythe 1980, 102
2 Ibid., 103
3 Evans, E. Estyn. op. cit., 301

had moved to another location. Other wells that have reportedly moved include St. Eoin's in Ireland which moved due to people washing their clothing in it and St. Peakaun's Well in County Tipperary which moved twice also due to clothes being washed in its water. In fact, St. Peakaun's Well wound up one mile from its original position. Another reason given for wells moving include the barring of public access to the well, which also may result in the loss of the well's healing powers.

In Wales, it is said that the Shee Well once "ran away." The legend tells of a band of robbers who lived nearby and who preyed upon travelers, often murdering them. The waters of the rivers flowing near their den became tainted with blood and the Shee Well disappeared into the hills until the thieves pledged to till the fields and mow the meadows. At that the Shee Well returned, its water pure once again. St. Fillan's Well in Scotland is another that moved on its own. Supposedly, the spring originally spurted from the top of a hill, "but removed itself to the base of a rock about a quarter of a mile farther south."[1]

St. Nunn's Well, mentioned previously, was also the object of pin offerings, said to placate the "Piskies" or Pixies of the site. Today St. Nunn's Well is also known as Piskie's Well and by such offerings of pins, it is said that the Piskies will help farmers be successful.[2] Another "Pixy Well" was said to exist at Crowcombe in Somerset with the associated pin offerings. A not-so-nice spirit was said to reside in the River Tees in Durham near Pierse-bridge. Called "Peg Powler," the spirit or water nymph would drag children into the depths of the river if they were naughty, especially on Sunday. It would seem that this myth was more a means used by parents to keep their children out of the treacherous river rather than a true and ancient legend.

Piskies, Pixies, Elves, Faeries and Nymphs are common residents of sacred wells and waterways. Sometimes these Sprites and Faeries also became Christianized by the new religious order in Britain. St. Neot was said to be only 15 inches tall. He spent his days immersed in the well praying and performing miracles with birds and other animals.

Faeries were also thought to reside at the Virtuous Well, also known as St. Anne's Well located near Trellech Village in Wales. One story is that a local farmer dug up a "faery ring" around the well to prove to others that he did not believe in "them silly tales." However, the next day when he attempted to draw water out of the well, it was dry! But it was only dry when he tried to obtain water. A little old man, presumably a faerie, was seen sitting on the well one day and told the farmer that he was very irritated about the destruction of the faerie ring and that the water would never be available to the farmer until the ring was restored. As soon as the farmer put the ring back, the water once again flowed freely.

---

1 Anon. "Our Hagiology," in *Blackwood's Edinburgh Magazine*, Vol. 82, October 1857, 454
2 Anderton, Bill. *Guide to Ancient Britain*. Berkshire: W. Foulsham & Co., Ltd., 1991, 199

As far back as 860 CE, according to the Archbishop of Rheims, people claimed to see images of entities on the surface of well water and to even speak with these beings. As expected, the Archbishop called these entities "demons." In addition lost "fairy cities" were also seen in the waters of Lough Neagh in Ireland. It was said that St. Mary's Well at Grampian was associated with the white witch Dame Aliset who cured a faery child with the well's healing water.

"Water maidens," water spirits in Slavic lore said to embody both life and death, fertility and destruction, were thought to live in the rivers and springs during the winter and in forests and groves during the spring and summer. Called "Rusalka" in Russian lore, they were comparable to the Greek Sirens, luring young men to watery depths.[1]

Puck's Well is another that has retained its original character through time. Today merely a muddy and foul-smelling bog, its legends speak of a much more active history. While most holy wells have been Christianized over time and renamed for particular saints, Puck's Well has escaped the gradual shift from Pagan to Christian. Originally called puca-wielle, or "spring of the goblin,"[2] Puck's Well is also regarded as the Devil's Well. However, Puck was not the Devil that the Christians thought. Puck was associated with Faery rings and dancing and mischievous goings on — he was a goblin. Goblins actually were beneficent to the local population. Old legends tell of these beings performing drudgery work such as drawing water, cutting wood, cleaning houses and even leaving money in shoes. However, one had to maintain the good will of the goblin or bad luck would occur. Puck was also said to haunt places of heinous crimes with howling, mad laughter or strange lights. Puck has long been associated with wells. Puck Wells are found also in Somerset, Wiltshire, and Northamptonshire as well as in Ireland.

Another well with associations to the Devil is Chattle Hole south of Warminster. Here, it is said, while a chapel was being built, each morning the workers would return to find all of the stones, which had been used the prior day, returned to the bottom of the hill. In addition, the well at Ffynnon Gloch in Cardinganshire, Wales is said to be a spot where the devil "rested." The bells of the nearby church are said to ring silently due to the evil that surrounds the area.

Some wells, which are located near standing stones, have different tales. Our Lady's Well located at Lower Swell in the Cotswolds has a legend that at midnight the "Wittlestone" (one of the standing stones nearby) walks to the well to drink.[3] This is not an isolated tale. There have been 39 tales of standing stones moving, dancing or bowing to nearby wells in England and Wales in the 20th

---

1 Andrews, Tamra. *A Dictionary of Nature Myths: Legends of The Earth, Sea, and Sky.* Oxford: University of Oxford Press 1998, 165
2 Jordan, Katy. "Wiltshire Wells," www.bath.ac.uk/~liskmj/wellsweb/wellstxt.htm, 1999
3 Hope, op. cit.

century. Twenty of those 39 tell of stones going to the nearest well to drink or bathe and 27 of the 39 are said to go into action at midnight.

Dragons also have a long history of lurking about wells in Europe. Named after the Anglo-Saxon/Viking water goblin Nykr, Nykerpole, or *nicor-pool*[1] is one such place. First recorded in 1272 near Marlborough, but now lost, the well was home to a monster similar to a sea serpent. Another similar place is Knucker Holes in Sussex where a great monster was said to crawl up out if the depths to terrorize the local population. Other sites that carry the Nykr name include Nicker Wood near Rotherham. *Nykur* in the original Icelandic language and *niccor* in Old English means "water monster" as well as "river horse." An associated water spirit is the *nack*, which was a male entity that ruled over a specific waterway.[2]

In County Durham at Penshaw, a well still exists at the foot of Worm Hill, the home of the Lambton "worm."[3] Supposedly this terrifying serpent was caught by a fisherman who, when he caught it, "flung it into a well close by." Over the years, it continued to grow until it filled the well. It moved to the river where it made periodic attacks on the local populace, "worried the cattle, devoured the lambs, and committed every sort of depredation in the helpless peasantry."[4] When the "worm" did not receive the food it desired it would "break out into a violent rage," tearing trees up by their roots. The local good knight consulted a "sibyl," or witch, who instructed him on the best methods to defeat the beast. The knight, who cut it in two, eventually killed the monster. "Worm Well," as it was known in the 1890s, was a wishing well which received pins as a votive offering. In Longwitton (also written as Long Witton), Northumberland, a monster kept people from three holy wells until it, too, was slain. A lone knight, Guy, Earl of Warwick, valiantly fought the Longwitton Dragon but no matter how many times he caused severe wounds to the beast, they healed instantly. For three days they fought until the knight saw that the dragon kept the tip of his tail in one of the wells — ensuring that its wounds would close due to the healing waters of the well. The knight retreated step-by-step until the monster, closely following, was free of the well and was able to be killed.[5] These stories are somewhat contrary to other traditions, which said that to kill or remove these guardians would result in dire consequences, usually a widespread epidemic. Other wells and pools with dragons, serpents or Griffin's are Griffydam, (also known as Griffy Well) in Leicestershire, the spring of Ares near Thebes, Greece, Llyn-yr-Afanc (the Monsters Lake) in Pembrokeshire and, of course, Loch Ness in Scotland. According

1 Jordan, op. cit.

2 Lindow, John. *Swedish Legends and Folktales.* Berkeley: University of California Press 1978, 38

3 "Worm" (Middle English) or "Wyrm" (Anglo-Saxon) meaning "serpent" or "dragon"

4 Hunt, Laurence. "Some Ancient Wells, Springs & Holy Wells of the Cotswolds," in *The Source,* Issue #2, Winter 1994

5 Briggs, Katherine. *British Folktales.* New York: Pantheon Books, 1977, 147-149

to Sir James Frazer[1] during the 16th century in Burford, Oxfordshire, the effigy of a large dragon was carried up and down the streets during the Midsummer Eve festivities.

It is possible that the slaying of dragons by Christian knights was symbolic of the Christian Church's domination over pagan ways. The dragon is symbolic of earth energy, thus the Earth Mother, and was thought to have power over the rains and the waters of the earth.

Rumors of hauntings near holy wells are also common throughout Great Britain. In Devonshire, at Cranmere Pool, weird wailing is heard supposedly from unhappy spirits who have been confined there as a punishment[2] and, at Cat's Well at Bratton (named after St. Catherine), a huge black dog is said to haunt the area. Another black hound is at Dean Combe, in a well known as the Pool of the Black Hound. At this site, a spirit was condemned by the parish Vicar to scoop out the pool with a shell with a hole in it and was told that it could not rest until the pool was emptied. Hope wrote, "at mid-day or at midnight, the hound may still be seen at its work."[3]

The three deep pits known as Hell-Kettles in Darlington Parish, England are also said to contain the "soules of sinfull men and women in them." These three pits were reported to be bottomless with hot water and that the souls of these "sinfull" men and women "have oft beene harde to cry and yell about them."

It is said that ghostly knights led by Arthur himself ride out of a hillfort, thought by some to be Camelot, at Cadbury on certain nights and disappear at Arthur's Well. These special evenings occur at the Solstice and Equinox. When I visited Cadbury, I was told by our guide that he and some of his friends had slept out on the broad expanse of the hillfort one solstice night. They were awakened by the thundering sounds of hoof beats as a large contingent of invisible riders swept past the campsite. Arthur's Well, by the way, was not a healing well (although an early 20th century poem says that if one washes his or her eyes in the well water, a "sleeping army" can be seen), but was regarded as a wishing well also and was used to water the King's horses.

The waters of some wells are said to have the power to turn ordinary items into stone. Gerald of Wales wrote of a well in Norway:

> If wood...flax or a linen web be placed in it [the well] for a year, it becomes very hard stone. Because of this, a certain bishop of Norway was able to bring back to Waldem'ar, king of Denmark in our time, a napkin which he had taken from him the year before for the purpose of proving

---

1 Frazer, Sir James. *The Golden Bough*: A Study in Magic and Religion. Hertforshire: Wordsworth Editions, 1993, 655

2 Cleaver, Alan. "Holy Wells: Wormholes in Reality?" part I in *The Source*, Issue #3, November 1985 and part II, *The Source*, Issue #4, March 1986

3 Hope, op. cit., 64

the fact referred to....The middle part, having been placed in the well, was a stone, but the rest of it remained as before...[1]

In 1664, M. Mackaile noted in his *The Oyly-well or, A Topographico-Spagyrical description of the Oyly-well, at St. Catherines-chappel in the Paroch of Libberton*[2] that water from a certain well in Scotland "should, in a short time, be converted into a stone."

It has been previously mentioned that some stones at wells refuse to be moved by humans without returning to their original positions. So too some carved images appear to have a "homing" instinct. Jean Markale described in his book *The Great Goddess* a statue supposedly uncovered during an excavation of a Temple of Mars at Saint-Lizier which "after being taken to the main church, returned to its original place each night." Another is that of Notre-Dame-du-Roncier (Our Lady of the Brambles) which was an ancient statue thought to be of the Virgin Mary discovered next to a fountain. Markale noted "that it returned there every night after having been moved to a safe place."[3] A similar occurrence has been recorded at St. Maelruan's Well in Ballynaleck. W.H. Grattan-Flood told the first story concerning this well in a talk at St. Peter's College in Wexford in 1902:

> In the year 1750 a man who lived in the neighborhood had a striking dream in which he was urged by some superior spirit to go and explore St. Maelruan's well in which there was something remarkable concealed. This dream recurred on three nights. The man visited the well, and in the course of his explorations, he came across a strange looking statue or effigy of a person carefully hidden in the well.

According to Grattan-Flood, who examined the statue, it was carved of black oak and even after repeated attempts no one has been able to be remove the statue from the boundaries of the parish where it was discovered.

The Brennemans, in their study of Irish holy wells,[4] record several instances beginning in 1985 of religious statues at certain holy wells that were allegedly seen to move. The first was at the village church at Asdee, County Kerry where a seven-year-old girl saw a statue of Jesus beckon to her; she also saw the eyes move in a statue of the Virgin Mary. This event occurred on St. Valentine's Day. The next month a group of children reported seeing a statue of Jesus move in St. Patrick's Church in Ballydesmond. In July of the same year, two women reported seeing a statue of Mary, which was modeled after the apparition of Lourdes,

---

1 Gerald of Wales, op. cit., 62

2 Mackaile, M. *The Oyly-well: Or, A Topographico-Spagyrical description of the Oyly-well, at St. Catherines-chappel in the Paroch of Libberton*. Edinburgh: Robert Brown, 1664

3 Markale, Jean. *The Great Goddess: Reverence of the Divine Feminine From The Paleolithic to the Present*. Translated from the French by Jody Gladding. Rochester: Inner Traditions, 1999, 92 & 157

4 Brenneman, Walter L. & Mary G. *Crossing the Circle at the Holy Wells of Ireland*. Charlottesville: University Press of Virginia 1995, 110-123

move in its outdoors setting. An additional 30 reports of moving statues would be filed by September of 1985.

The village of Wark, located in Northumberland, has three wells, Upper or High Well, Lower or Riverside Well, and the old Kirk Well. It was the practice of the residents of Wark to visit the wells on New Year's morning to be the first to drink of the wells on the first day of the year. It was believed that the individual, who did drink the "Flower of the Well," as the first drink was called, would gain supernatural powers that would last the whole year. Among those powers was the ability to pass through keyholes and to take nocturnal flights. The fortunate person who accomplished the feat would throw flowers, grass, hay or straw into the well so that the others, less fortunate, would know that the Flower of the Well had already been won.[1]

Ghostly "women in white" are also associated with holy wells and marshes. Marie Trevelyan noted in her book *Folk-lore and Folk-stories of Wales* published in 1909, that Wales, in common with England, has innumerable white ladies, and every county of the Principality has several of these apparitions." Markale wrote that "marshes are strange places where life and death are continually mixing with each other and delicate exchanges between dissolution and regeneration take place....It is in caves near springs or rivers, where likewise the atmosphere is humid and full of water vapor, that the mysterious "white ladies" appear...."[2] Markale believes that natural radioactivity, magnetic currents or other natural phenomenon are responsible for these apparitions. Whatever the cause, natural or supernatural, St. Julian's Well in Wellow, Somerset has a history of visitations by "the White Lady" when a calamity was about to happen to the former owners of the well. More than likely, these "White Ladies" are not the products of a natural phenomenon but create it. They are archetypal images of pagan goddesses, which periodically become evident near sacred sites.

The legend of Melusina speaks of a hunter in France coming across such Ladies in White. Baring-Gould wrote of a meeting between a mortal and the Ladies in White:

> Presently the boughs of the trees became less interlaced and the trunks fewer; next moment his horse, crashing through the shrubs, brought him out on a pleasant glade, white with rime, and illumined by the new moon; in the midst bubbled up a limpid fountain, and flowed away over a pebbly floor with a soothing murmur. Near the fountain-head sat three maidens in glimmering white dresses, with long, waving golden hair, and faces of inexpressible beauty.[3]

1 Hope, op. cit., 106
2 Markale, op. cit., 33, 34
3 Baring-Gould, S. *Curious Myths of the Middle Ages.* New York: John B. Alden, Publishers 1885, 205

Like the White Lady of St. Julian's Well, Melusina, who in reality was a mermaid, also appeared to "utter the most heart-rendering lamentations" prior to the death of her descendants or the king of France. Mermaids, according to Hope, "appear to have the preference for appearing on Easter Day and at daybreak."[1] Baring-Gould noted several instances when supposed mer-people had been captured. One such instance was the capture of a "Marmennill" or merman off the Icelandic island of Grimsey in the early 14th century and one washed up on the beaches of Suffolk in 1187. Baring-Gould notes other cases of mermen being seen and caught in 1430 in Holland, 1531 in the Baltic, 1560 on an island west of Ceylon, and 1714 in the West Indies.[2] California Indians also had mermaids, or rather "Water Women" and "River Mermaids," in their mythology. Called *He-Há-Pe*, these beautiful fish-women had long black hair and lived in deep pools and rivers. The "River Mermaids" reportedly pulled victims to their deaths in these deep waters.

In two instances, these mysterious Ladies in White have been seen scattering flowers or seeds in fields. In both instances, the flowers or seeds had turned to golden coins the next morning.

Ladies in White were also known in Estonia where "one of the commonest shapes for a water spirit is a woman with exceptionally long and dark hair, often sitting on a rock near a body of water or at the very edge of water, combing her hair, crying or lamenting. More detailed descriptions mention a silk scarf or a white shift as the characteristic attribute of a water spirit."[3]

In Germany, the goddess Sirona was widely venerated. A wooden carving of Sirona was found in a Roman well at Pforzheim. The holy waters at Alzay were dedicated to Venus, Sirona and the sun god Grannos in 223 CE. Other wells and springs were dedicated to Minerva and the goddess of the Black Forest, Diana Abnorba.

Another ghostly woman in gray or white has been recorded at St. Dene's Well near Cardiff, Wales. She reportedly would follow drovers for about a mile through the Llanishen neighborhood before she would return to the well. It was thought that she had done evil in her time and was in bondage to the well as punishment.

St. Patrick is credited with turning a woman into one of the white ladies at Llyn Gwyn, a lake in Wales. According to Trevelyan, St. Patrick and another un-named saint, were arguing about religion when St. Patrick became enraged. He saw several people standing nearby who had overheard the argument and turned them into fish but another woman he turned into a white lady whom "was often seen accompanied by flashes of light."[4]

---

1 Hope, op. cit XXii

2 Baring-Gould op. cit., 224-235

3 Merriam, C. Hart, editor, *The Dawn of the World: Myths and Tales of the Miwok Indians of California*, University of Nebraska Press, Lincoln 1993, pg. 228-230

4 Västrik, Ergo-Hart. "The Waters and Water Spirits in Votian Folk Belief," in *Folklore*, Vol. 12, December 1999, 23. Institute of the Estonian Language.

Not only Ladies in White or Gray have been reported, but Ladies in Green as well. One such Green Lady was reported to watch pilgrims place rags on a thorn bush at the Eye-Well near St. Donat's in Marcloss, Wales. Another was seen in the village of Woodrow in Buckinghamshire. According to the witness, a wraith-like figure dressed in green was seen gliding across a meadow leaving a path of green phosphorescent light until she disappeared suddenly. The witness pressed himself through the underbrush at the spot and found an ancient grotto — but no Lady was in evidence. Another mysterious Lady in Green was said to haunt the banks of the River Conon in Scotland. The strange apparition was that of a tall woman dressed in green that had a "malignant scowl" and who "would leap out of the stream at the side of travelers and point a skinny finger at them or beckon them to follow." She would then drag the traveler into the depths where they drowned.[1]

A number of goddesses are directly associated with holy wells in Ireland. Among them are Aibheaog whose sacred well had powerful healing properties effective against toothaches; Brid, or Bridget, whose ancient shrine is still maintained at Kildare; Finchoem, who is more a guardian of wells but who is associated with childbirth (she swallowed a worm crawling over a magickal well and conceived a child); Liban, another guardian of Ireland's wells who was able to take the form of the sacred salmon, and Sionnan, Queen of Wells and namesake for the River Shannon. Momu was the goddess of Wells in Scotland.

Water goddesses are certainly not confined to Great Britain. Chalchiuhtlicue, the virgin-mother goddess of the Aztecs, was known as a "Lady of the Lake," a goddess of streams and of the sea"[2] and the related water plants. There are also gods of the water as represented by Poseidon, "god of horses and lord of springs and salt water," Neptune, Noden, Burmanos, the god of seething water and hot springs, and Nectan, the Celtic god of waters and healing. Enki was the Summerian "god of sweet waters" as well as the god of wisdom, fertility, magick and the arts and crafts of civilization. The elements of Enki's character are identical to the sacred characteristics of holy wells and streams — fertility, life and wisdom.

Symbols of this goddess are the snake and frog (which is a common theme in holy wells in Britain and usually said to represent the devil) and an ancient water pot. This water pot is symbolic of the goddesses life-giving powers. Chalchiuhtlicue, like other goddesses of water, was also a healer. She is depicted with herbs in the Codex Borgia and a mountain called Yauhqueme ("covered with mugwort") was said to be her home. Chalchiuhtlicue was also known as the goddess of running water and was the wife of the rain-god Tlaloc. She was also the protective

---

1   Trevelyan, op. cit.

2   MacKenzie, Donald A. *Pre-Columbian America: Myths and Legends*. London: Senate 1996, 197 (a reprint of the 1923 publication, Myths of Pre-Columbian America, published by The Gresham Publishing Company)

goddess of pregnant women as are many of the other goddesses associated with springs and rivers.

Fish, especially trout and salmon, have a special association with holy wells. These fish living in holy wells were thought to possess both eternal life and wisdom; they were the holders of the knowledge of the gods and the Otherworld. We should remember that the fish is and was a universal symbol of the Great Goddess. Scholar Franz Cumont, in his book *Oriental Religions in Roman Paganism*, noted that the Syrian goddess Atargatis (the goddess of the seas, who was normally depicted in a mermaid form) held fish to be sacred. All were forbidden to touch, much less eat, the sacred fish except for priests who partook of it during certain rituals as a symbol of eating the divine flesh of the goddess herself. Cumont wrote "that worship, and its practices, which were spread over Syria, probably suggested the ichthus symbolism in the Christian period."[1]

The fish was also symbolic of the goddesses Venus, Aphrodite, Salacia, Kali, Kwan-yin and Isis. Isis was known as Abtu, the "Great Fish of the Abyss." In ancient Rome Friday's were known as *dies veneris*, or the Day of Venus during which fish were "orgiastically" eaten as an aphrodisiac in honor of the goddesses Venus and Aphrodite. The fish symbol, the association of eating fish on Friday, the linking of the fish symbol with the god(s), were all assimilated by the early Church in a continuing effort to take the pagan symbols and meanings to further build the foundation of Christianity which the Church rests on today.[2]

According to Celtic tradition, fish were thought to be the spirit of a transformed human being that had been trapped in a well and turned into the magical salmon or trout — transformed to become the guardian spirit of that well throughout time.

Salmon were believed sacred and immortal not only among the Celts but among Native Americans. Ethnologist Philip Drucker notes that the salmon was universally regarded as immortal among California Indian groups. Many California tribes had elaborate "first salmon" rituals, which preceded the salmon run each year. According to Drucker, "the general belief was that the salmon were a race of supernatural beings who dwelt in a great house under the sea. There they went about in human form, feasting and dancing like people. When the time same for the 'run', the Salmon-people dressed in garment of salmon flesh, that is, assumed the form of fish to sacrifice themselves."[3]

---

1 Cumont, Franz. *Oriental Religions in Roman Paganism.* New York; Dover Publications 1956, 117 (A reprint of the 1911 edition published by G. Routledge & Sons, Ltd)

2 Varner, Gary R. "Sacred Symbols: The Fish," in *Bright Blessings*, Vol. I, Issue 7, September 2000, 4

3 Drucker, Philip. *Indians of the Northwest Coast.* New York: The Natural History Press 1963, 154-155

Other wells with magical fish are St. Neot's in Cornwall and St. Corentine's Well in Brittany, Kilbride on the Isle of Skye, Gleneig of Iverness, St. Bean's Well in Argyle, Llandelay in Pembrokeshire and at Ffynnon Weneg at Cardiganshire.

Charles Squire noted that only the Salmon had the privilege of "knowing everything that was in the world. [The] divine salmon who lived in the well, and swallowed the [hazel] nuts as they dropped from the trees into the water, and thus knew all things, and appear in legend as the 'Salmons of Knowledge.'"[1]

Today in some of the small villages of Ireland, a fish in a well is still regarded as a good omen. Messenger, in his ethnographic study of the people living on a small Irish island, wrote "those who come to the spring always seek a tiny fish or eel in the water, which, if observed, is merely a good omen to some but an assurance of reaching Heaven to others."[2] The salmon, along with the eel, trout and other water creatures, embodied the wisdom of the goddess as well as Her healing powers. Fish or eels residing in such wells provided the healing power and without them the power would fade. Some legends indicate that these sacred fish only became visible at midnight and those lucky enough to see them were granted their prayers. Similar Christianized traditions state that only for one hour after midnight on St. Brigid's feast day were the healing wells of Ireland able to cure any form of disease. Three mysterious trout were said to inhabit St. Ciaran's Well in County Meath but were only visible for a few seconds at midnight on the first Sunday in August when they disappeared until the same time the next year.

If the sacred fish at Tyn Y Ffynnon appeared while someone bathed in or drank the well's water a cure was believed to be inevitable, but if the fish stayed hidden, no change would occur in the individual's condition.

Guardian fish were thought to be in the Golden Well near St. Peter's Church in Herefordshire (a carving of the fish is still located on the wall inside the church), and Bromere Pool in Shropshire. Human-like guardians also appear to be common at many wells and they may, in fact, be the spirits of those wells.

Stories of the guardians of wells are common throughout England and are based of some historical fact. Cunning men and women, also known as witches, did act as guardians for some of the holy wells into the 19th and early 20th centuries and probably were acting as guardians had for thousands of years.

The Wychwood Forest of Oxfordshire has two or three wells known for their healing properties that also had attendant guardians up through the early part of the 20th century. Long time resident T.L. Miles, in an article entitled *Springs, Wells & Witches*,[3] wrote, "in a clump of beech trees was a small dell. One side of the dell rose vertically and in the limestone face was a cave. Here for

1   Squire, Charles. Celtic Myths & Legends. New York: Portland House, reprinted 1994, 55
2   Messenger, John C. Inis Beag: Isle of Ireland. New York: Holt, Rinehart and Winston, Case Studies in Cultural Anthropology 1969, 97
3   Miles, T.L. "Springs, Wells & Witches," in *Cotswold Life*, May 1983, 38

generations lived a succession of old women, all regarded as witches, who were the guardians of the well."

Among the many legends surrounding this particular well is that the last guardian, known as Mother Shipton, was able to foretell the future, shape change into various animals, and create very strange atmospheric anomalies nearby which were witnessed by many people including the local constables. "Earth tremors" in 1893 reportedly ruined the old well but, "by some freak, a supply of water appeared in the fork of a large beech tree near the witch's cave...which was said never to overflow but always to remain at the same level."[1] This beech tree-well survived until the 1950s when the trunk rotted away and the water supply disappeared. The cave and original well site, according to Miles, now are several feet below a rubbish heap.

Other wells with reputed guardian priests or priestesses were St. Maree's Well on the island of Maelrubha in Loch Maree and at Ffynnon Eilian in Wales, whose guardian was a Mrs. Hughes. Mrs. Hughes' successor, a John Evans also known as Jac Ffynnon Elian, was imprisoned twice for reopening the well after authorities had closed it.[2]

"Boiling wells" are wells that seem to actually "boil" for no apparent reason, the water bubbling at certain times of day or when specific votive offerings are dropped into them. In addition, water taken from some wells will either never boil or will boil at different rates depending on how the water is used for divining the future. Boiling wells may in fact be mineral wells. I visited many mineral wells in California and they all bubbled or "boiled" at certain intervals. Another such boiling well is located at Ludlow, England beside the River Corve. Here, legend says, a scullery maid was cured of sore eyes after an "old man" blessed the waters and "bade it have power to heal all manner of wounds and sores...as long as the sun shines and water runs."[3]

Another form of well anomaly is that of ebbing and flowing. Many wells have legends associated with them that the water in the wells will rise and fall at certain times of the day or season of the year. Two such wells are those of Binsey in Oxfordshire and Giggleswick in Yorkshire. Of Giggleswick, Hope remarked "sometimes the phenomenon may be observed several times in the course of one hour, and on other occasions once only during several hours."[4] One explanation for this phenomenon is simply a fluctuation in the water table. However, other wells with similar stories evidently rose and fell much faster than a normal seasonal fluctuation and have been linked to the actual tidal action set in motion by the gravitational pull of the moon. Chris Whetton, contributing editor of Hydrocarbon Processing, has offered another explanation for this phenomenon:

1 Ibid., 39
2 Pennick, Nigel. *Celtic Sacred Landscapes.* London: Thames and Hudson 1996, 73
3 Hope, op. cit., 143
4 Ibid., 201

> In Britain's north Yorkshire, there is a curious well in which the water regularly — and mysteriously — rises and falls. Not surprisingly, it is known as the *Ebbing and Flowing Well*. While no one has seen the underground structure that feeds this well, and engineer can hypothesize a system to account for this phenomenon. The most likely possibility is an underground rock chamber and siphon arrangement...[1]

Such a siphon, according to Whetton, may be an animal burrow or some manmade item that would allow for the periodic exiting of water. What this explanation does *not* do is account for the regularity of the ebbing and flowing.

Many sacred wells have certain powers at certain times of the year. The well at Stoole in Ireland is said to have healing properties that cures the blind and the maimed but only on Midsummer Eve, likewise some springs in Sweden have medicinal value but only on St. John's Eve.[2] An old Welsh tale says that water collected from springs at midnight on St. John's Eve will stay fresh for a year and will also have the ability to heal.

A darker aspect to sacred rivers is the belief that some require periodic sacrifice. Referred to as "Hungry Rivers" by some, these waterways claim the lives of people on a regular basis. The Radfords relate that the Saale and Spree Rivers in Germany "are believed to require a victim on Midsummer Day." In addition, the Scottish river Ross was believed to require one person a year be drowned in its waters.[3] The American River is a small but treacherous river in Northern California near my home. It takes at least 2-3 lives a year, each year unfailing. The rapids on this river seem to call continually for sacrifice. Do we ascribe to the Native American belief that River Mermaids live in these rivers and pull victims to their deaths? Or, do we regard these myths simply as explanations for sudden and untimely deaths? Rivers have long been regarded as boundaries between the world of the living and that of the dead and it is a small step to cross that boundary.

The Radfords wrote, "It is a lamentable fact that as late as 1928 people in the West of Ireland allowed a man to drown because of their firm belief that the sea or river must claim a victim a year...."[4] Such a belief existed in Scotland, the Orkneys, China and Russia as well, with fishermen and others refusing to allow any rescue of drowning victims so that the river would be satisfied. It was also thought that to rescue someone drowning was contrary to the will of the gods. Knowlson wrote, "The idea seems to be this: that when a man is drowning it is the intention of the gods that he should be drowned; and that the rescuer, if successful in rescuing him, must be the substitute and be drowned himself later on."[5]

---

1 Whetton, Chris. "The mysterious underworld," in *Hydrocarbon Processing*, Journal of the Society of Hydrocarbon Engineers, February 2000, Vol. 79, No. 2

2 Radford, E. and M.A. *Encyclopaedia of Superstitions.* New York: The Philosophical Library 1949, 250

3 Ibid.

4 Ibid., 106

5 Knowlson, T. Sharper. *The Origins of Popular Superstitions and Customs.* London: T. Werner Laurie Ltd. 1910, 231

Among these Hungry Rivers is the River Dart in Devon, said to claim a victim each year, as the following rhyme speaks:

> River of Dart, oh River of Dart,
> Every year thou claim'st a heart.[1]

The River Ribble, which passes through Lancashire, is another said to require a life every seven years "to appease the anger of the river spirit."[2] It is possible that the legends surrounding the River Ribble are ancient ones since the river was regarded as sacred in Roman and pre-Roman times. The Ribble was sacred to the Celtic goddess Belisama, similar to Minerva a goddess of Battle. Belisama or a darker personage called Peg Powler may have demanded these annual "victims." As noted earlier, Peg Powler, also called Peg Powler of the Trees, was a water spirit with long green fangs who "lurked under the weeds to catch unwary children."[3] Similar evil figures were the Rusalkas of Russia who also had green hair and teeth and dragged children to their watery graves.

Not necessarily a myth, or a legend, a well in Shropshire was said to burn. According to *The Annual Register* for 1761, the well was four to five feet deep and six to seven feet wide with a puddle of "brown water" at the bottom. According to a report filed by a Reverend Mason, the brown water was

> "continually forced up with a violent motion, beyond that of boiling water, and a rumbling hollow noise, rising or falling.... Upon putting down a candle at the end of a stick, about a quarter of a yard distance, it took fire, darting and flashing in a violent manner, for about half a yard high, much in the manner of spirits in a lamp, but with great agitation.

> "It was extinguished by putting a wet mop upon it, which must be kept there a small time; otherwise it would not go out. Upon removal of the mop there succeeded a sulphurous smoke lasting about a minute, and yet the water was very cold to the touch."[4]

This well was located near the Severn River along the English–Welsh border. While it is possible that methane gas caused such an effect, the well has been lost since that date with no explanation given.

Myths and legends about wells and mystical waters are abundant around the world — attesting to the ancient and universal beliefs that humankind has collected through time and the powers that these places have in the world and in our hearts.

---

1 Westwood, op. cit., 20

2 Ibid., 391

3 Ibid., 393

4 Mason, Reverend. "An account of a burning well at Brosley in Shropshire..." in *The Annual Register, or a View of the History, Politics, and Literature for the Year 1761.* 92-93

CHAPTER 6. HEALING WELLS AND SPRINGS

When we think of holy wells, we think of healing wells. While many of the myths and legends in the previous chapter are concerned about mystical beasts, dragons, hauntings and strange occurrences the overriding quality of all of these stories is that the particular well was so special that normal events simply did not happen there. The obviously pagan origin for most of these wells has contributed much to the lore surrounding them. Almost all of the holy wells mentioned in this book have one theme in common — they have, or had, healing qualities. It is possible that the popularity of seeking cures for physical and mental ailments at wells was simply because holy wells were one of the very few forms of health care that the poor were eligible to utilize and could afford.

That people received cures by bathing in or drinking the water from these wells cannot be contested. Why this happens is still unknown but as a writer to Blackwood's Edinburgh Magazine wrote in the February 1858 issue, "there must be some miraculous power of healing attached to it (holy wells) in order to attract its devotees." Many of the wells tested for water quality have some large amounts of iron, sulfates, bicarbonates, and other minerals that are known to be effective in the treatment of certain ailments such as rheumatism, skin diseases, etc. Reports of miraculous healings throughout history suggest that something more is at work. Obviously, a psychic effect in addition to a physical one is manifested in these individuals. It is the total experience, including the preparation undertaken, the ritual, meditation, etc., which produces profound changes.

Stories about healing wells are universal. In Australia among the people of the south-coast is a story about the Bubbling Spring[1] that was said to gush out of the ground.

---

1 The legend of the Bubbling Spring can be found in *Australian Legends* by C.W. Peck, published in 1933. The full text may be found on www.sacred-texts.com/aus/peck.htm

Noted for healing properties useful for the treatment of such ailments as rheumatism, the Bubbling Spring was also known to "teem with eels " — a common feature of sacred, healing wells. When Juan Ponce de Leon searched for the Fountain of Youth in the 16th century, he was searching for a holy, healing well. It is probable that stories of several healing wells in the area of his exploration contributed to his belief that a single, magical well could be found that would prolong life and youth. Other sacred wells were also believed to confer eternal youth. The fountain of Pon Lai in China was said to bestow a thousand lives to those who drank of it.

The hot springs at Bath have had continuous usage for the last 7,000 years. The various votive offerings discussed previously were placed at or in the wells as an exchange for hoped for cures, as thanks giving for cures received, and to obtain wished-for desires. A great many wells and springs have been renamed for Christian saints but were sought out by earlier people who revered them for the qualities which they attributed to the older pagan gods and goddesses.

Photo 37: Personal altar erected by "the son of Novantius," Bath, England. The Latin text reads "the son of Novantius set this up for himself and his family as the result of a vision."

Today in many parts of the world, especially Great Britain, people continue to practice many of the old traditions associated with holy wells. Many of these traditions have lost their original meaning but are continued as folkways. At times, as related by John Messenger in his ethnography, *Inis Beag*, the local priests have attempted to stop these customs because they are too closely associated with paganism.

Many wells required certain rituals to activate the healing process. Many required a visit during certain times and certain days of the year. St. Euny's required the individual to visit and wash in the well water on three successive Wednesdays in May. At Baglan Well in Wales, the individual was required to visit on the first three Thursdays in May. Obviously, the month of May was important, probably due to the festivals that revolved around Beltain, as was the number of days — three — that the individual had to visit the specific well. St. Euny's, as previously stated, required that children could only be healed if they were dipped three times in the well and then dragged three times "widdershynnes" around it. Some required the visitant to arrive at or before dawn and to finish his/her washing, prayers, offerings, etc. before sunrise. Strangely enough not all healing-wells are regarded as holy wells although the terminology at times is interchangeable. Of the 19 healing wells known in Wiltshire, according to researcher Katy Jordan, only three are regarded as "holy."[1] The vast majority of healing wells were known for the treatment of blindness and other eye diseases, however wells also were known to heal the mind and the spirit.

Healing wells were also recorded in the Bible. It was written in the book of St. John,

> "There is at Jerusalem by the sheep market a pool, which is called in the Hebrew tongue Bethesda, having five porches.

> "In these lay a great multitude of impotent folk, of blind, halt, withered, waiting for the moving of the water.

> "...an angel went down at a certain season into the pool, and troubled the water: whosoever then first after the troubling of the water stepped in was made whole of whatsoever disease he had."[2]

The wells at Beersheba were dug by followers of Abraham and Isaac and were individually named by Isaac as Esek, Sitnah, Rehoboth and Shebah. Isaac also set up an altar near the well of Beersheba.[3] The Pools of Bethesda, near the Temple Mount, were also popular healing centers. Many of these sites became the holy "high places" that were later condemned and desecrated as being sites of goddess worship.

Jewish law during the *tannaitic* period, which followed the destruction of the Temple in the first century, required that menstruating women must be purified

---

1 Jordan, Katy. "Wiltshire Healing Wells and the Strange Case of Purton Spa," in *Living Spring Journal*, Issue 1, May 2000.

2 King James Version, *Holy Bible*, John, 5:2-4

3 Bord, Janet & Colin. *Earth Rites: Fertility Practices in Pre-Industrial Britain*. London: Granada Publishing Limited 1982, 100

through total immersion in a ritual pool. The water to be used in the pool had to have been collected naturally without it being drawn and poured. Among the Ethiopian Jews, even today, a menstruating woman must purify herself in "living waters," such as a river or flowing spring.[1] This ritual immersion is not done to cleanse the body; rather it is to purify the spirit.

The people of ancient Crete re-enacted the annual Mysteries at the Spring of Naruplia. Here, it was believed, after her marriage to Zeus the goddess Hera bathed in the spring and regained her virginity. The sacred healing capability of water is as old as humankind and universally found in the world's religious texts and oral traditions.

Some healing wells are known to cure many diseases while others only certain, specific conditions. For some unknown reason, the treatment of eye diseases, including blindness and soreness of the eyes, appears to be the most recorded attribute of healing wells. One reason that eyes were a constant worry in the past with many "eye-wells" drawing large groups of pilgrims is that commoner's did not receive sufficient Vitamin A in their diets, resulting in xerophthalmia. Lady Wilde wrote in the 19th century that "the most efficacious treatment for diseases of the eye is a pilgrimage to a holy well, for the blessed waters have a healing power for all ophthalmic ailments, and can even give sight to the blind."[2] Folklorist Wayland D. hand wrote in his study, *Magical Medicine*, "water as a natural cleansing and curing agent is fairly widespread in tales where the curing of the blind is involved. For this purpose water is applied to the eyes from springs, brooks and streams, wells, and fountains...." One bit of folk lore from Utah states "the first time you hear the swallow in the spring...if you go to a stream or fountain and wash your eyes, at the same time making a silent prayer, the swallows will carry away all your eye troubles."[3] Other ailments reported cured by healing wells and springs are rickets, whooping cough, lameness, palsy, skin diseases and leprosy, headaches, paralysis and insanity.

There appeared to have been an equal popularity for wells, which made a woman fertile, and wells, which made a woman barren. One local parson upset with the pilgrimages to one such well, which was often sought after for its contraceptive powers, had it filled and sealed.[4]

---

1 Anteby, Lisa. "There's Blood in the House:" Negotiating Female Rituals of Purity among Ethiopian Jews in Israel, in Women *and Water: Menstruation in Jewish Life and Law*. Edited by Rahel R. Wasserfall. Hanover: Brandeis University Press 1999, 174

2 Wilde, Lady. *Irish Cures, Mystic Charms & Superstitions*. New York: Sterling Publishing Company, Inc. 1991, 17

3 Hand, Wayland D. *Magical Medicine: The Folkloric Component of Medicine in the Folk Belief, Custom, and Ritual of the People of Europe and America*. Berkeley: University of California Press 1980, 298, 312

4 King James version, *Holy Bible*, Genesis 26: 15-33: "For all the wells which his father's servants had digged in the days of Abraham, his father, the Philistines had stopped them, and filled them with earth."

WELLS OF HEALING DREAMS

As previously discussed, St. Madron's Well in Cornwall is one of those wells that was known as an Asclepieum, or "dream temple." Named for the Greek god of healing, Asclepius, these healing centers were very popular with the ancient Greeks and Romans combining traditional medicine with the healing waters of nearby wells and springs with dream therapy. Patients, called "incubants," would sleep near the water and wait for dreams that would either identify their ailments or tell the patient how to heal them, or provide an outright cure. The Asclepieum located at Pergamum, Turkey has been determined to be mildly radioactive — as has St. Madron's — due to radon in the earth.[1] It is possible that the radon combined with the effects of the healing water and the spirit of the location created an atmosphere conducive to the healing of mental and physical diseases.

Willetts wrote, "incubation in the sanctuaries (in Crete) was a normal part of a cure. After bathing and offering sacrifices, the patients entered the temple and lay down. The god appeared to them in their sleep or in a waking vision, healed the disease or recommended treatment."[2] In addition, Willetts noted that during the 1st and 2nd centuries BCE, as indicated by votive tablets, diseases including infertility, blindness, ulceration's, inflammations, sciatica and chronic coughing/vomiting were cured by the Savior god Asklepios during incubation induced sleep at these sanctuaries.

The Asclepieum at Pergamum is still visited for its healing powers by contemporary Turks who also continue to use traditional eye-shaped glass amulets for protection against evil and sickness.

There were over 300 Aesculapian healing centers in Greece alone with their own wells and reservoirs. Many of these centers were also oracular centers that had been used throughout ancient history even before the Greek Empire rose to power.

IRELAND'S HEALING WELLS

Most of the Irish will not acknowledge that they still believe in "pagan" traditions, however most of the old ways still survive in one form or another, often cloaked in Christian terms. As Messenger noted in his 1969 study of the residents of a small Irish island which comprises the Irish Gaeltacht, "the water in the spring is not considered holy, but capable of 'bringing the grace of god and the saint,' and if it is drunk during prayer, it is believed to be especially efficacious for curing sterility, among other afflictions."[3] The well at Inis Beag has also been

1 Brown, Dale Mackenzie. "Sick? Try Sleeping," *in Archaeology*, March/April 2001, 92

2 Willetts, R.F. *Cretan Cults and Festivals*. Westport: Greenwood Press Publishers 1980, 226-227

3 Messenger, John C. Inis Beag: Isle of Ireland. Holt, Rinehart & Winston, Case Studies in Cultural Anthropology 1969, 97

said to cure blindness. While not willingly referred to as "holy" the distinction is mute in that the practice indicates a prevailing sense of holy and "special."

In Ireland, as in Wales and England, stories about the saints and wells abound. It would appear that most female saints were always daughters of kings, always young Christian converts living in a pagan land, and always pursued by a pagan prince who either cut their heads off or in some other way maimed them. For the most part, they were also cured by healing water. St. Bridget is said to have evaded a suitor who gouged her eyes out, but her sight was miraculously restored when she washed her eye sockets at Faughart stream (now St. Bridget's Well) in County Louth. Today pilgrims continue to visit the well seeking its healing power. While today's pilgrims may seek relief from blindness or other eye diseases and irritations, the healing offered at these eye wells is not necessarily one of physical problems. It is, rather, a regaining of inner sight, wisdom and spiritual awareness.

Many of the healing wells of Ireland were named for the goddess Bridget in pre-Christian times. Bridget, a solar deity associated with fire, was also known for her healing powers. After the "conversion" of Ireland these wells were renamed "Lady Wells." When the goddess Bridget became "Saint Bridget," by Catholic Church decree, these wells once again were called by their original names. Today we find a mixture of "Our Lady" wells and "Bridget" wells still visited for their healing powers. The attraction of holy wells in 19th century Ireland was tremendous. Philip Hardy wrote of St. Patrick's Well on the island of Lough Dergh:

> It is almost incredible what crowds visit this island annually, during the months of June, July, and August — it being no unusual thing to see from 900 to 1000 persons of both sexes upon it at one and the same time — an extraordinary circumstance, when it is considered that the island does not measure more than three hundred paces in any direction. They are ferried across in a boat, which can carry seventy or eighty persons at once, for which they are charged 6 ½d; each and yet so inadequate is this conveyance to the purpose, that the shores of the lake are frequently covered with persons waiting their turn...[1]

Among the other healing wells of Ireland are St. John's Well, on the Dingle Peninsula which was known for its ability to heal both headaches and toothaches and St. Catherine's Well at Drumcondra in County Dublin. St. Catherine's was also known to cure toothaches, but only if the water is drunk from a skull. Patrick Logan wrote that a similar method to treat toothaches is observed at an old church well at Kilbarry:

> In a hole in a wall of the old ruined church.... A skull is still preserved: I saw it there recently. Sufferers from toothache take the skull, and apply it to the tender area which is rubbed gently with the skull, and I was assured that it is still used successfully.[2]

---

1 Hardy, Philip Dixon. *The Holy Wells of Ireland.* Dublin: Hardy & Walker 1840
2 Logan Patrick. *The Holy Wells of Ireland.* Buckinghamshire: Colin Smythe 1980, 85

County Dublin also is host to other wells known to cure toothaches, St. Movee's Well at Grange (also known to cure headaches and sore throats) and St. Senan's Well at Slade. Other "toothache" wells in Ireland are St. Fiachra's at Ullard which is also known to cure arthritis, and St. Columcille's at Sandyford which is said to effectively treat sore throat and hoarseness. Arthritis was also treated and cured by the healing waters of St. Bernard's Well in Limerick, Tobar Finnain in County Kerry and Tobar an Ratha Bhain in County Cork.

Mental illness was said to be relieved by drinking the waters of Tobar na aGealt, or "The Well of the Lunatics." In the early 19th century, two individuals said to be "rabidly mad" journeyed to the Well of the Lunatics and returned home "sound in mind and stout in health."[1]

Father Moore's Well in County Kildare is named after Fr. John (Iohannis) Moore who was reported to have healing powers. Father Moore was accused by his superiors of using occult means to heal however he was exonerated however when he blew upon two candles that immediately ignited and could not be blown out. While this would seem to substantiate the charge, the Church felt otherwise. Like other wells, Father Moore's Well required "activation" by a relic (the priest's hat), which has recently disappeared, kept by a guardian family.[2] However, the well associated with the good Father was holy long before Father Moore became the well's patron in the early 19th century. Believed to have been dedicated to Brigid and called the "Black Well" in the 16th century, Father Moore's Well continues to draw pilgrims seeking its curative effects.

The practice of visiting the many holy wells in Ireland fell into decline after a law was passed which forbade all gatherings and celebrations associated with the holy wells. People did, of course, visit individually and secretly. Over the years, holy wells have again become popular religious symbols and efforts are being made to protect those that still exist and to find and revenerate those that have been lost. One of these rediscovered wells is St. Columba's Well. Located at the foot of Mt. Pellier hill it was rediscovered in 1914 by a local postman Jimmy Murray. Murray began to clean the site up and eventually people started to revisit the well to pray. Students from a nearby seminary became the caretakers and a new entranceway was constructed. A statue of St. Columba was erected in 1919 with a shrine built of nearby granite.

On June 9, 1920, the shrine and well were officially opened and blessed by visiting Bishop John Heavey. Festivities including music, dancing and singing brought the site back to life with pilgrimages following soon after. Over the years, cures were reported with offerings of crutches, canes and other items becoming common. Annual celebrations are now held at St. Columba's Well on the Sunday nearest June 9th.

---

1 Ibid., 72

2 Brenneman, Walter L. & Mary G. *Crossing the Circle at the Holy Wells of Ireland*. Charlottesville: University Press of Virginia 1995, 99

Poorman's Well in Tulligoline North was named after an old poor man who dreamed that his blindness would be cured if he visited the well. He did visit and was cured and the well became known for its healing of eye ailments. It is here also that a legend exists of two women in cloaks who could be seen at the well just before dawn. Another nearby well, the Ha'penny Well, also became known for its cure for blindness. A similar story about a blind man's dream is also connected with the Ha'penny Well.

HEALING WELLS OF WALES

While there are thousands of holy wells in Ireland, Wales also has its share of these sacred sites. One ancient healing well is that of the "Shrine of Our Lady of Penrhys" (also known as Ffynnon Fair Penrhys and St. Mary's Well) located in the Rhondda Valley in South Wales. Purchased by the Catholic Archdiocese of Cardiff in 1938, this site has a long and troubled history.

Legend has it that a beautiful statue of the Virgin miraculously was delivered from heaven and was found between two branches of a massive oak, which had grown around the statue. Because of the miraculous statue, a nearby well also came to be regarded as holy. Tradition says that the statue could not be removed from the clutches of the oak until the Catholic chapel was built near the site.

In the 16th century, September 14th, 1538 to be exact, the statue was removed from the well site and taken to Thomas Cromwell. Cromwell was advised by Bishop Latimer of Worcester, a Church of England bishop, to destroy the icon under the pretense to "avoid idolatry." The intent of the destruction was to destroy Catholic artifacts as part of the "dissolution" of the Catholic Church. Cromwell, as vicar-general to Henry VIII, had the statue burned publicly along with other statues of the Virgin on September 26, 1538.

It is probable that the statue of Our Lady of Penrhys was an image of a Celtic goddess left in the oak by Druids who placed the image in a sacred grove, next to a holy spring. Many wooden carvings such as this have been found over the years throughout the Celtic world. The obvious age of the relic, having become part of the Oak through the tree's growth, would indicate that Cromwell had destroyed a pagan icon, not a Christian one.

Since that day in 1538, pilgrims have continued to visit the Penrhys Holy Well seeking the cures said to be tokens of the Lady's love. In 1595, a large number of pilgrims were apprehended by the authorities and brought before Morgan Jones of Tregib, the local magistrate. Jones refused to bring charges against them, stating that these were only ailing people hoping to find a cure at the well. In May 1977, the first "Pilgrimage of the Sick" since the Reformation was undertaken with 2000 people in attendance.

The well's ability to heal was first recorded in 1460 when Gwylim Tew, a bard, was cured of "the ague and fever." Another bard, Lewis Morganwg, reported that the "mad were baptized and became sane, the blind recovered their sight, cripples bathed and afterwards ran, and the deaf obtained their hearing" at Ffynon Fair.[1] According to Margaret Milliner of the Rhondda Civic Society, "people still come to the mountain for their relief."[2] Eighty thousand pounds sterling had been raised in 1999 for the restoration of the sacred well.[3]

Ten holy wells exist in north Carmarthenshire in the Parishes of Penboyr and Llangeler. One well, Ffynnon Celer, is a dream well like St. Madron's. According to legend, the sick were to bath in the well and then sleep to ensure that the cure being sought would occur. Rebecca's Well, also in north Carmarthenshire, offered healing for sore eyes and "gravel" (also known as gallstones or kidney stones). The healing water was said to be most powerful before sunrise.

The Capel Erbach well in Llanarthney parish is said to cure spasms and the water of Pistyll Giniwil at Llansaint cures both eye and stomach ailments as did Rebecca's Well mentioned above. The water of Pistyll Teilo well not only causes bruises to disappear but is also home to a wailing ghost.

In Pembrokeshire, near St. David's, is St. Non's Well. Reportedly, the waters of St. Non's cures eye ailments, children's diseases and labor pains. Tradition says that the young Nonnita found herself on the wild coast of Wales one night, alone, when she went into labor. The spot where her son was born, who later came to be the Welsh St. David, instantly became a spring. The birth is said to have occurred on March 1st, 500 CE. St. Non's has been a healing well for centuries and most likely dates back into the pagan past. This is obvious due to a nearby stone circle and the linguistic evidence that St. David was in reality Dewi, the Welsh sea god. "Nonnita" was a derivative of "nonne" which meant a priestess healer. It is noteworthy that the word "nun" was the Egyptian word for the primal ocean and the Hebrew letter "nun" meant "fish."[4] It would appear that St. Non's Well was originally dedicated to the goddess and then Christianized.

St. Anne's Well located on the eastern edge of Trellech Village is an ancient well with curative powers. Referred to as the "Virtuous Well" because of these powers, it has been tied to the Druids as a site sacred to them. Highly impregnated with iron, the water of the Virtuous Well was greatly renowned for its healing of eye ailments and "complaints peculiar to women."

Probably the most visited and revered holy well in Wales is that of St. Winifred's at Holywell. There has been a continuous record of healing at this well for over 900 years.[5] The legend of the creation of St. Winifred's Well has already been discussed in Chapter Five and reflects the possible connection with the

---

1 Bowen, Dewi. "The Holy Wells of Glamorgan," in *The Source*, Issue 8, Autumn 1988
2 "Medieval Miracles Shrine Restored" in *BBC News*, December 16,1999. //news.bbc.co.uk
3 Ibid.
4 Walker, Barbara G. *The Women's Encyclopedia of Myths and Secrets*. Edison: Castle Books 1983, 731
5 Fry, Roy and Tristan Gray Hulse. "The Holywell Cure Records" in *The Source*, Issue #1, Autumn 1994

Celtic Head Cult in pre-Christian Britain. The numbers of cures reported at St. Winifred's Well are so many that it has become known as "the Lourdes of Wales." Cures have been reported for blindness, sores of the mouth and tongue, deafness, paralysis, and a variety of internal ailments.

Newspaper accounts of cures were common in the local press the *Flintshire Observer* and *The Courier*. One such article in the *Flintshire Observer*, dated July 13, 1933, sported the following headlines:

"'IT FELT LIKE SOMEONE WAS STROKING MY LEG'
CHORLEY GIRL CURED AT ST. WINEFRED'S WELL
AN AFFLICTION WHICH VANISHED"

A 25-year-old named Nellie Gore, suffering from a blood clot in one leg, visited the holy well in search of a cure. Her knee was swollen and quite painful as she immersed herself in the water. She reported "I had not been in the well long before I felt my knee getting better and I could feel the pain leaving it. It felt like someone was stroking down my leg. I stayed in the water and said a short prayer, and when I came out I knew that I was cured." The reporter noted, "she looked wonderfully fit and well." Another newspaper report from the *Courier* dated August 6, 1923, reported that thousands of people witnessed a 12 month old blind baby have her sight restored "at once" after being immersed in the water.

HEALING WELLS OF SCOTLAND

As discussed earlier, Scotland is the home of "clootie wells," wells that have rags or strips of cloth left as offerings, usually tied to nearby tree branches. Clootie wells in Scotland were normally visited to make wishes[1] while in Southern England rag wells are visited for their healing and spiritual powers. However, Scotland also has a number of healing wells. Legend has it that St. Columba blessed over 300 wells and springs in Scotland in his effort to christianize pagan holy sites.

St. Aidan's Well in Angus was effective for the treatment of sore eyes, diseases of the chest and deafness. Asthma and whooping cough were cured at St. Medana's Well in Galloway. Skin diseases were treated with water from St. Catherine's Well in Edinburgh. Children suffering from "wasting diseases" were covered in plaid and tied to a stake near a well on the faery knoll of Therdy Hill where they spent the night alone. It was believed that the ill child was a "changeling" which the faeries had substituted for the real child. By placing the ill child on the hill it was thought that the faery would return the real child the next morning that would bear no evidence of illness.

---

1 Clootie wells in Scotland are still frequented for their powers to grant wishes. Recently a friend visited a clootie well on Black Isle where she hung a strip of cloth among others and made a wish as is the custom.

Gwyned Well in Abered was visited not for its cure but for the purpose of divination. It was said that by throwing a garment of a sick person into the well one could determine if an individual would recover from an illness or not. According to Marie Trevelyan, if the garment "sank to the right he would get well, but if it went to the left he would surely die."

Foretelling the future health of an individual was also an important reason to visit the well at the sanctuary of Demeter at Patrae in ancient Greece. After prayers were said and incense burned as offering to the goddess Demeter a mirror was tied to a cord and lowered to the water's surface. The diviner would then be able to see the face of the specific individual in the mirror and determine if they would live or die. Another sacred well or spring with powers of divination in ancient Greece was located at the Kassotis spring at the Temple of Apollo at Cyaneae in Lydia. It was here that the Oracle of Delphi bathed and drank of the sacred waters before she would conduct her rituals. Pegomancy, the practice of foretelling the future by using waters of pools or springs, was one method used by the Armenians, the Irish and by the British. In England the river Ouse, Maiden's Well and the Fairy's Pin Well, Gulval and Nantswell in Cornwall, Boughton and Oundle in Northamptonshire, are examples.

The well at Gulval evidently had an old woman guardian who could divine from the well's waters the health of individuals who were not present. Hope wrote, "On approaching this intelligent fountain, the question was proposed aloud to the old woman, when the following appearances gave the reply: If the absent friend were in health, the water was instantly to bubble; if sick, it was to be suddenly discoloured; but if dead, it was to remain in its natural state." Hope refers to the old woman as the "old priestess."

Insanity was cured at St. Maelrubha's Well on an island in Loch Maree. Reportedly, the "patient" was dragged behind a boat and rowed twice around the island, then plunged into the well and made to drink the water — all of which produced the cure. However, drinking from Borgie Well near Cambusland, Scotland caused insanity.

Fertility was sought at St. Winifred's Well at Holywell and Ffynnon y Filiast and Ffynnon y Brenin that were both located at Gwynedd in Llaniestyn parish. Janet and Colin Bord report, "The traditional pagan worship of mother goddesses at holy wells, the natural interpretation of the well as a secret entrance into the body of the Earth Mother or even as her womb, the belief in the life-giving or procreative powers of water — all combined to instill in people the certainty that the holy well was the source of fertility."[1] There are additional holy wells known for their gifts of fertility on the Isle of Skye, one, which ensured the birth of twins, and one that ensured the fertility of cattle.

---

1 Bord, Janet and Colin., op. cit 98

The waters of St. Mary's Well at Grampian were said to cure whooping cough, sore eyes and joint diseases and were also reputed to have cured a "faery" child through the efforts of a witch.

Those seeking relief from toothaches would go to a healing well in North Uist. They were required by tradition to remain silent and not to eat or drink until they reached the well where they then drank three handfuls of the healing water and said "the Father, the Son and the Holy Ghost."

Epilepsy was cured at the Well of the Head in Wester Ross where individuals would drink from a skull kept by a "guardian." This practice continued into the 20th century.

HEALING WELLS OF ENGLAND

Most of the sacred wells of England are found in the western part of the country although a few are known to exist in the London area. Many have undoubtedly been destroyed over the years and were most likely spread throughout the English landscape. One of those wells located in Kent, in the far southeastern section of England is the Abbess's Well at Minster Abbey. There are actually two wells at Minster Abbey; both have been in use for over 3,500 years. Queen Sexburga, Queen of Kent who became the abbess, constructed Britain's oldest nunnery at this site in 640 CE. Sexburga reportedly had a vast knowledge of healing wells and waters, which is why she built the abbey near the two sacred wells. Over the years, the waters healed the wounds of Crusaders, baptized new converts and cured the sick. For her healing work the Abbess Queen, as she became known, was sainted. Legend has it that St. Augustine in 598 CE conducted a mass baptism of over 12,000 converts near the wells in the River Swale.

During the Reformation when Henry VIII dissolved the Catholic Church and ordered many of the holy wells in Britain filled in, the Abbess's Well survived due to the local populations reverence for it. The well has never failed even in the most severe drought although its underground source remains a mystery.

In 1991, local historian Brian Slade undertook an excavation of the wells. Among items recovered were late Bronze Age, Iron Age and Norman pottery, Anglo-Saxon dress pins, a cross, coins (dating back to the Roman settlement), a 400-year-old shoe (ladies size 5), five medieval gold pins, and glassware. The most important item, however, was a figure of a three-headed goddess found in deep silt at the bottom of the well. A book published in 1904 entitled *A History of the Isle of Sheppey* reported that a temple dedicated to the Roman gods Apollo and Diana once stood on the site. It is probable that the statue discovered in 1991 was from that temple, which may have been in existence prior to the Roman occupation.

After the statue's discovery, "miraculous" happenings began to occur. The wife of one of the excavators became pregnant and gave birth to a healthy girl — this was particularly miraculous in that the woman had had a series of miscarriages over the years. Since that time hundreds of pilgrims from as far away as Australia, Germany and Mexico have traveled to the Abbess's Well to drink the water and to touch the statue of the Three-Headed Goddess. They come seeking cures for ailments as diverse as cancer, blindness, lameness and infertility.

Analysis of the water reveals that it is completely pure with trace elements of potassium and magnesium.

London itself has a few healing/sacred wells although most of these have been covered over. One known as "Camberwell" ("camber" is a word meaning "cripple" in Welsh) was sacred to the original Celtic residents. Chesca Potter in an article called *The River of Wells* wrote, "The River Fleet in London was once called the 'river of wells' due to the numerous healing wells which 'sprung up' along its banks."[1]

Increasing pollution from the 13th century until the end of the 19th century resulted in the destruction and, ultimately the disappearance of Fleet River along with its holy wells. Other London wells are Ladywell in South London, which has been paved over, Wells Park which is the site of seven wells — one still in existence at 26 Longton Avenue, Brideswell and Chad's Well in Central London, Clerkenwell, and St. Pancras Well.

St. Pancras was part of St. Pancras Church; the oldest church in London being constructed in 314 CE. St. Pancras still exists as part of St. Pancras Gardens near King's Cross. A beautiful temple like structure stands near the road with several larger-than-life goddess figurines serving to hold aloft the temple roof. At one time, the Fleet River ran past this site. St. Helen, Emperor Constantine's mother, had the church built on the site of an older Roman ruin that was constructed on top of an ancient pagan sacred site. The healing water of St. Pancras was advertised as being "in the greatest perfection and highly recommended by the most eminent physicians in the Kingdom." The general destruction of pagan sites by the Midland Railway in the 19th century brought an end to the pilgrimages. Today St. Pancras stands beside a busy thoroughfare with congested traffic and thousands of pedestrians. However, some people still discern a sense of holiness and mystery in association with this area today.

While insanity was treated in a rather rough manner in Scotland one well in Leicestershire, Sketchley Well, was reported to have a reputation "to brighten the intellect" simply by drinking the water.[2] In Perthshire, at St. Fillan's Holy Pool, an insane individual was led three times "sunwise"[3] around the pool first in

---

1 Potter, Chesca. "The River of Wells," in *The Source*, Issue #1, March 1985

2 Bilson, Charles. *Vestiges of Paganism in Leicestershire*. Loughborough: Heart of Albion Press, 1994, 16 (A reprint of the 1911 edition published by George Allen)

3 The tradition of walking "sunwise" around holy wells is an ancient one associated with the inauguration of a high king of Ireland who would circuit around the holiest site of the kingdom, Tara. This tradition dates back to the pre-Christian times when chieftains would circle their ritual center that would have included a sacred well or spring.

the name of the Father, second in the name of the Son, and lastly in the name of the Holy Spirit. The individual was then submerged in the pool in the name of the Holy Trinity.

Animals too had specific wells where they could be cured of certain ailments. At Hampshire's Iron's Well, formerly known as Lepers' Well, dogs were cured of the mange. Hope wrote, "The spring has a little wooden structure, over and round it, with a board wanting at the top, by which you may drop your dog into the chalybeate water; and a convenient arrangement exists by which, after he has finished his ablutions, he may scramble out on the other side."[1] This well was known at one time as a healing well for lepers until, for some unknown reason, the curative powers of the water changed and became effective for dogs but not for humans.

In 1756, Doctor J. Wall wrote of the healing properties of the Malvern Well in Worcestershire. In his account, the Malvern waters cured a woman's fistulous ulcer, another woman's "phagedenic ulcer of the cheek," a terrible skin disease and "internal cancer" in one year. All, according to Dr. Wall, being examples of the waters "remarkable instances of their great effects."[2]

ICELAND'S HEALING WELLS

One normally doesn't think of Iceland in regard to its wells and springs but Iceland has a long pagan past with holy and healing wells in abundance. Many of the same traditions and rituals observed in Ireland and the rest of Great Britain are also seen in Iceland.

A few of the healing wells in Iceland are at Roenaes, Sommested (including Skrave Church), and at Hellevad and Holmstrup. The two wells at Sommested were said to lose their healing powers when farmers washed their horses in the holy water. This same legend is also found in England, Wales and Ireland. Trevelyan noted that in Wales "if a person washed or sprinkled any kind of animal in one of the fountains of healing, the water lost its virtue."[3] Likewise at Tobar na Sool and Our Lady's Well in Ireland, two wells known to cure blindness, lost their healing powers when blind horses were treated with the healing water. At Our Lady's Well in Limerick County, the horse was cured but the horse's owner became blind.

Iceland's hot springs are bountiful but today only two commercial establishments are in operation. One used as an outpatient clinic by the Ministry of Health is called the Blue Lagoon that is a thermal salt-water lagoon situated on a

---

1 Hope, Robert Charles. *The Legendary Lore of the Holy Wells of England.* London: Elliot Stock 1893, 77 (A facsimile reprint by Llanerch Publishers, Felinfach Wales, 2000)
2 Wall, Dr. J. "Extract of a Letter of J. Wall, M.D. to the Rev. Dr. Lyttelton, Dean of Exeter, and F.R.S. concerning the good Effects of Malvern Waters in Worchestershire," in *Philosophical Transactions of the Royal Society*, Vol. 50, December 1757, 23-24
3 Trevelyan, Marie. *Folk-lore and Folk-stories of Wales.* London: Elliot Stock 1909

lava bed. This lagoon is rich in sodium silica, calcium, potassium and other minerals and is noted for its treatment of psoriasis. The other is the NLFI Health and Rehabilitation Clinic at Hveragerdi, which has been shown to be effective in the treatment of stress-induced ailments, post-trauma conditions and rheumatism.[1]

The Healing Wells of France

France, known for the sacred healing well at Lourdes, has many other healing wells and springs as well. Perhaps the most famous is that of Vichy. Founded by Caesar's invading army at the Roman settlement of Vicus Calidus, or "hot town," Vichy was the summer residence of Emperor Napoleon III. The mineral waters are high in calcium carbonates and carbon dioxide with effective treatments of migraines, rheumatism, diabetes, obesity and disorders of the digestive tract, reported.

France has taken the medical value of mineral springs seriously. There are over 100 thermal spas [2] in France and they are all under the supervision of the Ministry of Health. Many of these spas have research centers nearby. One of these is Aix-les-Bains, which, like Vichy, is high in bicarbonates as well as sulfur. One of the research centers at this spa specializes in rheumatism. Bagnères-de-Bigorre, another center known for its treatments of rheumatism, depression and stress-related disorders, has an amazing 60 springs with calcium, iron, and magnesium sulfates present in the waters.

Saint Honoré has only three springs, with bicarbonates, chlorides, carbon dioxide and arsenic, but the water appears to be effective for diseases of the ear, nose and throat as well as rheumatism and respiratory ailments.

Another healing well much like that at Lourdes, is at Chartre in the Eure valley. A Neolithic engraving of a goddess is located here and the nearby well is said to have cured Fulbert, the builder of the Chartre Cathedral. Since that time, the sick and infirm have made regular pilgrimages to the sacred well seeking cures of the Goddess/Virgin Mary.[3]

North America's Healing Wells

As previously mentioned, there are few widely known holy/healing wells in the Americas compared to Europe, and Great Britain in particular, although there are some worth discussing. Some rather ancient excavated wells have been found in the American Southwest near Clovis, New Mexico dating back to 3,000

---

1 Altman, Nathaniel. *Healing Springs.* Rochester: Healing Arts Press 2000, 227
2 "Spa" comes from the Latin term *Sanus Per Aquam*, a term used by the Roman legions meaning "health by water." Spas were a creation of the Roman soldiers who used them extensively after battle and long marches.
3 Markale, Jean. *The Great Goddess: Reverence of the Divine Feminine From the Paleolithic to the Present.* Rochester: Inner Traditions 1997, 141. A good reference book on present day spas in France is *Healing Springs* by Nathaniel Altman.

BCE and Cienega Creek dated to 2,000 BCE.[1] Archaeologists have not found any offerings in these wells and they are assumed to be utilitarian in nature but it is unknown if a religious purpose was also associated with them. It is possible that there are many more such sites but they have retained their local character and are not readily known to the general population. One well worthy of discussion is known as the "Lourdes of America" located at the little adobe village of San-tuario de Chimayo near Espanola, New Mexico. Here on a Good Friday in the early 19th century a farmer saw a "burst of light" rising from the ground. Upon examination, the man found a crucifix and a "darkened Christ figure."[2] Although a spring nearby has healing properties the most sought after material here is the soil from the area where the light was seen. Since that day, people have taken the soil home in bottles, rubbed the soil onto their bodies and ingested it seeking a cure for their ailments. The numerous canes and crutches left at the "little well room" attest to the numerous successes.

The water of Manitou Lake in Saskatchewan, Canada is said to have cured three Cree Indian men of smallpox in the early 1800s, and Lac St. Anne in Al-berta has been a pilgrim site since 1889 when missionaries learned that the lake was considered sacred and healing by the Indians living nearby. Located 50 km east of Edmonton this small lake becomes host to thousands of pilgrims for five days each July who come seeking the healing powers of its waters. It has been reported that, although the lake has healing properties all year long, "the waters are said to take on special curative properties" during these five days.[3]

Another healing spring is that of Great Pagosa Hot Spring in southern Colo-rado. Used by the Ute Indians who both bathed in the water and drank of it, the hot springs were effective in the treatment of arthritic conditions. The word "pa-gosa" is a derivative of the Ute word *pagosah*, meaning "healing waters." After the white man came across the springs in 1859, Ft. Lewis was established nearby and the springs fell victim to American capitalism, becoming a resort.

The Native Americans universally considered rivers, springs, lakes and other natural features to be animate and alive. So too certain springs were considered sacred with healing powers, the majority of hot springs today that are used as re-sorts were used first by Native Americans for similar purposes. It is unfortunate

---

1 Woodbury, Richard B. and Ezra B.W. Zubrow. "Agricultural Beginnings, 2000 BC–AD 50" in *Handbook of North America n Indians: Vol. 8, Southwest*, edited by Alfonso Ortiz. Wash-ington: Smithsonian Institution 1979, 52

2 Swan, James A. *Sacred Places: How the Living Earth Seeks Our Friendship*. Santa Fe: Bear & Co. 1990, 36. Buried images have been uncovered in many places in Britain and Europe and were presumably images of various saints or the Virgin Mary. However, they were most likely images of the ancient Earth Goddess. As Pennick noted, "images that were discovered in the earth by chance, were believed to have appeared in the world by means of divine grace." See Nigel Pennick, *The Celtic Saints*. New York: Sterling Publishing Co., Inc. 1997, 31

3 Joseph, Frank. *Sacred Sites of the West: A Guide to Mystical Centers*. Blaine: Hancock House Publishers 1997, 35

that many ethnographers ignored the many details about these sites and rarely offer more than a footnote. The Northern Pomo situated in what is now Mendocino County, California used a spring that they called "child water" to facilitate pregnancy. It was thought that if a married woman desired a child she should drink from this spring. The Central Pomo also utilized a spring that they referred to as "child water," the mud from this spring was taken and rubbed on the body of the woman wishing to become pregnant.[1]

The hot springs and mineral springs of Vichy Springs, Harbin Hot Springs and Calistoga in California are perhaps a few of the more famous American healing springs.[2] The hot spring waters of Calistoga come from deep inside the earth, warmed over a huge, 13-mile in diameter magma pool. These waters are effective in the relief and treatment of rheumatism, arthritis and stress induced ailments. Harbin Hot Springs, which has four types of waters including arsenic (used only for skin treatments and never ingested), sulfur, magnesia and iron. Combined, these waters are useful for the treatment of skin ailments, intestinal distress, kidney troubles, rheumatism and other joint diseases and circulatory problems.

Perhaps the most famous American healing springs are those at Saratoga Springs in New York State. Once referred to as the "Queen of American Spas" it was the inspiration of Calistoga's developers. An old story is told in Calistoga that Sam Brannan, who founded the resort, wanted to call Calistoga "Saratoga of California" but in a drunken stupor said "Calistoga of Sarifornia" — and the name stuck. Saratoga was, as most healing springs were, a primordial spring used by the Native Americans long before being taken over by the white man. The Iroquois used the waters for healing and were able to keep its location concealed until 1767. The Mohawks referred to these springs as the "Medicine Springs of the Great Manitou" and believed that the springs were a gift to all from the Great Spirit. [3] The spring became an object of a tug of war with those who wanted to exploit it commercially, until it was declared to be in the public domain. The waters were useful for indigestion and as a laxative, with such notable visitors as George Washington and Alexander Hamilton frequenting the spot. Since those days, the waters have been used for the treatments of asthma, heart disease and rheumatism.[4]

Other healing spas "appropriated" in early North America by the westward expanding European culture include the Bow Valley Springs in Western Canada used by the Assiniboine Indians until taken over by wealthy whites. Hot Springs, Arkansas, has 47 thermal springs which "percolate" at 6040 feet below ground and rise at the rate of 940,000 gallons a day at 143 degrees. This water has been

1 Heizer. Robert F. "Natural Forces and Native World View," in *Handbook of North America n Indians: Volume 8-California.* Washington: Smithsonian Institution 1978, 652

2 See Chapter 2 for detailed descriptions of these sites.

3 Altman, op. cit., 41

4 Claims for specific health benefits are no longer given at Saratoga due to several malpractice lawsuits

dated to 4000 BCE. Containing calcium, bicarbonates, silica and sodium, its waters were claimed to cure "almost everything, from syphilis to melancholy."[1] Hot Springs was considered sacred and a place of peace for all surrounding tribes but was located in Tunicas Indian territory. Spanish explorer Hernando DeSoto was the first European to see these springs in 1541.[2]

White Sulphur Springs in West Virginia has been well known since the late 1700s by white settlers and much longer to Native Americans. White Sulphur Springs became famous in 1778 when a woman who was crippled with rheumatism was taken to the springs by her family. They had heard that the Shawnee Indians believed the springs to have miraculous healing powers. The woman was laid out in a hollowed out log and her family filled the hollow log with spring water, which they heated with stones. After a few weeks she had reportedly recovered so well that she rode home on her own horse.[3] There were really three springs at this location. One, the white sulfur spring, gave the spa its name but another, a clear water spring, appears to be the healing spring. These water sources became very popular with America's new aristocracy. Thomas Jefferson frequented the area often and attempted to get the Commonwealth of Virginia to purchase it for public use. Other famous visitors were Daniel Webster, Davy Crocket, Francis Scott Key, Robert E. Lee, Henry Clay and seven US presidents. The waters are rich in sulfates and hydrogen sulfide and have been effective in the treatment of rheumatism, stress-related disorders, liver problems and gastrointestinal diseases.[4]

Healing Springs in County Barnwell, South Carolina, is another site that was held sacred by Native Americans. Today the Healing Springs Baptist Church stands next to the four springs that bubble up out of the ground offering delicious drinking water containing sodium carbonate, potassium sulfate, iron sesquioxide, ammonia and silica. Reportedly, vegetables watered with this spring water stay fresher much longer. During the Revolution, the springs gained notoriety when six wounded British soldiers were left there to tend to their wounds. After bathing in the spring water, their injuries miraculously healed and they returned to their units fit to fight. Over the years, a series of owners traded and bought the springs until 1944 when the last owner, L.P. Boylston, died. In his will, he stated that the healing springs belonged to God and that no earthly owner should again possess them.[5]

---

1 Croutier, Alev Lytle. *Taking the Waters.* New York: Abbeville Press 1992, 154. It should be noted that the United States Public Health Service operated a clinic and bathhouse at Hot Springs for the treatment of syphilis and gonorrhea around 1918 until the development of penicillin in the 1940s.

2 Altman, op. cit., 40

3 Olcott, William. *The Greenbriar Heritage: White Sulphur Springs West Virginia.* Haarlem: Arndt, Preston, Chapin, Lamb & Keen, Inc. n/d, 5

4 Altman, op. cit., 182

5 Barnwell County Chamber of Commerce. "Healing Springs" (www.barnwellcounty. com/healing_springs.htm 2001)

CHAPTER 7. ANCIENT AND CONTEMPORARY RITUALS OBSERVED AT HOLY WELLS

R.J. Stewart wrote, "The therapeutic power of wells remained into histori-cal Christian times, with saints taking over but never quite disguising pagan functions. Rituals were preserved in folklore deriving from pagan worship; these include processing around wells, making offerings...and ceremonies involving drinking from skulls."[1]

A rich tradition of specific observances and rituals has evolved over the years at many of these sacred wells. It is believed that if these "patterns" are observed an individual's wish or cure would be granted. Many of these practices will seem rather odd unless the antiquity of such practice is considered. Because most all of these "patterns" have occurred in Catholic or Anglican countries such rituals in the past resulted in religious ridicule from the Protestant quarter and were used as ammunition in anti-Papal broadsides. This was most common in the 19th century. A typical example of this type of propaganda is a statement in the No-vember 18, 1854, issue of the English publication *Notes and Queries*:

> The Irish peasantry are...so thoroughly persuaded...of the sanctity of those pagan practices, that they would travel, bareheaded and barefooted, from ten to twenty miles for the purpose of crawling on their knees round these wells and upright stones, and oak trees, westward as the sun travels, some three times, some six, some nine, and so on in uneven numbers, until their voluntary penance was completely fulfilled.

It is obvious that *some* of these "folk-ways" are survivals of very ancient pagan rituals that pre-date Christianity by many hundreds and thousands of years. Just as holy wells became Christianized, so too the ancient religious traditions be-came absorbed into the new religion.

---

1 Stewart, R.J. *Celtic Gods Celtic Goddesses.* London: Blanford 1990, 41

This section will offer a wide variety of examples that will indicate how these rituals are related and how they tie into traditional pagan beliefs.

The number "3" is a very magical number in many religious traditions. It represents the triad of body, mind and spirit. It also symbolizes the triune Mother-Goddess whose figurines are common in ancient Europe. The number three is also represented among Roman triad of Minerva, Mercury and Apollo, the Greek Fates, Gorgons and Furies as well as the Holy Trinity of Christianity. The continuation of working with three's in rituals involving sacred waters attests to the history of these ancient prescriptions.

There are very many accounts of pilgrims walking three times around a holy well as part of a ritual. The minister of the Scottish parish where St. Fillan's Well is located wrote in the late 1700s:

> It is still visited...especially on the 1st of May and 1st of August....The invalids, whether men, women, or children, walk or are carried round the well three times in a direction *deishal*, that is, from east to west, according to the direction of the sun. They all drink the water, and bathe in it. These operations are accounted a certain remedy for various diseases.[1]

On the small, 37-acre sacred isle of Inis Gulaire, situated off County Mayo in Ireland, it was customary to go around each of the seven *leachta* (stone cairns) near the holy well, three times on the knees and an additional three times walking, while saying seven Paters, seven Aves and a Creed. The well on Inis Gulaire was dedicated to St. Brendan with access prohibited to women.

At Lough (or *Loch*) Dergh, also in Ireland, pilgrims would "go around the stones standing in the water three times to satisfy for the sins of our will, memory, and understanding..."[2] Another account of the particular "pattern" at Lough Dergh states that the pilgrim would "go right-handwise round the well reciting... prayers. This circuit is made three times."[3] It is possible that the origins of this particular pattern date back to the legend of the Irish goddess Boann. Boann had been forbidden by her husband, King Nechtan, to go to the well for no woman was allowed near it. However, Boann ignored the king and went to the well where she also walked three times around it widdershins. This was a direct pagan challenge to the ancient law of patriarchy.[4] The well was so angered that its waters rose up and swept Boann out to sea; she thus became the River Boyne. It is interesting to note that the Celts knew Nechtan as a god of the waters; they also called him the Daghda — the "good god." Another point of view is that the *pattern* of crawling or walking three times around a holy well is not rooted in paganism at all but is a self-imposed penance:

---

1 Anon. "Our Hagiology," in *Blackwood's Edinburgh Magazine*, Vol. 82, October 1857, 454

2 Hardy, Philip Dixon. *The Holy Wells of Ireland.* Dublin: Hardy & Walker 1840

3 Logan, Patrick. *The Holy Wells of Ireland.* Buckinghamshire: Colin Smyth 1980, 21

4 Straffon, Cheryl. *The Earth Goddess: Celtic and Pagan Legacy of the Landscape.* London: Blandford 1997, 195

The people who collect about these wells, and went round them on their knees, did not do so for the benefit of the souls of their departed friends, but for the purpose of performing penance for their own offenses, or pay some secret vow made to the Creator, either in way of thanksgiving for some benefit, or in atonement for some sin. These penances or thanksgivings were always self-imposed, and had nothing whatever to do with any dogma of religion or rule of the Church.[1]

The cure of John Trelille at St. Madron's Well in 1640 was one of the best documented cases. Trelille had been partially paralyzed for 16 years when he visited the well. Witnesses reported that Trelille crawled three times around the well before "dipping" himself three times in the water. He then fell asleep near the well and upon awakening he was cured. A similar ritual used to be practiced at St. Euny's which required children to be dipped three times in the well and then dragged three times "widdershynnes" around it in order for cures to be effective. At the Well of the Weathers, also known as Tobar na Mult and An Tubrid More, in County Kerry, the practice is not to immerse oneself in the water but to take three sips and to drip some of the water three times on the face.

St. Boniface and Craigie Wells on the Black Isle were two healing wells where the custom was to take three handfuls of water which were then spilled on the ground. The individual would then tie a piece of cloth to a nearby tree accompanied by the sign of the cross. Finally the person would take a drink from the well — all this a ritual to secure healing.

To cure the mumps in Ireland Lady Wilde recorded the following:

> Take nine black stone gathered before sunrise, and bring the patient with a rope around his neck to a holy well — not speaking all the while. Then cast in three stones in the name of God, three in the name of Christ, and three in the name of Mary. Repeat this process for three mornings and the disease will be cured.[2]

For smaller children a halter was tied around the child's neck, he was then lead to a brook where he was bathed and dipped "three times in the name of the Trinity."[3]

Pilgrims continue to visit Holywell, also known as St. Winifred 's, in Wales for its curative powers. The pilgrims walk three times through the small, inner bath while saying the Rosary. Those seeking comfort then "dip" three times in the bath. This same process has been in place at least 1350 years.

In Wales, according to Marie Trevelyan, "it was customary in the first half of the nineteenth century for farmers to throw three ears of wheat, drawn from the

1 Redman, S. "Ceremony for the Souls of the Slain in Battle," in *Notes and Queries*, Vol. 72, April 16, 1859, 322

2 Wilde, Lady. *Irish Cures, Mystic Charms & Superstitions.* New York: Sterling Publishing Company, Inc. 1991, 24

3 Ibid.

first wagon-load to leave the harvest-field, into the nearest running water...this was done for luck."[1]

At St. Fegla's Well in Carnarvosnhire, Wales it was the practice to wash ones hands in the well, drop a coin (a fourpenny-piece) into it and then walk around the well three times while repeating the Lord's Prayer. If the individual seeking the healing was a male, he would also carry a cock, and a woman a hen, in a basket to the local church where he or she would remain until daybreak. If the cock or hen died during the night then it was known that the sickness had been transferred from the man or woman to the bird. This was done to seek cure of "falling sickness."

People with epilepsy would often visit the Well of the Head in Wester Ross, Scotland where, after the sun had begun to set, they would solicit the well's guardian for permission to approach the well. In silence, the individual would climb the hill to the well, take the ritual skull from its silver casket and walk three times deosil (sunwise) around the well. The guardian then dipped the skull in the water and handed it to the individual in the name of the Trinity. At that time, the guardian assigned "prohibitions" to the person. If everything was done according to plan, a cure would be forthcoming.[2]

Certain wells also had specific visitation schedules, which had to be observed for healings to be effective. At St. Euny's Well in Sancreed, one had to visit and wash in the well on the first three Wednesdays in May for an effective cure. Rickets was cured at Baglan Well in Glamorgan but only if visited the first three Thursdays in May. At St. Madron's Well in Cornwall, rickets was cured if pilgrimages were made during the morning on the first three Sundays in May. Children's skin diseases were also treated and cured at St. Madron's if the following ritual was observed:

> Here, on the first three Wednesdays in May, children...were plunged under the water three times against the sun. and carried nine times round the spring, going from east to west. After this, a piece of the child's clothing was torn from a garment and hung on the thorn tree which grew near the baptistry or left between stones.[3]

At St. Mary's Well at Orton, Grampian, Scotland it was the practice to visit the well on the three Saturdays before and the three Saturdays following Lammas. Barren women were assured of being fertile if they walked three times sunwise around healing bodies of water while bathing their abdomens with the healing water and chanting a sacred eola, or incantation. Crowds used to gather at Caernarvonshire's Ffynnon Dduw well the first three Sundays in July to dance and to

1 Trevelyan, Marie. *Folk-lore and Folk-stories of Wales.* London: Elliot Stock 1909
2 Livingstone, Sheila. *Scottish Customs.* New York: Barnes & Noble 1996, 87
3 Radford, E. and M.A. *Encyclopaedia of Superstitions.* New york: The Philosophical Library 1949, 256

play games and at Ffynnon Erfyl in Montgomeryshire on Whit Sunday, Trinity Sunday and Easter Monday.

Wells dedicated to the Celtic saints were visited on those days thought to be most powerful — the particular saint's day, such as St. Elijah's Day in Estonia, Ascension Day, New Year's Day and Palm Sunday. Official pilgrimages were conducted in Cornwall to the holy wells of Gulval, Nantswell and Roche. After spending the day at these wells, drinking the water and meditating, the pilgrims would spend the night next to the well in prayer. In the morning, just after sunrise, the pilgrims participated in *bowsenning*, a ceremony in which they immersed themselves in the sacred water "to receive the blessing of the saint."[1] This ceremony is still observed in Ireland and Brittany.

If one was lucky enough to be at Gulval Well in Cornwall on St. Peter's Eve a question could be asked of the well if a beloved one was sick or well, living or dead. If the water bubbled and boiled the person was well, if the water remained calm, it was bad news.

The time of day was also regarded as being specifically important in visiting wells for cures, wishes and divining the future. As previously noted, some wells were visited at midnight and others at sunrise or sunset. These times appear to have been universally recognized as propitious. Ergo-Hart Västrik noted in his paper *The Waters and Water Spirits in Votian Folk Belief* that in Estonia "in olden times" when doctors were scarce, individuals would go to "people who taught things" for advice as to where and when holy water sites should be visited. He noted, "those who were afraid to go alone took a companion with them. They were afraid because you had to go after sunset. Or early in the morning when the sun rises..."[2] Many of the rituals were carried out "at the springs and streams further away from villages which were considered extraordinary/sacred because they flowed 'counter-clock-wise'...literally 'against the day.'"[3]

In North Kelsey, England, girls would walk three times backwards around Maiden's Well and then look into the water to seek an image of their future husband. Thomas remarks that pilgrims to St. Winifred's Well would ask St. Beuno three times for a cure. He wrote, "if he had not done so by the third time of asking, they would die, but this only meant that he had chosen to grant them extra spiritual rewards instead."[4]

Other numbers were also very important to pilgrims but for the most part were multiples of three. At times, an individual would take three sips of the water, walk three times around the well and then say nine Hail Marys. At St. Buonia's Well, also at County Kerry, the pilgrim walks nine timed around the well, each

1 Pennick, Nigel. *The Celtic Saints*. New York: Sterling Publishing Co., Inc. 1997, 104
2 Västrik, Ergo-Hart. "The Waters and Water Spirits in Votian Folk Belief," in *Folklore*, vol. 12, December 1999, 30. Institute of the Estonian Language.
3 Ibid.
4 Thomas, Keith. *Religion and the Decline of Magic*. London: Penguin Books 1971, 768

time stopping to pray near an ancient cairn. On top of the cairn is a flagstone that has a circular hole in the middle through which pilgrims pass their votive offerings of pins, buttons, etc. It is interesting that nearby is a standing stone upon which people have scratched a cross figure deep in the stone with pebbles.

Domestic animals, especially cattle, have been part of Celtic and pagan ritual for thousands of years. At Beltane, the Celts drove their cattle between huge bonfires to purify them and some of this tradition has survived into the twentieth century. Frazer wrote "in the Hebrides (during Beltane) every fire was put out and a large one lit on top of the hill, and the cattle driven round it sunwards (*dessil*), to keep off murrain all the year."[1] Almost identical practices were observed in the Slavic countries as well as Italy. At Loch Iona, a small lake in County Clare, it was the practice to drive sick cattle across the lake (but only on Mondays or Thursdays) to ensure their recovery. In Morocco, it was also a practice to wash cattle in rivers on St. John's Eve to keep illness and bad luck at bay. On Lammas Sunday at Croagh Patrick in Ireland, wells were dressed with fresh flowers and cattle driven through streams. Lumps of butter had been tossed into the streams in the belief that the animals would have a better chance to survive and prosper through the year. This tradition was continued into the 1950s as a group ritual and while it may still continue, today it is done so privately. Legends of milk, rather than water, flowing from the well of St. Illtyd in Wales during mid-summer, were common in the past. Such legends indicated a belief that the "milk" flowed directly from the breasts of the Earth Mother. This is an ancient belief that wells are both life giving and life nurturing. In Estonia, where the goddess of waters, lakes and rivers was worshipped in former times, a priest would sprinkle holy water on the cattle and sheep once a year. This would ensure that they would remain healthy and fertile for the following year.[2]

Until the middle of the 19th century, cattle were driven around the St. Herbot church near Huelgoet, Brittany, "then led to his holy well to drink the water. Bottles of water were taken home by participants who needed to treat sick cattle."[3]

In the 19th century, Lady Wilde began to compile Irish customs and myths, many involving holy wells. One of these "Irish cures" was for cattle that no longer gave milk. Wilde wrote that such cattle are probably "bewitched by the fairies." The recommended cure was that "the owner must lead her three times round one of the ancient stone monuments near a holy well, casting an elf stone each time on the heap."[4]

---

1 Frazer, Sir James. *The Golden Bough: A Study in Magic and Religion.* Hertfordshire: Wordsworth Editions Ltd. 1993, 620

2 Västrik, op. cit

3 Pennick, op. cit., 22

4 Wilde, Lady. *Irish Cures, Mystic Charms & Superstitions.* New York: Sterling Publishing Company, Inc. 1991, 12

While many wells were thought to lose healing and magickal properties when animals, specifically horses, were washed in them,[1] other wells were used extensively to protect and heal animals. The waters of Stot Well in Scotland were said to cure a wasting disease in cattle. Katy Jordan noted in her book *The Haunted Landscape* that Hancock's well at Luckungton not only was used to treat and cure human sprains but sick dogs. Net Well on Net Down was considered a "cattle well" as was the Salt Spring at Wooton Bassett. In addition to these animal wells, Hog's Well near Warminster was known for its powers to strengthen piglets.[2]

Kildar is the home of the goddess Bridget's Well and shrine. A flame has been kept burning (off an on) since antiquity and the Catholic Diocese has continued an obviously pagan ritual in the form of a "Celebration of the Christlight." As part of the Jubilee 2000 Ireland, the parishioners gathered clay from their local wells, rivers and lakes and took the clay back to their local church. At sunset on May 20th a large "vigil fire" was lit at Curragh with "firekeepers" tending it through the night. As pilgrims arrived, they would place embers from their own parish fires into the vigil fire. As the fire died down they would mix the clay from the wells, rivers and lakes with the ashes, which were then scattered in a garden, proposed for "renewal and harmony." At the end of the Jubilee, fires were rekindled from the vigil fire and returned to the local churches.

This is an important mixture of ancient pagan festivals and Christian celebration. By combining the sacred elements of fire and water from the holy wells, a communal event has been created that perpetuates the sacred flame and gives back to the earth. Part of Ireland's Jubilee was the National Day of Local Pilgrimages in which almost every Catholic parish in the nation organized to "take to the hills, wells, rocks...in a jubilee pilgrimage." Among those events was one in which "every parish (in Killala) is being asked to bring a stone from a local holy site to put on a cairn inside the abbey at Moyne."[3] The offering of stones and the construction of cairns is an ancient practice of creating or marking shrines. Cairns have been built by almost every culture in every land. They are still used by Native Americans, as seen at Panther Meadow on Mt. Shasta, and Australian Aborigines among others. This combination of ancient practices and modern day Catholicism affirms our connection to a universal, but subconscious, ritual memory.

Another ancient tradition that mixed Christian and pagan elements were the sacrificial rites at Kotko Village in Estonia. Here during the Spring, well into the

---

1   Marie Trevelyan wrote in her book, *Folk-lore and Folk-stories of Wales*, "if a person washed or sprinkled any kind of animal in one of the fountains of healing, the water lost its virtue."

2   Jordan, Katy. *The Haunted Landscape: Folklore, Ghosts & Legends of Wiltshire*. Bradford on Avon: Ex Libris Press 2000, 193

3   McGarry, Patsy. "Jubilee pilgrimages abound as matches are sidelined," in *The Irish Times*, May 20, 2000.

19th century, a ram was slaughtered to the "mother and father" (*enne* and *ata*). By doing so the rest of the village's herd would not drown in the springs, rivers and bogs. Västrik wrote "the sacrifice to the water spirit was integrated into church practice: a small wooden chapel was located near the sacrificial site, the ceremony was conducted by a priest."[1] A similar ritual was conducted in Lancashire, England where every seven years, on a specific night, the Ribble River would take a life. To combat this tragedy the residents would drown a bird, dog or cat in the river to satisfy the need for a sacrificial life.

The holiest water in India is that of the Ganges River. Although terribly polluted by raw sewage, including floating corpses, devout Hindu's believe that the sins of a lifetime will be removed by drinking a few drops from the Ganges. Several pilgrimages are undertaken each year as they have for centuries. One of the most popular known is the Panchakroshi. The Panchakroshi is a 50-mile trek over five days with stops at 108 shrines. Pilgrims rise at dawn the first day to bathe in the river and then proceed clockwise over the 50-mile course. Another popular pilgrimage is called the Panchatirthi. During this pilgrimage, the pilgrims are required to stop and bathe at five spots thought to be spiritual crossing places. These are areas where an individual may cross between the physical world and one of spiritual liberation.[2]

One of the oldest continuous sacred water festivals in the world is the Maha Kumbh Mela, also held on the Ganges River in India every 12 years when the planets align. Two-thousand-one was a special year for the festival because not only did the planetary alignment occur, but also a lunar eclipse. This unusual celestial alignment-eclipse last occurred 144 years ago.

As the planets reach their maximum alignment, huge crowds gather on the Ganges and Yumuna Rivers. It is said that the mythical underground river Saraswati begins to boil and merge with the blue waters of the Ganges and the green waters of the Yumuna.

Part of the ritual performed during Maha Kumbh Mela is the "churning of the ocean" that mimics the primordial churning of the oceans by the Devas (angles) and the Asuras (devils). The Devas and Asuras worked together in this task so that they could uncover the Nectar of Immortality. In myth, one of the Devas flew off with the nectar, spilling a few drops into the river transforming the waters into a holy place for pilgrims.

Large crowds have celebrated the Kumbh Mela since at least 500 CE when a traveling Chinese merchant first recorded the event. During the festival people bathe in the sacred waters and make offerings of small statues, usually of the elephant god Ganesha. Ganesha is a god who has powers specifically to help an

---

1 Västrik, op. cit., 35

2 Harpur, James. *The Atlas of Sacred Places: Meeting Points of Heaven and Earth*. New York: Henry Holt and Company 1994, 192

individual overcome obstacles and to provide good luck. Votive offerings made to Vishnu include grain, butter, incense and water.

One of the "patterns" held at various sacred wells and other sites include the use of licorice. Licorice by its nature acts as an expectorant, a laxative, is good for coughs and arthritis and is used as a natural sweetener. How did it become associated with holy wells? The origin is unknown however since the 18th century until the 1970s children used go to these spots and dip a licorice stick into a cup containing well water and sip the water-licorice mixture. Researcher Alison Maloney noted that the practice at the Liquorice Wells in Wychwood Forest may have been to "promote good health" since the mixture "created a sort of internal disinfectant.[1] Wychwood Forest resident T.L. Miles, in his article *Springs, Wells & Witches*, wrote "On Palm Sunday, people from the villages bordering the forest visit the spring as the water is supposed to have curative properties...for maximum effect the water has to be mixed with Spanish liquorice and some of the visitors take away bottles of the water for future use....As children, on Palm Sunday we always wore a sprig of the willow known to us as "palm" and drank a little of the liquorice mixture....In my own village the custom died out during the First World War when liquorice wasn't available. When peace returned, like so many old ways, it was never revived."[2] The "Healing Well" near Wye in Derbeyshire was also part of the licorice tradition.

Palm Sunday was also a time for the traditional fair at Silbury Hill, a huge man-made mound 4500 years old. Silbury Hill, located in Wiltshire, was probably constructed as a temple dedicated to the Earth goddess. During the fair, local residents would gather to have picnics featuring figs, and to drink water from the nearby Swallowhead Spring — often mixed with licorice.

A similar tradition is that of "sugar-cupping." Hope noted, "on Easter Day young people and children go to the Dropping Well, near Tideswell, with a cup in one pocket and a quarter pound of sugar (? Honey) in the other, and having caught in their cups as much water as they wished from the droppings of the Tor-spring, they dissolved the sugar in it."[3] It used to be a tradition at Giant's Cave in Cumberland, "from time immemorial," for adolescent boys and girls to get together on the third Sunday in May to drink sugar-water. This, of course, often resulted in further activities at the local public house that would result in parental displeasure. This day was called "Sugar-and-Water Sunday."[4] Other wells frequented for this activity were St. Margaret and St. Helena's wells in Yorkshire and Woden's well in Gloucestershire. Hope noted that young people

---

1 Maloney, Alison. Wells-And-Spas@JISCMAIL.AC.UK April 26, 2001
2 Miles, T.L. "Springs, Wells & Witches" in *Cotswold Life*, May 1983, 39
3 Hope, Robert Charles. *The Legendary Lore of the Holy Wells of England.* London: Elliott Stock 1893, 61 (A facsimile reprint by Llanerch Publishers, Felinfach Wales, 2000)
4 Ibid., 40

visited these wells every Sunday with similar events in Cumberland, Derbyshire, and Shropshire.[1]

While there may be some medicinal value to this practice, it would appear that the association of Palm and Easter Sunday also brings with it an ancient religious tradition. Russet Well and Lady Well in Castelton, also in Derbyshire, were part of the "sugar cupping" tradition. There is only anecdotal information concerning this ritual and it is unlikely that the true meanings behind this old custom will be revealed. However, Hope implies that the use of sugar may be tied to rituals that utilized the prophetic powers of certain wells:

> The wells in England, as elsewhere, had not all the same virtues attrib-uted to them. Some were blessed and used for baptisms, to others were attributed curative properties...while others possessed mystical and pro-phetic powers, at which offerings of cakes, pins, needles, and small coins were made, and sugar and water drunken.[2]

However, Buckley noted that this custom might have had a more utilitarian origin in that the sugar masked the metallic taste of some well water, which had a high mineral content. "Nevertheless," he adds, "the waters of Ffynnon Stockwell and Pistyll Giniwil (in Wales), which both taste absolutely pure, have each been subject to this custom."[3]

As noted earlier, some wells were utilized to foretell the future or to obtain favorable signs for important events in an individual's life. St. Madron is one of these wells. Cornish historian Dr. Borlase, as quoted by Hope, stated, "By drop-ping pins or pebbles into the fountain, by shaking the ground around the spring, or by continuing to raise bubbles from the bottom, on certain lucky days, and when the moon is in a particular stage of increase or decrease, the secrets of the well are presumed to be extorted."[4]

Alev Croutier, in her book *Taking the Waters*, wrote of her childhood in Istanbul in the 1940s and 1950s:

> We often traveled to the tomb of Kuyu Baba, a Sufi saint, who was re-puted to grant just about anything. We would tie rags next to hundreds of others that were dancing in the wind around his tomb, which was by a spring, and then would make wishes, offering him a sacrifice if our wish was granted. Once a rooster gave its life because I passed my exams. After that, I stopped going to the saint.[5]

One of the most interesting and complex patterns I have heard is practiced at the Toothache Well in County Leitrim, Ireland, which is also known as St. Bridg-id's Well. Pilgrims are required to say five Paters, five Aves and a Creed, make a

---

1 Ibid., xv

2 Ibid., xxi

3 Buckley, Kemmis. "Some Holy wells of South Carmarthenshire," a talk given to the Llanelli Art Society, February 3, 1971

4 Hope, op. cit., 10

5 Croutier, Alev Lytle. *Taking the Waters*. New York: Abbeville Press 1992, 66

promise to the saint that he or she will not shave or polish shoes on Sunday, bless him or herself with water from the well and also put some of the water on the effected tooth. After this, the pilgrim adds a stone to the nearby cairn and leaves a stone, pin or coin at the well. Should the individual forget and shave or polish shoes on any Sunday the toothache will be back in full force.[1]

As discussed earlier, ancient standing stones and sacred waters have a common ancestry. Their existence is intricately interwoven. One such megalith with a long history of connected ritual is the dolmen called La Pierre à Berthe located in a field next to the village cemetery of Pontchâteau, in Brittany. According to Aubrey Burl, it was believed that the dolmen would cure gout if one approached it on one's knees. "Up to the 19th century," wrote Burl, "pilgrims would go from the fountain by the church to make their devotions at the stone."[2] The fountain, or well, connection to the standing stone had an important part in the perceived cure received at the dolmen. Unfortunately, the dolmen was blown up in 1850 by a treasure seeker.

Among traditional and Orthodox Jews it has been a ritual practice since the 2nd century BCE for women to purify themselves in either a ritual pool or in a "living water" source, such as a flowing spring or river. Algerian Jewish women also conducted a ritual of evil transference involving the careful concoction of a beverage that, after eight days, was thrown with much ceremony into a running spring. The result hoped for was the cure of an illness. Writer Joëlle Allouche-Benayoun summarized the use of water ritual among Algerian Jews:

> The rites of water embody the passage from the profane to the sacred, the passage from the "outer" to the "inner," the passage from the state of nature (undisciplined urges, out of control) to the state of culture (state of sublimated urge or state of the Law). But above all....(they) seem to be a symbolic way of casting out the existential anguish inherent in the thinking human being.[3]

1 Logan, op. cit., 84
2 Burl, Aubrey. *Megalithic Brittany.* New York: Thames and Hudson Inc., 1985, 102
3 Allouche-Benayoun, Joëlle. "The Rites of Water for the Jewish Women of Algeria," in *Women and Water: Menstruation in Jewish Life and Law.* Edited by Rahel R. Wasserfall. Hanover: Brandeis University Press 1999, 213

CHAPTER 8. AN HISTORICAL PERSPECTIVE ON HOLY WELLS

Throughout this book, I have shown that sacred wells, rivers, lakes and streams have been objects of reverence throughout history from the Neolithic to the 21st century by pagans and Christians alike. The legends, myths and rituals discussed have a shared history as well. While some of these legends, myths and rituals have been slightly modified to reflect the currently accepted religious traditions, they continue to exist. They exist today as they have since these sacred sites began to attract people with their healing powers and supernatural characteristics.

Because religion and cultural traditions are so important in maintaining a society, they are also the most vulnerable to attacks by those forces wishing to monopolize them and to use them as objects of control. This did not occur until the conflict between the "Old Ways" and Christianity came to a focal point. Some early Christian leaders were so taken aback with the concept of baptism, due to the ancient powers imbued in water, that they had to repeatedly remind their followers of the differences between pagan and Christian worship. Tertullian wrote, "witness all shady founts, and all unfrequented brooks, and the ponds in the baths...or the cisterns and wells which are said to have the property of 'spiriting away, through the power, that is, of a hurtful spirit."[1] In fact, the message in those days was that pagan spirits and demons inhabited the waterways and they should be avoided at all costs.

When the early Christian missionaries began their conversion of the pagan populations of the British Isles they immediately began to bless the wells that

---

1 Flint, Valerie. "The Demonisation of Magic and Sorcery in Late Antiquity: Christian Redefinitions of Pagan Religions," in *Witchcraft and Magic in Europe: Ancient Greece and Rome.* Philadelphia: University of Pennsylvania Press 1999, 336

were already held sacred and to re-name them for Christian saints. This of course allowed the populace to continue to visit the wells as they always had as long as they gave credit to the new gods and saints.

As Christianity evolved, and split into factions during the Reformation, things began to change. Laws were enacted to prohibit people from making pilgrimages to wells or to visit them for spiritual, physical or divination reasons. Protestants began to publish broadsides that claimed that the Catholic priests were creating holy wells and associated rituals to control people and to profit from them. Holy Wells became a political issue between these two religious factions. This section will focus on the struggle that Christianity has had in accepting these sacred sites as well as how ruling politics have used them as pawns in the manipulation and control of the population.

During the first few centuries of Christianity, the early Catholic Church adopted a method to include previously pagan holy sites into Christian legend so that Christianity would be easier for the "heathens" to accept. Pope Gregory in 601 CE instructed the clergy to destroy all pagan idols they found in Britain but to "purify" any temples and wells and to use them in Christian service. This is one reason that many of the ancient Christian churches in Britain contain many pagan images including the famous Sheela-na-gig figures. It is also the reason that many Churches have wells, long unused, located in the recesses of their structures. Holy Wells were perhaps the most difficult of all pagan symbols to eradicate. The life giving water that naturally bubbled from the earth was a constant feature not only representing religious belief and values, but also supplying the actual water needs. As one historian wrote, "sacred springs were renamed in honor of saints and churches built over the sites of pagan temples, yet the nature of reverence and worship remained the same."[1]

Martin of Braga, in his work *On the Castigation of Rustics* written in 574 CE, said, "many demons, expelled from heaven, also preside either in the sea or in rivers or springs or forests; men ignorant of god also worship them as gods and sacrifice to them." [2] Martin went on to ask "to put bread in a spring, what is it but the worship of the Devil?"[3]

St. Augustine is quoted as warning the Roman's "lest any one during the festivity of St. John should dare to wash himself in springs, ponds, or rivers, by day or by night, since this wretched custom has remained till now from pagan custom." His efforts to stop the veneration of springs and other sacred waters were ineffective as evidenced by the continuation of the custom today.

During the 4th and 5th centuries, Christian fanatics threw huge amounts of pagan figurines, statues, reliefs and altars into deep wells in an attempt to

---

1 Ellerbe, Helen. *The Dark Side of Christian History*. Orlando: Morningstar and Lark 1995, 53
2 Hillgarth, J.N. *The Conversion of Western Europe, 350-750*. Englewood Cliffs: Prentice-Hall, Inc. 1969, 57
3 Ibid., 61

rid the world of pagan influence. Interestingly Merrifield pointed out "precisely the same methods seem to have been used to dispose of unwanted pagan images as had been used to make offerings to the deities of earth and water that they represented."[1] Merrifield cautions, in fact, that we should not jump to conclusions about findings in wells being votive offerings as they may have been the result of early Christian acts of vandalism.

While the wells themselves were more or less protected during this time, the priestess-guardians were not. The Christian monks began to prohibit women from visiting many of the wells. Priestesses who remained were subject to organized attacks, raped and robbed of the sacred implements of the wells, in acts of defilement. These acts of organized violence were effective tactics in the destruction of the pagan religious institutions and traditions that had existed for so long. As one medieval French document relates, "never any more from the wells did appear maidens, nor did they serve any more..."

Holywell remains the primary holy well in Britain and has been in continuous use since pre-Christian times. It too has had a resident guardian-priest through the ages until 1688 when Protestants attacked the chapel and drove the guardian out.[2]

Such violence, so pronounced and decisive in its destruction of pagan culture and tradition, resulted in the disappearance of the spiritual center of society — which in turn resulted in the creation of a spiritual wasteland. The very idea that people could no longer worship the Old Gods or celebrate the harvests invited disaster of unknown proportions.

The Theodosian Code, XVI, 10, 25, written around 435 CE, bluntly equated paganism with the "criminal mind:"

> We interdict all persons of criminal pagan mind from the accursed immolation of victims, from damnable sacrifices, and from all other such practices that are prohibited by the authority of the more ancient sanctions. We command that all fanes, temples, and shrines, if even now any remain entire, shall be destroyed by the command of the magistrates, and shall be purified by the erection of the sign of the venerable Christian religion. All men shall know that if it should appear, by suitable proof before a competent judge, that any person has mocked this law, he shall be punished by death.[3]

Theodosius, in his zeal, ruled that those who did not embrace the Catholic -Christian faith without question, "We adjudge demented and insane."

Charlemagne himself ruled in 789: "with regard to trees, and rocks and springs, wherever ignorant people put lights or make other observances, we give notice to

1 Merrifield, Ralph. *The Archaeology of Ritual and Magic.* New York: New Amsterdam Books 1987, 99
2 Pennick, Nigel. *Celtic Sacred Landscapes.* London: Thames & Hudson 1996, 70
3 Hillgarth, op. cit., 48

everyone that this is a most evil practice, execrable to god, and wherever they are found, they are to be taken away and destroyed."[1]

Archaeological evidence of the destruction of holy wells exists in several locations in Britain. In Gloucestershire and Southwark religious items including altars had been dumped into wells and, in Roman London, limbs broken from religious statues have been found at the bottom of ancient wells. As mentioned above, statues of pagan deities were often thrown into abandoned wells in an effort of "sending them to the underworld of demons where Christians thought they belonged."[2]

During the 8th century, St. Willebroad is said to have visited an island situated between Denmark and Frisia. The island had a holy well that was regarded as so sanctified that water could only be drawn from it in silence. During this visit, he went to the holy well where he baptized three men and then slaughtered a cow on the spot, thus defiling the holy well. Because he intentionally violated the well, King Radbod pursued Willebroad but the saint was able to escape death.[3]

That these wells, rivers, streams and lakes were considered sacred to the pagan inhabitants of Europe is obvious. However, what about the fact that these wells are still regarded as holy by some Christians? As previously shown, the early Christian missionaries blessed and "converted" many of the wells to Christian use. This was normally done by naming them after early saints. The desired outcome may have been to easily persuade the pagan to worship the new god, but it also may have been to preserve the resident mystical and healing powers in the wells for use by Christians. It is doubtful that all of the sacred wells had a continuous history of use from pagan traditions through modern day Christianity. However, the fact remains that holy wells have existed under both pagan and Christian society. The fact that small wax or carved figures of arms and legs have been in continuous use as votive offerings from pagan times, at least as early as 500 BCE by the Greeks and Etruscans, through modern Catholicism, indicates that a continuity of tradition associated with wells has occurred. These small figures were used to solicit cures for diseases afflicting specific body parts.

A series of church canons and laws were promulgated between the 7th and 12th centuries, which forbade pilgrimages and worship at wells and other holy water sites. King Egbert ruled "if any keep his wake at any wells, or at any other created things except at god's church, let him fast three years, the first on bread and water, and the other two, on Wednesdays and Fridays, on bread and water; and on the other days let him eat his meat, but without flesh."

---

1 Smith, John Holland. *The Death of Classical Paganism*. New York: Charles Scribner 1976, 240-241

2 Merrifield op. cit., 97

3 Davidson, H.R. Ellis. *Gods and Myths of the Viking Age*. New York: Bell Publishing Company 1964, 171

In the 13th century, the Bishop of Lincoln attempted to use threats of excommunication to stop pilgrimages to wells in Buckinghamshire. Reports of "unapproved" miracles at holy wells and the Bishop's belief that the local vicar was profiting from offerings left at the wells were some of his reasons for resisting the practice.

The conflicts between Christian groups (Catholic vs. Protestants) also used the holy wells as focal points for attack. As noted earlier, the chapel at St. Madron's Well in Cornwall was partially destroyed during the English Civil War by Puritan fanatics. Other wells faced similar fates. St. Margaret's Well at Binsey was another destroyed during the English Civil War but was restored in the 19th century by the vicar of Binsey.

The Protestant Reformation lead by Martin Luther was instrumental in the overzealous destruction of pagan and Catholic holy sites, especially in Ireland where much of the old folkways were considered superstition based upon demonology. The 17th century English Penal Codes made Catholicism and its associated traditions, many based on paganism, outright illegal. The advancement of fanatical Puritanism resulted in the destruction of many Catholic churches and school as well as ancient and contemporary places of worship. What this actually did, however, was to force practicing Catholics back into the fields and woods where once again the remaining sacred sites of centuries past became popular meeting places. One historian noted "by undermining the healing power of saints' relics and images as well as the protective power attributed to holy words and consecrated objects, the Reformation deprived men and women of the prospect of supernatural aid which could help them with the problems they encountered in their daily lives...it is impossible to know whether, as a result, the demand for popular magic increased."[1] It is probable that the old pagan traditions became much more popular during this time due to the increased deprivation of religious liberty. Even so, the Protestant Reformation did not do away with holy wells altogether. Keith Thomas noted in his treatise *Religion and the Decline of Magic* "of course, this new Protestant attitude to ecclesiastical magic did not win an immediate victory; and some of the traditions of the Catholic past lingered on. Many of the old holy wells, for example, retained their semi-magical associations, even though Protestants preferred to regard them as medicinal springs working by natural means."[2] In fact, the divine presence around these wells was unquestioned when, in 1630, a man who had belittled the powers of St. Winifred's well was found dead at the well. The investigative authority ruled his death "by divine judgment."[3]

---

1 Luxton, Imogen. "The Reformation and Popular Culture," in *Church and Society in England: Henry VIII to James I*, edited by Felicity Heal and Rosemary O'Day. Hamden: Archon Books 1977, 71

2 Thomas, Keith. *Religion and the Decline of Magic*. London: Penguin Books 1971, 80

3 Ibid., 81

The 19th century ushered in a series of renewed attacks on holy wells. Philip Dixon Hardy, writing in 1840, regarded holy wells and the traditions associated with them as "superstitious and degrading." Hardy believed that they were purely the result of the Catholic Church manipulating the local populations. The Church, according to Hardy, was able to control the people and extort money from them through the various pilgrimages that were promoted.[1] Hardy wrote "while one or two slight, though apparent sincere attempts, have been made to suppress them, by some Roman Catholic hierarchy, the simple fact of numerous Holy Wells, Patterns, and Stations, being still not only sanctioned but patronized by the priests of the Roman Catholic Church, must appear proof positive, that they are still considered by such, as part...of the machinery with which they maintain their dominion over the minds of the ignorant and uninformed."[2] Other writers attempted to draw the reader to the conclusion that the "heathens" corrupted wells and that Christian saints were needed to sanctify them:

> They (the heathens) had put a demon of theirs into it (the well) to such effect, that any unfortunate person washing himself in the well or drinking of its water, was forthwith stricken with paralysis, or leprosy, or blindness or an eye, or some other corporeal calamity. The malignant powers with which they had inspired this formidable well spread far around the fear of the Magi,[3] and consequently their influence. But the Christian missionaries were to show a power of a different kind — a power of beneficence, excelling and destroying the power of malignity....The saint, after a suitable invocation, washed his hands and feet in the water, and then drank of it with his disciples...the saint and his followers came away uninjured; and the demon was driven out of the well, and it became ever afterwards a holy fountain curing many of their infirmities.[4]

Hardy, and others, believed that the traditions associated with holy wells were manufactured by the Catholic Church to control the people and to gain monetary profits from the pilgrims. During the Middle Ages, profits from holy sites were a great boon to the Catholic treasury. The Church created an efficient bureaucracy to control access and to collect the offerings left by pilgrims. Collection boxes were installed near the wells and priests were employed as collectors — profits became huge. Some of the miraculous tales of Saints and sacred wells undoubtedly were manufactured to keep pilgrims going from one holy site to another. Bob Brooke, in an article appearing in *British Heritage*, wrote of one such tale from the Cotswolds:

> A monk of Winchcombe Abbey invented a story that Prince Kenelm of Mercia was murdered by his sister Quendreda's lover, who buried Kenelm's head under a thorn tree. A white dove carried a scroll that de-

---

1 Hardy, Philip Dixon. *The Holy Wells of Ireland.* London: Hardy & Walker 1840
2 Ibid.
3 The writer states that these "ministers of the heathen system" were referred to as *Magi* and infers that they were Druids.
4 Anon. "Our Hagiology," in *Blackwood's Edinburgh Magazine*, Vol. 82, October 1857, 455

scribed the evil deed to the Pope in Rome, who ordered that the body be found. Local clerics used a white cow to locate it on the slopes of Sudely Hill, where a spring burst forth. Quendreda tried to curse the ensuing funeral procession by reading Psalm 108 backwards, but her eyes exploded. On the strength of this amazing tale, Winchcombe Abbey became a popular destination for pilgrims and one of the largest abbeys in England.[1]

This is an interesting tale in that it adds many of the traditional pagan themes to a Christian story. The cow is sacred to Bridget and is representative of the Great Mother and all moon Goddesses. The thorn tree also represents the horns of the crescent moon as well, in Christian symbolism, sin, sorrow and tribulation.[2]

When the Reformation demanded the elimination and confiscation of Church property, including the destruction of traditional holy sites visited by pilgrims, protests were "inspired not by religious motives but by concern that the (area) would be deprived of a source of income from the flow of pilgrims to the shrine."[3]

The efforts undertaken to rid the world of these sacred wells indicate how powerful they have remained in the lives and spirits of the people living near and far who have been drawn to them. Because they remain indicates that people have also fought to keep them, and to preserve them for future generations. Not all 19th century writers were opposed to the veneration of holy wells and spring, however. In a book review published by *Blackwood's Edinburgh Magazine* in the February 1858 issue, it was said, "if it could be wished that any superstition should remain among us, it is that which attached a peculiar sacredness to the pure spring. In one way or another we would have all men worship water — the giver of health, and the cleanser of all impurities."[4]

The fact remains that both pagan and Christian society have embraced sacred wells and springs for the same reasons. They reflect the mystical powers innate in what many regard as the divine. While continued use of these specific wells cannot be proven, the continued traditions associated with them can be. From the votive offerings and well dressing s, to making wishes, little has changed over the millennia. At Doon Well in County Donega, pagan and Christian traditions have come together. Christians have placed a 26-inch statue of Jesus, which has been covered with clooties, next to the hazel tree by the well.[5]

The continued reverence for sacred wells in Christian times and by Christians was cause for concern by many. An article in *The Gentleman's Magazine* published in 1811 complained that "on Beltane morning superstitious people go to this well

1 Brooke, Bob. "Treasure Hunting in the Cotswolds" in *British Heritage*, Vol. 21, Number 2, February/March 2000, 37

2 Cooper, J.C. *An Illustrated Encyclopaedia of Traditional Symbols.* London: Thames and Hudson, Ltd., 1978,170

3 Luxton, op. cit., 69

4 "Sullivan on Cumberland," in *Blackwood's Edinburgh Magazine*, Vol. 83, February 1858, 352

5 Brenneman, Walter L. & Mary G. *Crossing the Circle at the Holy Wells of Ireland.* Charlottesvill: University Press of Virginia 1995, 52

and drink of it; then they make a procession round it nine times; after this they in like manner go round the temple (stone circles nearby). So deep-rooted is this heathenish superstition in the minds of many who reckon themselves good Protestants, that they will not neglect these rites even when Beltane falls on the Sabbath."[1]

The universal practices discussed in this work indicate an archetypal memory, a collective unconsciousness at work. A memory that inspires each of us to look to these life sources for healing and communication with the Otherworld, and for comfort. Paul Broadhurst wrote over fourteen years ago:

> By quaint villages and isolated farms the thread of continuity that runs through both the Nature religions and the Christian tradition still exerts a potent influence over human beings and the countryside, now noticeably beginning to materialise in the current resurgence of interest in the old Holy Wells. On a deeper level, the development of 'well-consciousness' is a re-identification with the living body of the Earth, a re-establishment of the great feminine principle behind Life, as the polarities swing back to a delicate equipoise.[2]

The pendulum is still in motion, with gradual but important steps being taken by individuals and groups to preserve these sacred places all over the world. The recognition of the ageless archetypes and the roles that they play in our daily existence is also becoming commonplace.

---

1 Quoted in: Knowlson, T. Sharper. *The Origins of Popular Superstitions and Customs*. London: T. Werner Laurie Ltd. 1910, 194
2 Broadhurst, Paul. "Holy Well or Holy Grail ? The Mystic Quest in Cornwall," in *The Source*, Issue #4, March 1986

CHAPTER 9. HOLY WELLS AND DIVINE APPARITIONS

Over several hundred years, mysterious ladies in white and the Virgin Mary have been reported at or near many holy wells. From the Lady of Guadalupe in Mexico to the Virgin Mary at Lourdes to the apparition at Fatima, Portugal to the sighting of the Blessed Mary at the shrine of Inchigeela in Ireland, these paranormal occurrences have become commonplace at sacred water sites. What is it that links the sacred feminine to wells and springs? As previously discussed, there are also male gods and saints associated with sacred wells. However, these powerful male figures do not appear as ghostly images, or as three-dimensional figures seen at holy wells — only female images have appeared.

The sightings of female apparitions at wells have been reported from all parts of the globe. Some have appeared as a guide to locating healing water sources. One such image of the Madonna appeared on the wall of an Anglican Church located two hours from Adelaide, in the small Australian town of Yankalilla. A local dowser became interested in the story and found that a stream was running underneath the church. This stream led to drilling for water that resulted in a well being found two meters from the apparition's location. Since 1996, the well has become a focal point for pilgrims from all over Australia.[1]

The Virgin Mary has appeared before pilgrims seeking relief for eye ailments at St. Mary the Virgin Well at Dunsfold in Surrey. It is assumed that these appearances are the reason for the construction of the nearby church.[2] One of the most prevalent traditions, concerning the appearance of Mary at these sacred

---

1 Cassetta, Pasquo. "Image of Madonna and Child Leads to Discovery of Healing Water." http://www.mcn.org/l/miracles/pasquo.html 3/20/01
2 Baker, Rowland G.M. "Holy Wells and Magical Waters of Surrey" in *The Source*, Issue 1, March 1985

sites, is her request that a shrine or church be built at, or near, that location. This is also true of Lourdes. Bernadette quoted the Lady as stating, "Go and tell the priests to build a chapel on this spot. I want people to come here in procession... Go and drink in the spring and wash in it. I am the Immaculate Conception. I desire a chapel here."[1] A similar apparition occurred at the small village of Quer-rien, France on August 15, 1652, when the Virgin appeared to 12-year-old Jeanne Courtel. Jeanne was cured of deafness when she witnessed the apparition and was told that a sanctuary should be built on that location. Years earlier a spring mysteriously burst out of the ground here.

The Brennemans' research of holy wells in Ireland concluded that the ancient wells previously dedicated to Bridgid are in a decline. This is due, in the most part, because these wells "are taken out of the sphere of the sacred and placed into that of the secular. It is a matter of removing the well from the mythological realm to the realm of history."[2] This would appear to address the various tradi-tions of holy or healing wells losing their powers due to such mundane practices as the bathing of animals and children or washing clothing in the wells. The in-vasive nature of everyday labor nullifies the sacred. However, as the Brennemans also note, those wells dedicated to the Virgin Mary are prospering. In fact, new holy wells are being "born" in Ireland because of the growth in the power of wells dedicated to Mary. However, this is not due to the Christian nature of Mary, but to the combination of the powers intrinsic to Brigid/Mary. "What appears to be emerging," according to the Brennemans, "is a form of syncretism in which the loric, in the figure of Brigid, presents itself in a quiet or tacit manner, while the sa-cred, in the figure of Mary, plays a predominant role in terms of the overt symbols that are present at the well. Thus, it is not simply a matter of Mary taking over Brigid wells but rather a change in the relationship of Brigid and Mary...a change in the symbolic meaning of the holy well."[3]

I believe that we can safely say that Brigid *is* Mary as Mary *is* Brigid. The age old influence and perceived powers of the feminine spirit continue to be felt regardless of what terms are applied to it. This power simply *is* as it always has been but the effects ebb and flow in accordance to the amount of attention paid to it by the faithful at certain locations — Christian or pagan faithful. As the Brennemans summed up their study of Irish holy wells:

> We began to think that perhaps there was a connection between the appearances of the Virgin Mary in Ireland and the ancient lady at the well. Could the lady be appearing now in modern Christian form with a mes-sage not for the kings of ancient Ireland but for the entire world, a mes-sage that is grounded in the power of place, the well? Could these modern postindustrial apparitions be a survival of earlier myth and ritual modes

---

1 Cranston, Ruth. *The Miracle of Lourdes.* New York: Image Books 1988, 33

2 Brenneman, Walter L. & Mary G. *Crossing the Circle at the Holy Wells of Ireland.* Charlottes-ville: University Press of Virginia 1995, 109

3 Ibid., 110

appearing at a different point in history and thus presenting a universal-ized message?[1]

As Juan Diego saw in 1531 what he believed to be the Virgin Mary at Tepeya-cac, on the same site of an Aztec shrine dedicated to Tonantzin, the Aztec mother goddess, so do many of the modern apparitions occur in areas once recognized as holy to pagan goddesses. While the names of the religion change, the divine powers that be do not. The message also remains the same — a reminder of hu-mankind's ultimate connection to the land and the sacred powers that are sym-bolized in sacred wells.

Other wells recently reported to have had divine visitations include one at the small village of The Culleens in County Sligo, the Gortaneadin Grotto in County Cork, and at the Mount Melleray grotto in County Waterford. Both children and adults saw these apparitions of the Virgin Mary in the 1980s.

Other apparitions of note include that of "Mary of the Rosary" in San Nicolas Argentina that occurred in September 1983. Here the Virgin Mary appeared be-fore Gladys de Motta and said "I desire to stand on the bank of the Parana River.... And let them make me a sanctuary; that I may dwell among them."[2] Fifty-years before this appearance, Mariette Beco, who lived in the northern European vil-lage of Banneux in the Ardennes Mountains, saw the Virgin. Mariette stated, "the lady called for me to follow her to the spring. She asked me to put my hand in the water and when I did so she said, 'This spring is to be dedicated to me.'" The Virgin told Mariette that the spring would heal the sick.[3]

In September 1846, in the French Alps village of La Salette, eleven-year-old Maximim Giraud and fourteen-year-old Mélanie Mathieu saw an apparition. The Virgin's message to the two children was that unless the villagers kept the Sab-bath, children would die and crops would fail. Two years after the sighting a "dried-up spring there burst into life again" and people began to report cures due to the healing powers of the water.[4]

Another miraculous event occurred in 1557 near Rapallo, Greece. It was here that Giovanni Chichizola saw an apparition of the Virgin. The Virgin left a paint-ing of herself attached by a chain to a nearby rock. Tradition says that when Giovanni attempted to pick up the picture a stream of water began to run from beneath it. When the painting was removed from the site, it vanished, only to be found again later at the rock. The stream water cured many of those who drank from it. As in the other cases, a church was built at the site.

---

1 Ibid., 115-116

2 Mullen, Peter. *Shrines of Our Lady.* New York: St. Martin's Press 1998, 23

3 Ibid., 33

4 Ibid., 75. Jean Markale noted in his book *The Great Goddess* (pg. 155) that the apparition of La Salette "was only a setup propagated by an elderly nun nostalgic for the ancient régime."

Two apparitions seen in times that are more recent include an apparition at the small town of Betania in the Venezuelan rainforest. Again, the apparition appeared at a beautiful grotto where a healing spring gushes from the earth. Seen on March 25, 1976, on the Feast of the Annunciation it has reappeared each year on the same date. Others report seeing "mystical frogs" in the surrounding forest as well. Obviously, there are more than historic traditions present here. Another apparition took place at Tre Fontane (the Three Fountains) in Rome in 1947 and has reappeared every April 12 since then. This site also has a grotto with many cures reported when individuals have applied the earth from the grotto to their bodies.

The sociological studies of these various sightings have indicated interesting similarities. Most sightings were by teenage girls, or young adult women. Reports indicate that all of the witnesses were terrorized at first and all were treated harshly by their families and authorities when they first reported the apparitions. All of the witnesses had received some sort of message, usually involving the state of world peace or the un-Christian behavior of the local population. However, the more interesting similarities among some of the apparitions were the creation of streams where none had been and the miraculous healing at those streams. All of the apparitions were very similar in appearance, although many of these similarities may be due to the inordinate amount of publicity that other previous sightings had received. The similar reports may also have been due to the religious teachings received by the observers.

My hypothesis is that *something* out of the ordinary was seen. A vision of a supernatural female entity was observed at *most* of these times but they were not necessarily, or strictly, "Christian" visions. Many pagan aspects were obvious during these events; one in fact was the report of the Virgin appearing in a hawthorn tree, which has had a long history of importance among pagan traditions. As Markale noted, "perhaps they don't know that, traditionally, hawthorn bushes are the dwelling places of fairies, and that fairies are nothing other than folkloric images of this divine mother from whom they seek tenderness."[1] The importance of water to the apparition is difficult to explain unless we regard these events as visions of a primordial deity — one far older than the mother of Jesus. However, the specific messages appear to have been unintentionally created in the minds of the observers. The messages appear to be politically motivated or repetitive of nationalist voice during times of international tension that involved the country where the apparition was seen. Many times they also appear to be farfetched. For the mother of god to state that children would die, and crops fail,

---

1 Markale, Jean. *The Great Goddess: Reverence of the Divine Feminine From the Paleolithic to the Present.* Rochester: Inner Traditions 1999, 159

due to a village's failure to keep the Sabbath, would seem a bit unreasonable for one of such loving and divine nature.[1]

It would seem reasonable that the *power of place* was responsible for these manifestations through time and geographic location. The sacred wells and other sacred sites that I have seen do emanate a very strong feeling of mystery and power and unknown purpose. As noted earlier, Jean Markale believes that natural phenomenon, including radioactivity and magnetic currents may be responsible for these sightings as well as those of the mysterious women in white seen near many sacred wells. How these mysterious events are and were perceived by the witnesses, all of strong Catholic cultures, would indicate how the specific details of the phenomenon were logically assimilated in the mind. One purely *pagan* apparition occurred in the 19th century when local residents attempted to drain Black Mere Pool, which is located between the English towns of Leek and Buxton. When the workers began to drain the pool the "Goddess" in her mermaid form appeared to them and threatened to "drown the town of Leek" if the pool dried up.[2] Needless to say, the pool was left alone.

It is interesting that many of the apparitions seen were very small, between three and four feet and usually encased in a blinding orb of light. Perhaps we are dealing more with faery than we know.

---

1 An excellent book which delves into the deeper meaning of these sightings, including socio-political and economic as in addition to the prevailing religious teachings of the time is *Marpingen: Apparitions of the Virgin Mary in a Nineteenth-Century German Village* by David Blackbourn and published by Vintage Books 1995.
2 Straffon, Cheryl. *The Earth Goddess: Celtic and Pagan Legacy of the Landscape.* London: Blandford 1997, 135-136

CHAPTER 10 HOLY WELLS IN TODAY'S WORLD

Sacred wells have been with humankind for thousands of years. Their symbolism of wisdom, holiness, and healing and divine feminine power mixes with the darker aspects of life and death, the underworld and the underworld's denizens. There are thousands of holy wells, streams, rivers and lakes throughout the world, in some locations undoubtedly still secret. But what is the future for keeping these shrines, for preserving them against the daily onslaught of development, pollution, vandalism and neglect?

The days of the organized destruction of holy wells, and other ancient holy sites are over. However, perhaps a more insidious destruction of wells has occurred over the years in the form of indifference. "Development" has taken a huge toll of ancient sacred sites around the world. As mentioned previously the area around St. Pancras' in London had numerous healing wells that were destroyed in the 19th century by the Midland Railroad. Today numerous wells are in a state of disrepair, among them the Lion's Well at Long Crendon, the healing well at Bowden Lane Springs and St. Osyth's Well in Bierton — all in Buckinghamshire. St. Osyth's has been covered over with a concrete lid. Lady Well in Stirling was bulldozed to make room for a supermarket! These and many others are the victims of a society that has lost touch with its spirituality.

However, there are as many successes as there are losses. The British government has instituted a program of "Millennium Grants" to restore holy wells and other ancient sites of importance. In the last year or so, the MacArthur Foundation awarded a grant to Oleg Grigorievich in the Ukraine to continue work in "the tradition of preserving sacred wells as the effective method of protecting water sources."

Individual efforts are also becoming common. As mentioned previously, a well has recently been rediscovered in Cambridgeshire and efforts were undertaken by a local pagan and local History Society to restore the well and the tradition of Well Dressing.[1] Recently, I was given an update of the efforts to convince the local council that the well should be rededicated:

> Nobody said it couldn't be done, but nobody came through with the relevant permission or nod of the official head. So, after much frustration (which I think was organized by those who did not want something of this ilk as it smacked too much of paganism), I have said to hell with authority and I've gone ahead and placed flowers, candles, and a Goddess image by the well.

> I'll have to wait and see who gets to her (the Goddess) first, the local Methodists or the local vandals, one and the same really![2]

Other restoration attempts have met with more success. In Derbyshire, the *Ashbourne News Telegraph* on April 11, 2001, reported:

> After an interval of more than 80 years, the former Kniveton tradition of well dressings is to be revived together with another defunct local custom, Kniveton Field Day.

> ...the idea is to dress the school well, village pump and possibly the well in Chapel Lane. The blessings of the wells will take place at 10am on Sunday, June 24, starting at the church door, then school well, the village pump and progressing on to the monthly united services at the Methodist Chapel.[3]

Additional well dressing events were to take place during 2001 in Etwall, Endon, High Legh, Milford, Waingroves, Wirksworth, and Matlock Bath. Others were unfortunately canceled in Britain due to the outbreak of Foot and Mouth disease.

In the United States, holy wells are being created where they never existed before. In Sacramento, California a statue of the Virgin of Guadalupe has been erected a few dozen feet away from a Catholic Church with a small well-like structure at the foot, filled with water. This small "well" represents the spring near Tepeyacac[4] where Juan Diego saw the Virgin Mary for the third time on December 11, 1531. Nearby, candles, flowers and other votive offerings, including letters of requests tied with strings and ribbons, have been placed. It is this act of devotion that begins the process of creating sacred space.

---

1 Bamford, Ken. Personal Communication. December 8, 2000

2 Bamford, Ken. Personal Communication. May 1, 2001

3 *Ashbourne New Telegraph.* "Revival for Well Dressings After 80 Year's Break," April 11, 2001, p.3

4 The hill, known as Tepeyacac, had been the site of an Aztec shrine dedicated to the Aztec mother Goddess, Tonantzin. Many of the indigenous worshippers today continue to refer to the Virgin of Guadalupe as Tonantzin, the Earth Goddess.

The interest in sacred wells and springs has not abated over the centuries — only increased. While many rituals are conducted privately by a variety of people of different religious persuasions, the continuous pilgrimages made by groups and individuals testifies to the importance that these sites have had and continue to have in our lives. Due to government and civic support in Britain, these sacred sites are being renovated and re-venerated. They now figure importantly in the daily lives and celebrations of the small villages that dot the landscape. Just as importantly, many springs and wells in the United States which have been a part of the landscape for so long, and taken for granted for so many years, are also being recognized for their importance.

When I was a child living in Burlington, an Iowan town on the Mississippi River, I loved going to a secluded cave deep in the forest above the banks of the river. From the dark depths of this cave a clear spring ran, flowing into a small waterfall a few feet away. This spring is known as Black Hawk Spring in memory of the Sauk-Fox leader, Chief Black Hawk, who frequented the spot. Over the years, the spring has been neglected for the most part, although it remained an attraction for young boys. Today the water is no longer drinkable due to an old cemetery located above it, which has suffered from water leeching through the wooden caskets resulting in a polluting mixture. Recently I have become aware that the citizens of Burlington have come to recognize the need to renew the spring and a cleanup is underway. It is through these efforts that our sacred sites will continue to exist and to offer their magick to future generations.

What we must be careful with though, is becoming overzealous in our attempts to restore sites that have become modified over time. Certainly, we must protect and preserve sacred sites for everyone to use and to enjoy. We must also preserve our traditions without destroying those things which may have become part of our sacred landscape inadvertently. As noted in the section about Glastonbury's White Spring, an effort is underway to destroy the old Reservoir building erected in 1870, which was constructed over the original natural grotto. The intent is certainly honorable — to restore the grotto to its original natural state. At the same time do we determine what is worthy of our past to destroy? The Reservoir in itself is a part of Glastonbury's history and has its own character and ambiance. Can we today know how the original grotto appeared and would we, in our attempts at reconstruction, again alter the sacredness of this place beyond what is necessary? We must be cautious in our endeavors to replace the historical landscapes in our efforts to "restore" something that has been lost. Perhaps the best solution is the natural one. As Philip David says, "...the waters do meet. Somewhere. They always will, no matter what we do to prevent them. We might as well let them do it naturally..."[1]

---

1 David, Philip. Personal Communication. August 7, 2001

The greatest threat to our sacred wells and springs around the world is "land improvement." Perhaps the best example, or is it the worse, is Ireland. A Heritage Council survey of more than 1,400 archaeological monuments in Ireland, including holy wells, found that 34% of them have been destroyed since 1840. An article appearing in the September 6, 1999 edition of The Irish Times, noted, "the main cause of monument destruction was land improvement, much of it driven by intensive farming and development."[1] Recently, the plans to create a landfill as part of the Connacht Waste Management Plan for the Irish town of Ballinahistle created more than garbage space. According to the Irish Times on May 29, 2000, an area possibly as important as Newgrange was discovered at the site. The site consists of a ring fort; a Bronze or Iron Age ring barrow or mound; ritual sites; hilltop burial cairns; two villages and holy wells.[2] Fortunately, Irish Environmental Protection Agency regulations as well as archaeological guidelines by the European Union will help protect this important multi-faceted site.

Holy wells continue to be the main source of affordable health care by many people and cultures.

The many spas mentioned previously are as popular as ever to those who can afford the treatments available. However, we should remember that these are places that were frequented by the indigenous peoples in the past who also revered them for their spiritual qualities.

---

1 MacConnell, Sean. "Demolition of Historic Monuments Causes Alarm," in *The Irish Times*. September 6, 1999
2 Siggins, Lorna. "Waste plan 'threat' to ancient site," in *The Irish Times*. May 29, 2000

Chapter 11. Place Names and the Danger of Language

Names, especially ancient ones, must be approached cautiously. The evolution of language is such that local dialects even in written form, including local meanings and references, may lead one to believe that a word means one thing when, in reality, the opposite may be true. This is also true for terms, names and references for holy wells.

Many of the words associated with wells, springs and other waterways are commonly understood. A few of these ancient words, which still maintain some usage today, especially as word endings, are:

- *well* or *awelm* meaning a spring,
- *font* a word derived from Fons which means "well," also the name of the son of the god Janus, Fontus; and
- *-ville*, which is sometimes a corrupted form of "well" [1]

When one is discussing sacred wells and waterways, it is important not to take a word at its reasonable face value. Some examples include the use of the word "Cross" in geographical place names, such as the Welsh Y *Cryws*, or Three Crosses. While one would reasonably expect the word to designate a holy site, it may also simply refer to a three-way intersection on a road. Another is a spring in Marlborough located at the end of a lane called Treacle Bolley. One theory is that *treacle* referred to medicinal substances (a mixture of medicine and molasses) and, in fact, several healing wells in England are referred to as treacle wells. Another possibility is that "treacle" was a derivative of "trickle." However, well researcher Alison Maloney notes "the 'treacle' association with the holy well does not seem to date back much further than Lewis Carroll's mention of it in

---

1 Maloney, Alison. Wells-And-Spas@JISCMAIL.AC.Uk April 27, 2001, "Re: Licorice and Holy Wells"

'Alice.'[1] Another example previously discussed is St. Alkelda's Well. *St. Alkelda* is actually a reworking of the Old Norse words *halig kelda*, which means a spring of living waters.

Chattle Hole, a well associated with the Devil and discussed earlier, also has a long history connected to its name. Katy Jordan noted, "Goddard suggests a derivation from 'cetel,' an Old English word meaning cauldron. More likely, I suspect, is a derivation from the ubiquitous name chadwell, meaning cold spring. We have seen how -well suffixes often contract to -le; the consonant 't' is simply 'd' unvoiced, and Chaddle could easily change to Chattle in ordinary speech."[2] It is interesting that today the name has again evolved and the well is called "Chapel Hole."

"Holy" (*halig* in Old English) itself is subject to debate. There is some linguistic evidence that it originally meant "healthy" or "whole" while there is also evidence that it referred to "sacred."

Well names that seem to have a clear meaning may actually have a hidden one — although it may have been unintentional. One example is Sunday Well, which, according to researcher Francine Nicholson, may have evolved from the Old English prefix "*sound-*" meaning "a watering hole where game was known to gather."[3] Other examples of names with reversed meaning are Devil's Well in Wales, which was a "normal healing well," and Ffynnon y Pasq, or "the Easter Well" that was used for black magic.[4] One of the names most twisted through time is that of Honeychild Manor Farm in Kent, England. According to Stephen Furnival, current resident of Honeychild Manor Farm, *Honey* is a "corruption" of the name of the original owner, which was *Huna*. By 1150, Huna became *Hune* with the *e* sound further changing the name to *Honey*. *Child* came from the old Scandinavian word *Celde* that meant a spring. So, "Huna's spring" became "Honeychild."[5]

Another well with a mis-translation may be that of St. Anne's Well, also known as Our Lady's Well in Hempsted in Gloucestershire. A sculpture is located at this well, made from large limestone blocks, showing a large figure of a woman standing between two smaller ones. If it is a representation of St. Anne, then the two smaller figures most likely would be her daughter, St. Mary, and either an angle or St. Anne's husband. However, there is a linguistic similarity between the words "Anne" and "Wan," a pre-Christian reference to the god Woden.[6] Another well, called Woden's Well is actually located in the town of

1 Stucky, Frederick James. *The Holy Groves of Britain: Vol I*. Devon: Merlin Books Ltd. 1995, 42

2 Jordan, Katherine M. "Seven Wiltshire Wells and their Folklore" in *The Source*, Issue 6, Summer 1998

3 Nicholson, Francine. "Unholy wells," Wells-And-Spas@JISCMAIL.AC.UK June 20, 1999

4 Gray, Madelein. "Unholy wells, Wells-And-Spas@JISCMAIL.AC.UK June 21, 1999

5 Anon. "Honeychild Manor Farm," in *Farmers Weekly* (www.farmersweekly.net) July 21, 2000

6 Hunt, Laurence. "Some Ancient Wells, Springs and Holy Wells of the Cotswolds," in *The Source*, Issue #4, Winter 1995

"Wanswell," an obvious pagan designation. While the well has been called Our Lady's Well for sometime it is just as likely that "Our Lady" was the goddess Bridgid or Coventina. The sculpture depicting the goddess in her triad form, as she is depicted in other ancient reliefs such as that found at Bath, is clearly older than the Christian designation of the well as St. Anne's.

Chapter 12. What Makes Healing Water Heal?

We have spent a considerable amount of time in this book on the spirituality of sacred wells and waters, what cures were sought, what cures were obtained, the rituals performed at many of the wells, their mythology, history and associations with particular gods and goddesses. A short discussion of a more technical level is also warranted.

Many of these wells do, in fact, provide relief, if not outright cures, of physical and mental ailments. Previously, I noted that this is a result of a combination of a psychic/spiritual connection with the power of place. I still believe this. But there is more. The water itself, at least in the mineral and hot springs, which have been utilized for thousands of years, does contain a mixture of elements that have been found to be beneficial to one's health.

Each particular element, either mineral or gas, is discussed separately here.

Radon Gas

As mentioned previously in the sections on St. Madron's Well and Sancreed, radon gas is associated with some healing wells that have a history of putting people to sleep. During their sleep, they receive either instruction from the gods on how to treat their illnesses or they simply receive a cure. What is radon? It is an inert radioactive gas which has been ruled carcinogenic by the United States Environmental Protection Agency but is touted as a healing agent in several Japanese and European spas. Being easily absorbed through the skin and respiratory systems, bathing in radon water is nonetheless prescribed at Badgastein-Bockstein-Thermalstollen spa in Austria for rheumatism, gout, skin diseases, diabetes, gynecological ailments, asthma, gallstones and fatigue.

The Asclepieum centers throughout history normally called for a period of rest and sleep mixed with bathing in the healing waters of the nearby sacred well or spring. It was this combination of elements at these sites that affected healing treatments. Until further conclusive research is done which will address the safety issue of continuous exposure to radon it is advised that pilgrims refrain from these types of sites. Some of the healing waters visited today, which contain radon, includes Bath in Britain, Yalova in Turkey, Agua Hedionda in Mexico, Tabio in Columbia and Velingrad in Bulgaria.[1]

The gas itself is commonly found in soil and water from the natural decay process of uranium. While radon in water does pose some problems, the most dangerous exposure is through breathing the gas in indoor environments. The United States National Academy of Sciences issued a report on September 15, 1998, which stated, "radon is also found in ground water tapped by wells, which supply about half the drinking water in the United States. Ground water moves through rock containing natural uranium that releases radon into the water. Water from wells usually has higher concentrations of radon than does surface water such as lakes and streams."[2] The possible harmful effects of radon in water located in the outdoors, such as sacred streams and wells, is minimal. However, harmful effects of radon contained in quantities located in indoor spa areas may be much higher. The NAS report indicated that up to 160 deaths a year in the United States can be attributed to a combination of radon gas inhaled from indoor water supplies and the effects of smoking.

Paul Devereux believes that radiation in certain doses may be conducive to healing and to achieving altered states of mind, and this effect may have been used by shamans and healers in the past.[3]

ARSENIC

The next rather questionable ingredient in some healing wells and springs is arsenic. Known around the world as a formidable poison, arsenic does have some curative properties. As in most cases, organic arsenic, as found in some mineral springs, is not as toxic as that produced from copper smelting. Today it is also found in pesticides and preservatives, animal feed additives (!) and in semiconductor manufacturing, thus winding up in ground water through polluting runoff. For the most part arsenic found in water is inorganic in nature, which is

---

1 Altman, Nathaniel. *Healing Springs: The Ultimate Guide to Taking the Waters.* Rochester: Healing Arts Press 2000, 72

2 Doull, John et al. *Risk Assessment of Radon in drinking Water.* Washington: The National Academy of Sciences 1998

3 Devereux, Paul. Places of Power: Secret Energies at Ancient Sites: A Guide to Observed or Measured Phenomena. London: Blandford 1990, 184-190

more toxic than organic forms.[1] In fact, organic arsenic is, according to the World Health Organization, "readily eliminated by the body."[2]

Naturally occurring arsenic was used, prior to penicillin, for the treatment of venereal diseases and dysentery. Today arsenic containing waters at various springs and spas are used for treating athlete's foot and other skin-fungal ailments in addition to venereal disease. Soaking one's hands and feet in these waters is certainly beneficial — just don't drink it!

The World Health Organization has included Argentina, Australia, Bangladesh, Chile, China, Hungary, India, Mexico, Peru, Thailand and the United States as nations where drinking water containing arsenic concentrations higher than the 0.01 mg/l standard has been detected.

IRON

Many healing wells are famous for their red-coloration, which is the result of heavy iron content. Chalice Well at Glastonbury is one of the most famous with its associations with the blood of Jesus and of the goddess. Iron is an important mineral in our bodies, it helps to nourish our blood and immune systems and keeps our metabolism in balance. The iron rich waters of these holy wells have been sought out for hundreds if not thousands of years being effective in the treatment of anemia, tuberculosis, nervous conditions and mental fatigue.

CALCIUM

Another very important mineral to our bodies is calcium. While it is found in many food sources, as is iron, the poor eating habits of our present day society, as well as those of our ancestors, has resulted in many people not having sufficient quantities of calcium. Calcium is important in the function of the liver, its helps our muscles to contract, including the heart, and regulates the density of our cell membranes. Found in milk, green vegetables, soy, sea kelp and wheat germ, calcium is also found in many wells and spas around the world. Calcium sulfates are also commonly found in healing springs and help intestinal ailments, associated with food and medication allergies, and colitis.

BICARBONATES

Bicarbonates are most commonly found in mineral springs. Bicarbonates are useful in effective treatment of gastric disorders, diabetes (through the increased utilization of blood sugars by the body), pancreatitis (through the stimulation of the pancreas), and bile duct disorders. Drinking water containing bicarbonates also improves the metabolism and digestion. Bathing in hot pools with bicarbon-

---

1   Anon. "Drinking Water Priority Rulemaking: Arsenic." Washington: United States Environmental Protection Agency, 7/23/2001 (*www.epa.gov/safewater/ars/arsenic.html*)

2   Anon. "Arsenic in Drinking Water," Fact Sheet No. 210, Revised May 2001. Geneva: World Health Organization

ates helps improve the blood's circulation and is helpful to those suffering from hypertension and cardiovascular diseases. Anyone with these conditions should only bathe in these hot spas under the supervision of a licensed medical practitioner. The water at Hot Springs, Arkansas; Saratoga, New York; Palm Springs, California and Thermopolis, Wyoming contains bicarbonates.

SULFUR

Most mineral springs are noted by their sulfurous smell — likened to "rotten eggs." This smell is common in springs located near volcanic activity but may also be found in other areas which are not volcanic. As mentioned previously, the waters of Harbin Hot Springs, Vichy Springs, Calistoga and Castle Rock Mineral Springs are all sulfuric and all located in volcanic areas.

Sulfur springs are very beneficial in healing. Sulfuric gas is antibacterial and is an expectorant. Bathing in warm water rich in sulfur and breathing in the vapors can be very conducive to relief of respiratory ailments as well as digestive and urinary problems, skin diseases and venereal disease.

SODIUM CHLORIDE

Another common and important mineral found in healing springs is sodium chloride. As indicated by its name, sodium chloride is very heavy in salt content, a result of water leaching salt from subterranean rock salt. Utilizing salt waters should be done carefully. As many of us are over consumers of salt in our foods it shouldn't be ingested lightly. However, bathing in salt waters can be an effective treatment for rheumatism, nerve diseases and gynecological diseases among others.

MAGNESIUM

Magnesium is important for its ability to regulate the functions of the body. It helps to produce energy and protein, as well as assists the heart, nerves and muscles in their proper functioning. It normally occurs in trace amounts in mineral springs but can be easily absorbed by the body by either drinking it or bathing in hot springs over a prolonged period.

OTHER MINERALS

Silica, lithium and potassium are three other minerals found in many healing waters, which also have beneficial qualities. Lithium can be deadly if ingested in large amounts. However, lithium has been used in the treatment of depression and has been shown to be effective in the treatment of mood swings and sleep disorders. Potassium is another mineral that helps to regulate body metabolism, maintaining proper blood pressure, mineral and fluid balances and proper nerve impulse transmission.

The final mineral we shall discuss here is silica — silica also more widely known as beach sand. Silica not only exists as beach sand but also as a small part of the human body's makeup. Silica is important for its part in the formation of proper bone density as well as healthy skin and hair.

It is no wonder that healing wells and springs have been visited for countless years for their miraculous cures. The minerals noted above, combined with the very important spiritual link to the particular site itself, do result in physical and mental health improvement. However, it is doubtful that the minerals themselves would be as effective without the added connection made to the "spirit of place."

The following table is only a partial listing of holy wells located throughout the world and discussed in this book. The table is organized by well name, type of well (i.e., wishing, healing, etc.) and then more specifically by location and description. Each well is given an alpha coding to indicate what the well is known or thought to have been used for. For example, healing wells are designated with an (H), wishing wells with a (W), etc. Each well may have more than one designation.

Name	Type	Location	Description
BRITAIN			
Chalice Well	P, x, h	Glastonbury, UK	Iron-rich waters with healing characteristics, said to hide the Holy Grail
White Spring s	p, x, h, o	"	clear, white water, representative of fertility
St. Madron's Well	f, p, x, h, o, d, w	½ mile west of Madron Village, Cornwall	a "dream temple" well, healing and also used for divination
St. Nectan's Well	f, p, x, h, o, wa	Cornwall, Tintagel	gorgeous waterfall, healing pool, faeries in residence
St. Piran's Well	X, h, o	"	marked by a stone pyramidal structure

Sancreed	p, x, o	¼ mile west of Sancreed Church, Penzance, Cornwall	Located underground, this well is situated on a pig farm — regarded as "weirdly prehistoric"
St. Euny's Well	X, h, w	"	also underground, this well is reported to have miraculously healing waters
Coventina's Well	p, o, h, s	Northumberland	a well dedicated to the goddess Coventina by Roman soldiers with thousands of offerings found
St. Ninian's Well, also known as St. Nunn's or the Piskies Well	x, h, o, f	Northumberland	Pins offered to the faery to keep them happy, the faery are said to maintain the well
Alsia Well	H, d, o	St. Buryan, Cornwall	a holy well which at one time was known to cure rickets, young girls used to toss pin into the water to determine the number of years before they met their future lover
Gulval Holy Well	d	Cornwall	a famous divining well, used to determine if a friend was alive or ill
Bath	p, t, o, c	Bath, UK	known mostly as a spa used by the Romans, Bath also was home for hundreds of curse tablets
Robin Hood's Well, aka St. Ann's Well	x, h	Nottinghamshire	named after Robin Hood in the 15th century, this well was later seized by a monastic order which dedicated it to St. Ann
St. Bridgid's Well	o, p, x	Kildare, Ireland	an ancient Celtic pagan site and holy well
Tobar Lastra	m	Donnaghmoyne, Ireland	"Well of Light," a moving well
Pistyll Teilo	h, ha, x	Kidwelly, Wales	a pool near the chapel of St. Teilo said to heal and to be haunted
St. Anne's Well, aka the Virtuous Well	f, p, x, h	Trellech Village, Wales	an ancient healing well associated with the Druids and faery, said to cure eye ailments

Nykerpole, or nicor-pool	dr	Marlborough, England	a lost well said to have been inhabited by a water goblin /dragon
Cranmere Pool	ha	Devonshire	said to be haunted, sounds of wailing have been heard here
Arthur's Well	ha	Cadbury, England	said to be visited by the ghosts of Arthur and him men during certain times of the year
Marlow's Holy Well, aka Queen Elizabeth's Well	h, o, ha	Brisham, Berkshire	a healing well noted for apparitions of ladies in white
Our Lady's Well	p, x, h	Hempsted, Gloucestershire	Dedicated to St. Anne but possibly a pagan well dedicated to Woden
St. Julian's Well	ha	Wellow, Sommerset	Apparitions of "women in white" here
Black Mere Pool	p	Near Leek and Buxton, England	an apparition of a pagan goddess in the 19th century. She appeared in a Mermaid form to protect a pool from being drained
Eye-Well	ha, o, h	near St. Donat's, Marcloss, Wales	an area noted for apparitions of the Green Lady
Butterby Springs	mn, h	County Durham	a mineral spring near the River Wear 1st recorded in 1607
Llyn-yr-Afanc	dr	Pembrokeshire	in Welch the name means the "Monsters Lake"
Griffydam	dr	Leicestershire	also called the Griffy Well, historically noted for its serpent
Boiling Well	h	Ludlow, England. Near the River Corve.	a boiling well noted for its healing of eye diseases, sores and wounds
Court Well	p, h	Oxfordshire	An ancient well possibly associated with the Norse god Woden
St. Helen's Well	p, x, o, h	Gargrave, Yorkshire	a continuously used well from pagan times to the present
Pin Well	p, x, o	County Tyrone	A pin well with a nearby beech tree stuck with thousands of pins and nails

EUROPE			
Banneux	x, g, h	Ardennes Mountains	an apparition appearing near a sacred and healing spring
Lourdes	x, g, h, o	Lourdes, France	a healing spring discovered under direction of the goddess /Virgin Mary in 1858. 66 "miracle cures" have been documented here
Querrien	x, g, h	Querrien, France	an apparition of the Virgin Mary with an associated healing spring
La Salette	x, g, h	French Alps	an apparition appearing with a renewed healing spring
Rapallo	x, g, h	Rapallo, Greece	an apparition with an associated healing spring
Kassotis Spring	d, o, h	Greece	located at the Temple of Apollo, home of the Oracle of Delphi
Cave of Psychro	o	Lyttos, Crete	a series of caves with an underground pool, votive offerings of figurines, skulls of various animals, weapons, lamps, cups and vases as well as jewelry
Ares	d	near Thebes, Greece	a spring with a legendary serpent or dragon
Grand	p, x	France	a continuously used sacred well from Celtic to modern times
Lake Enare	o	Ukonsaaru Island, Finland	a sacrificial site
Rag well	p, c, o	Vinnitsa, Ukraine	A holy, healing well where the ill hang their shirts from nearby trees
AFRICA/ MIDDLE EAST			
Abini-Teti	p, o	Sardinia	Votive offerings of bronze figurines, jewelry and other imported items
Enzayimarku	p, x, h, o	Chelga, Ethiopia	a healing spring used by the Qemant, various rituals conducted here

Pools of Bethesda	h, p, x	near Temple Mount, Jerusalem	the Biblical healing center later condemned as a site of goddess worship
UNITED STATES			
Panther Meadows Sacred Spring	p, o, h	Mt. Shasta, California	still regarded by four California tribes as a holy spring, headwaters of McCloud River
McCloud Falls	p, wa	McCloud, California	Sacred to the Shastan Indians
Burney Falls	p, wa, f	40 miles east of McCloud	sacred to Native Americans and used for vision quests, said to be the home of water spirits
Castle Crags Mineral Spring	p, h, mn	Near Dunsmuir, California	used by the Wintu Indians prior to 1855, commercially bottled through the 1920s
Harbin Hot Springs	p, t, h, mn	Middletown, California	hot springs used by the Miwok and surrounding tribes, now a commercial spa
Vichy Springs	p, t, h, mn	Ukiah, California	same but used by the Pomo Indians
Sacramento River	p, h, f	Mt. Shasta City, California	the start of the Sacramento River visited today by people seeking healings, said to have faeries present
Zaca Lake	p	Santa Ynez Valley, California	Regarded as the doorway to the celestial realm of the Chumash souls, sacred to the Chumash Indians
Humqaq Pool	p	Point Humqaq, California	Sacred to the Chumash, believed to be the place where Chumash spirits waited to ascend to heaven
Montezuma's Well	p, o	Near Flagstaff, Arizona	A sacred cenoté situated near the cliff dwellings of the Hohokam Indians
Lourdes of America	x, h	Near Espanola, New Mexico	A healing spring discovered in the 19th century when a "burst of light" was seen rising from the ground

Great Pagosa Hot Springs	p, h, t	Southern Colorado	Used by the Ute tribe before being discovered by the white man. "Pagosa" is derived from "Pagosah" meaning "healing waters"
Saratoga Springs	p, h, t	New York	Used originally by the Iroquois and Mohawk, Saratoga Springs is the most famous healing springs in America
Hot Springs	p, h, t	Arkansas	47 thermal springs originally used by the Tunicas Indians
White Sulphur Springs	p, h, t	West Virginia	A Shawnee sacred site still utilized for its healing properties
Healing Springs	p, h, mn	County Barnwell, South Carolina	Four healing springs used by Indians until 6 wounded British soldiers from a Revolutionary battle were healed. Still used today.
ARGENTINA			
Mary of the Rosary	x, g, h	San Nicolas, Argentina	an apparition appearing in September 1983 near the Parana River
VENEZUELA			
n/a	x, g, p, h	Betania	an apparition with heavy pagan undertones near a healing spring
MEXICO			
Chichen-Itza Sacred Cenoté	p, d, o	Chichen-Itza, Yucatan	human and material sacrifices made, used to divine the future
Tepeyacac	p, x, g, h	Near Mexico City	apparition of the Virgin Mary appeared at an ancient shrine dedicated to the Aztec Mother Goddess, Tonantzin
Balankanché	p, o	Near Chichen-Itza	a cavern shrine with a stalactite-stalagmite World Tree with an underground water source
ASIA			
Lumbini	p	Nepal	Birthplace of Buddha

AUSTRALIA			
Yankalilla	x, g, h	Near the town of Yankalilla	Apparition of the Virgin Mary appeared and acted as a guide to a healing stream
Bubbling Spring	p, h	south coast of Australia	a healing spring steeped in legend utilized by the Aboriginal peoples

Legend:

C = cursing

D = divination

DR = dragons

F = faery well

G = Goddess/Mary apparitions

H = healing

Ha = haunted

M = moving wells

MN = mineral springs

O = offerings present

P = prehistoric/pagan

S = skulls present

T = thermal/spa

W = wishing well

WA = waterfalls

X = Christian

Chapter 14. Resources

Archaeologists, folklorist, historians and a variety of individuals who are simply fascinated with the history, mythology and spirituality of these sacred sites have seriously undertaken holy well research. Many publications on specific wells and research projects are listed in the bibliography; however, there are also on-line resources available that may aid the researcher. I have listed those resources below which I have found to be most beneficial.

The Living Springs Journal – an electronic journal for the study of all aspects of holy wells and waterlore: www.bath.ac.uk./lispring/journal/home.htm

Archives of Wells And Spas – an on-line discussion forum for students and researchers of sacred wells and lore: www.jiscmail.ac.uk/lists/wells-and-spas.html

SOURCE – the on-line archive of the Holy Well Journal. www.bath.ac.uk/lispring/sourcearchive/front.htm

Holy Wells Web – Katy Jordan's excellent website. www.bath.ac.uk/~liskmj/holywell.htm

Derbyshire Well Dressing – provides history and schedules for well dressing events in Derbyshire: www.welldressing.com

The Wellspring Fellowship: The Lodge, Penpont, Brecon, Powys, LD3 8EU, Wales, UK

BIBLIOGRAPHY

Alcock, Leslie. *Was This Camelot? Excavations at Cadbury Castle 1966-70.* New York: Stein and Day 1972

Allouche-Benayoun, Joëlle. "The Rites of Water for the Jewish Women of Algeria," in *Women and Water: Menstruation in Jewish Life and Law.* Edited by Rahel R. Wasserfall. Hanover: Brandeis University Press 1999

Altman, Nathaniel. *Healing Springs: The Ultimate Guide to Taking the Waters.* Rochester: Healing Arts Press 2000

Anderson, John. Kuta Teachings: Reincarnation Theology of the Chumash Indians of California. Kootenai: American Designs Publishing 1998

Anderton, Bill. *Guide to Ancient Britain.* Berkshire: W. Foulsham & Co., Ltd., 1991

Andrews, Tamra. *A Dictionary of Nature Myths: Legends of the Earth, Sea, and Sky.* Oxford: Oxford University Press 1998

Anon. *The Chalice Well.* Glastonbury: Chalice Well Trust n/d

Anon. "Honeychild Manor Farm," in *Farmers Weekly* (www.farmersweekly.net) July 21, 2000

Anon. "Our Hagiology," in *Blackwood's Edinburgh Magazine,* Vol. 82, October 1857

Anon. "St. Nun's Well, Etc.: With A Notice of Some Remains of Ancient Well Worship," in *Notes and Queries.* Nov. 18, 1854

Anon. "Sullivan on Cumberland," in *Blackwood's Edinburgh Magazine,* Vol. 83, March 1858

Anon. "Drinking Water Priority Rulemaking: Arsenic." Washington: United States Environmental Protection Agency, 7/23/2001 (www.epa.gov/safewater/ars/arsenic.html)

Anon. "Arsenic in Drinking Water," Fact Sheet No. 210, Revised May 2001. Geneva: World Health Organization

Anteby, Lisa. "There's Blood in the House": Negotiating Female Rituals of Purity among Ethiopian Jews in Israel," in *Women and Water: Menstruation in Jewish Life and Law.* Edited by Rahel R. Wasserfall. Hanover: Brandeis University Press 1999

Avner, Uzi. "Sacred Stones in the Desert," in *Biblical Archaeology Review,* Vol. 27, May-June 2001

Baker, Rowland G.M. "Holy Wells and Magical Waters of Surrey" in *The Source*, Issue 1, March 1985

Baldwin, Neil. *Legends of the Plumed Serpent: Biography of a Mexican God.* New York: Public Affairs 1998

Baring-Gould, S. *Curious Myths of the Middle Ages.* New York: John B. Alden, Publishers 1885

Bauschatz, Paul C. *The Well and the Tree: World and Time in Early Germanic Culture.* Amherst: The University of Massachusetts Press 1982

Bilson, Charles. *Vestiges of Paganism in Leicestershire.* Loughborough: Heart of Albion Press 1994 (A reprint of the 1911 edition published by George Allen)

Blackburn, Thomas C. and Lowell John Bean. "Kitanemuk," in *Handbook of the Indians of California: Volume 8-California.* Washington: Smithsonian Institution 1978

Bonwick, James. *Irish Druids and Old Irish Religions.* New York: Barnes & Noble Books 1986 (a reprint of the 1894 edition)

Bord, Janet. "Cursing, Not Curing: The Darker Side of Holy Wells," in *The Source*, Issue #4, Summer 1995

Bord, Janet and Colin. *Earth Rites: Fertility Practices in Pre-Industrial Britain.* London: Granada Publishing Limited 1982

Bord, Janet and Colin. *Mysterious Britain:* Ancient Secrets of Britain and Ireland. London: Thorsons 1972

Bowen, Dewi. "The Holy Wells of Glamorgan," in *The Source*, Issue 8, Autumn 1988

Branston, Brian. *The Lost Gods of England.* New York: Oxford University Press 1974

Brenneman, Walter L. & Mary G. *Crossing the Circle at the Holy Wells of Ireland.* Charlottesville: University Press of Virginia 1995

Briggs, Katherine. *British Folktales.* New York: Pantheon Books 1977

Briggs, Robin. *Witches & Neighbors: The Social and Cultural Context of European Witchcraft.* New York: Viking Press 1996

Broadhurst, Paul. "Holy Well or Holy Grail ? The Mystic Quest in Cornwall," in *The Source*, Issue #4, March 1986

Broadhurst, Paul. "Secret Shrines: Strange Happenings a Stone's Throw From Tintagel," in *The Source*, Issue #7, May 1987

Broadhurst, Paul. *Tintagel and the Arthurian Mythos.* Launceton: Pendragon Press 1992

Brooke, Bob. "Treasure Hunting in the Cotswolds" in *British Heritage*, Vol. 21, Number 2, February/March 2000

Brown, Dale Mackenzie. "Sick? Try Sleeping," in *Archaeology*, March/April 2001

Buckley, Kemmis. "Some Holy Wells of South Carmarthenshire." A talk given on February 3, 1971 before the Llanelli Art Society, Wales

Buckley, Kemmis. "Llandeilo Llwydiarth — The Well and the Skull," in *The Source*, Issue 2, Winter 1994

Burl, Aubrey. *Megalithic Brittany.* New York: Thames and Hudson Inc., 1985

Capt, E. Raymond. *The Traditions of Glastonbury.* Muskogee: Artisan Sales 1983

Carroll, Father Pat. "Experiencing inner calm and cures at Lourdes," in *The Irish Times*, August 10, 1999

Cassetta, Pasquo. "Image of Madonna and Child Leads to Discovery of Healing Water." Http://www.mcn.org/l/miracles/pasquo.html 3/20/01

Catholic Online. "Ninth Apparition, Thursday 25 February 1858: Discovery of the Miraculous Spring," www.catholic.org/mary/ninth/html

Chambers, Rachel. "Ethiopia: Washing Away the Demons," in *BBC News*, October 18, 1999 (//news.bbc.co.uk)

Cleaver, Alan. "Holy Wells: Wormholes in Reality?," part 1 in *The Source*, Issue #3, November 1985, part II in *The Source*, Issue #4, March 1986

Cooper, J.C. *An Illustrated Encyclopaedia of Traditional Symbols*. London: Thames and Hudson Ltd. 1978

Courtney, R.A. *The Holy Well & The Water of Life*. Penzance: Beare & Son 1916

Cranston, Ruth. *The Miracle of Lourdes*. New York: Image Books, 1988

Croutier, Alev Lytle. *Taking the Waters*. New York: Abbeville Press, 1992

Cumont, Franz. *Oriental Religions in Roman Paganism*. New York; Dover Publications, 1956 (A reprint of the 1911 edition published by G. Routledge & Sons, Ltd.)

Davidson, H.R. Ellis. *Gods and Myths of the Viking Age*. New York: Bell Publishing Company, 1964

Delaney, Frank. *The Celts*. London: Grafton Books, 1989

Devereux, Paul. *Places of Power: Secret Energies at Ancient Sites: A Guide to Observed or Measured Phenomena*. London: Blandford, 1990

Devereux, Paul. *Earth Memory: Sacred Sites — Doorways into Earth's Mysteries*. St. Paul: Llewellyn Publications, 1992

Devereux, Paul. *The Sacred Place: The Ancient Origin of Holy and Mystical Sites*. London: Cassell & Company 2000

Doherty, Mary. "Holy Wells," a Clonmary School manuscript, 1938

Doull, John et al. *Risk Assessment of Radon in drinking Water*. Washington: The National Academy of Sciences, 1998

Downes, Joseph. "David the 'Telynwr;' Or, the Daughter's Trial: A Tale of Wales," in *Blackwoods Edinburgh Magazine*, Vol. 58 (357) July, 1845

Drucker, Philip. *Indians of the Northwest Coast*. New York: The Natural History Press, 1963

Eliade, Mircea. *The Sacred & The Profane: The Nature of Religion*. San Diego: Harcourt Brace & Company, 1959

Ellerbe, Helen. *The Dark Side of Christian History*. Orlando: Morningstar and Lark, 1995

Ellis, Peter Berresford. *The Druids*. Grand Rapids: Wm. B. Eerdmans Publishing Company, 1995

Evans, E. Estyn. *Irish Folk Ways*. Mineola: Dover Books 2000 (A reprint of the, 1957 edition published by Routledge & Keegan Paul, Ltd., London)

Elwell-Sutton, P. "The Two-Horned One," in *Legends of the World*. Edited by Richard Cavendish. New York: Barnes & Noble, 1994

Ferguson, Gary. *The World's Great Nature Myths*. Helena: Falcon Publishing, Inc., 1996

Ferguson, John. "Classical Greece and Rome," in *Legends of the World*. Edited by Richard Cavendish. New York: Barnes & Noble, 1994

Field, David. "Bury the dead in a sacred landscape," in *British Archaeology*, Issue 43, April 1999

Flint, Valerie. "The Demonisation of Magic and Sorcery in Late Antiquity: Christian Redefinitions of Pagan Religions," in *Witchcraft and Magic in Europe: Ancient Greece and Rome.* Philadelphia: University of Pennsylvania Press, 1999

Fish, Brenda. "The Legend of El Dorado," in *Legends of the World.* Richard Cavendish, editor. New York: Barnes and Noble, 1994

Frazer, Sir James. *The Golden Bough: A Study in Magic and Religion.* Hertfordshire: Wordsworth Editions, 1993

Freeman, Mara. "Sacred Waters, Holy Wells," in *Parabola*, Volumne XX, Number 1, Spring 1995, pgs 52-57

Friedman, Irving. "A River Went Out of Eden," in *Parabola*, Vol. XX, Number 1, Spring 1995, 66-72

Frontinus, Sextus Julius. *The Water Supply of the City of Rome*, trans. By Clemens Herchel. Boston: New England Water Works Association, 1973

Fry, Roy and Tristan Gray Hulse. "The Holywell Cure Records" in *The Source*, Issue #1, Autumn, 1994

Gamst, Frederick C. *The Qemant: A Pagan-Hebraic Peasantry of Ethiopia.* Case Studies in Cultural Anthropology. New york: Holt, Rinehart & Winston, 1969

Gerald of Wales. *The History and Topography of Ireland.* Translated by John O'Meara. London: Penguin Books, 1982

Gimbutas, Marija. *The Language of the Goddess.* New York: Harper Collins Publishers, 1991

Goldschmidt, Walter. "Nomlaki," in *Handbook of North American Indians: Volume 8—California.* Washington: Smithsonian Institution, 1978

Graves, Robert. *The White Goddess: A Historical Grammer of Poetic Myth.* New York: The Noonday Press, 1948

Green, Miranda. *The Gods of the Celts.* Gloucestershire: Allan Sutton Publishing, Ltd., 1997

Green, Miranda. *The World of the Druids.* London: Thames and Hudson, 1997

Green, Miranda. "The Religious Symbolism of the Llyn Cerrig Bach and Other Early Sacred Water Sites" in *The Source*, Issue 1, Autumn 1994

Griffyn, Sally. *Sacred Journeys: Stone Circles & Pagan Paths.* London: Kyle Cathie Limited 2000

Hand, Wayland D. *Magical Medicine: The Folkloric Component of Medicine in the Folk Belief, Custom, and Ritual of the Peoples of Europe and America.* Berkeley: University of California Press 1980

Hardy, Philip Dixon. *The Holy Wells of Ireland.* Dublin: Hardy & Walker, 1840

Harpur, James. *The Atlas of Sacred Places: Meeting Points of Heaven and Earth.* New York: Henry Holt and Company, 1994

Harte, J.M. "The Holy Wells of Somerset," in *The Source*, Issue #2, July, 1985

Heizer, Robert F. "Sacred Rain Rocks of Northern California," in *Reports of the University of California Archaeological Survey, No. 20*, March 16, 1953

Heizer, Robert F. "Natural Forces and Native World View," in *Handbook of North American Indians: Volume 8—California.* Washington: Smithsonian Institution, 1978

Hillgarth, J.N. *The Conversion of Western Europe, 350-750.* Englewood Cliffs: Prentice-Hall, Inc., 1969

Hope, Robert Charles. *The Legendary Lore of the Holy Wells of England.* London: Elliot Stock, 1893 (Facsimile Reprint by Llanerch Publishers, Felinfach Wales 2000)

Hunt, Laurence. "Some Ancient Wells, Springs and Holy Wells of the Cotswolds" in *The Source*, Issue #4, Winter, 1995

Hutton, Ronald. *The Pagan Religions of the Ancient British Isles: Their Nature and Legacy.* Oxford: Blackwell Publishers Ltd., 1991

Jones, Francis. *The Holy Wells of Wales.* Cardiff: University of Wales Press, 1954

Jones, Kathy. *The Ancient British Goddess: Her Myths, Legends and Sacred Sites.* Glastonbury: Ariadne Publications, 1991

Jones, Kathy. *In the Nature of Avalon: Goddess Pilgrimages in Glastonbury's Sacred Landscape.* Glastonbury: Ariadne Publications 2000

Jones, Prudence & Nigel Pennick. *A History of Pagan Europe.* New York: Barnes & Noble Inc., 1995

Jordan, Katherine M. "Seven Wiltshire Wells and their Folklore" in *The Source*, Issue 6, Summer 1998

Jordan, Katy. "Wiltshire Healing Wells and the Strange Case of Purton Spa," in *Living Spring Journal*, Issue #1, May 2000

Jordan Katy. *The Haunted Landscape: Folklore, ghosts & legends of Wiltshire.* Bradford on Avon: Ex Libris Press 2000

Jordan, Katy. "Wiltshire Wells," www.bath.ac.uk/~liskmj/wellsweb/wellstxt.htm, 1999

Joseph, Frank. *Sacred Sites of the West: A Guide to Mystical Centers.* Blaine: Hancock House Publishers, 1997

Joyce, Thomas A. *Mexican Archaeology: An Introduction to the Archaeology of the Mexican and Mayan Civilizations of Pre-Spanish America.* London: Philip Lee Warner, 1920

Kennedy, Conan. *Ancient Ireland: The User's Guide.* Killala: Morrigan Books, 1997

Keys, David. "4,700 year-old Oak temple found in Wales," in *The Independent*, November 26, 2000

Kivikoski, Ella. *Ancient Peoples and Places: Finland.* New York: Frederick A. Praeger, 1967

Klages, Ellen. *Harbin Hot Springs: Healing Waters Sacred Land.* Middletown: Harbin Springs Publishers, 1991

Kluckhohn, Clyde and Dorothea Leighton. *The Navaho.* New York: Anchor Books 1962

Knowlson, T. Sharper. *The Origins of Popular Superstitions and Customs.* London: T. Werner Laurie Ltd., 1910

Krickenberg, Walter et al. *Pre-Columbian American Religions.* New York: Holt, Rinehart and Winston, 1968

Lapena, Frank R. "Wintu," in *Handbook of North America n Indians: Volume 8-California.* Washington: Smithsonian Institution, 1978

Leighton, Ralph. *Tuva or Bust: Richard Feynman's Last Journey.* New York: W.W. Norton & Company, 1991

Levine, Donald N. *Greater Ethiopia: The Evolution of a Multiethnic Society.* Chicago: The University of Chicago Press, 1974

Lindow, John. *Swedish Legends and Folktales.* Berkeley: University of California Press, 1978

Livingstone, Sheila. *Scottish Customs.* New York: Barnes & Noble, 1996

Logan, Patrick. *The Holy Wells of Ireland.* Buckinghamshire: Colin Smythe, 1980

Luxton, Imogen. "The Reformation and Popular Culture," in *Church and Society in England: Henry VIII to James I,* edited by Felicity Heal and Rosemary O'Day. Hamden: Archon Books, 1977

MacAnTsaoir, Iain. "Sacred Precincts, The Nemeds." *Clannada na Gadelica,* 1999

Mackaile, M. *The Oyly-well: Or, A Topographico-Spagyrical description of the Oyly-well, at St. Catherines-chappel in the Paroch of Libberton.* Edinburgh: Robert Brown, 1664

MacKenzie, Donald A. *Crete & Pre-Helenic: Myths and Legends.* London: Senate Publishers, 1995 (A reprint of the 1917 edition originally titled *Crete & Pre-Helenic Europe* published by The Gresham Publishing Company, London)

MacKenzie, Donald A. *Pre-Columbian America: Myths and Legends.* London: Senate, 1996, 197 (a reprint of the 1923 publication, *Myths of Pre-Columbian America,* published by The Gresham Publishing Company, London)

Mallory, J.P. *In Search of the Indo-Europeans: Language, Archaeology and Myth.* London: Thames and Hudson, 1989

Mandeville, Sir John. *The Travels of Sir John Mandeville.* Trans. by C.W.R.D. Moseley. London: Penguin Books, 1983

Mann, Nicholas R. *The Isle of Avalon.* St. Paul: Llewellyn Publications, 1996

Markale, Jean. *The Great Goddess: Reverence of the Divine Feminine From the Paleolithic to the Present.* Translated from the French by Jody Gladding. Rochester: Inner Traditions, 1999

Mason, Reverend. "An account of a burning well at Brosley in Shropshire...," in *The Annual Register, or a View of the History, Politics, and Literature for the Year 1761.* 92-93

Mays, Buddy. *Ancient Cities of the Southwest.* San Francisco: Chronicle Books, 1982

McGarry, Patsy. "Jubilee pilgrimages abound as matches are sidelined," in *The Irish Times,* May 20, 2000

Merriam, C. Hart. editor, *The Dawn of the World: Myths and Tales of the Miwok Indains of California,* Lincoln: University of Nebraska Press, 1993

Merrifield, Ralph. *The Archaeology of Ritual and Magic.* New York: New Amsterdam Books, 1987

Messenger, John C. *Inis Beag: Isle of Ireland.* Case Studies in Cultural Anthropology. New York: Holt, Rinehart and Winston, 1969

Michell, John. *Sacred England.* Glastonbury: Gothic Image Publications, 1996

Miles, T.L. "Springs, Wells & Witches," in *Cotswold Life,* May 1983

Miller, Mary and Karl Taube. *An Illustrated Dictionary of the Gods and Symbols of Ancient Mexico and the Maya.* New York: Thames and Hudson, 1993

Molyneaux, Brian Leigh. *The Sacred Earth: Spirits of the Landscape, Ancient Alignments and Sacred Sites, Creation and Fertility.* Boston: Little, Brown and Company, 1995

Muir, Richard and Humphrey Welfare. *The National Trust Guide to Prehistoric and Roman Britain.* London: George Philip/The National Trust & The National Trust for Scotland, 1983

Mullen, Peter. *Shrines of Our Lady.* New York: St. Martin's Press, 1998

NicBhride, Feorag. "The Application of Archaeological Theory to the Study of 'Celtic' Water Cults, with Particular Reference to Holy Wells Studies," a talk given to the Perth Source Moot, 1998

Ogden, Daniel. "Binding Spells: Curse Tablets and Voodoo Dolls in the Greek and Roman World," in *Witchcraft and Magic in Europe: Ancient Greece and Rome*. Edited by Bengt Ankarloo and Stuart Clark. Philadelphia: University of Pennsylvania Press, 1999

Olcott, William. *The Greenbriar Heritage: White Sulphur Springs West Virginia*. Haarlem: Arndt, Preston, Chapin, Lamb & Keen, Inc., n/d

Peck, C.W. *Australian Legends: Tales Handed Down From the Remotest Times by the Autocthonous Inhabitants of our Land*. N/p: 1933. Electronic text at www.sacred-texts.com/aus/peck.htm

Pennick, Nigel. *Celtic Sacred Landscapes*. London: Thames and Hudson, 1996

Pennick, Nigel. *The Celtic Saints*. New York: Sterling Publishing Co., Inc., 1997

Pepper, Elizabeth. *Celtic Tree Magic*. Middletown: The Witches Almanac Ltd., 1996

Pepper, Elizabeth and John Wilcock. *Magical and Mystical Sites: Europe and the British Isles*. Grand Rapids: Phanes Press 2000

Peterson, Frederick. *Ancient Mexico*. New York: Capricorn Books, 1962

Potter, Chesca. "Madron Well: 'the Mother Well'," in *The Source*, Issue #5, July 1986

Potter, Chesca. "The River of Wells," in *The Source*, Issue #1, March 1985

Radford, E. and M.A. *Encyclopaedia of Superstitions*. New York: The Philosophical Library, 1949

Rappoport, Angelo S. *Myth and Legend of Ancient Israel Vol. 2*. New York: KTAV Publishing House, Inc., 1966

Rawlins, R. R. "On the Ancient Custom of Decorating Wells with Flowers, etc," reprinted in *The Source*, Issue #2, July 1985

Redman, S. "Ceremony for the Souls of the Slain in Battle," in *Notes and Queries*, Vol. 72, April 16, 1859

Ross, Anne and Don Robins. *The Life and Death of a Druid Prince*. New York: Summit Books, 1989

Rowan. "Buttons, Bras and Pins: The Folklore of British Holy Wells," in *White Dragon*, Lughnasa, 1996

Scullard, H. H. *Roman Britain: Outpost of the Empire*. London: Thames and Hudson, 1986

Sheldrake, Rupert. The Rebirth of Nature: The Greening of Science and God. New York: Bantam Books, 1991

Simpson, Jacqueline, trans. *Legends of Icelandic Magicians*. Cambridge: D.S. Brewer Ltd., for the Folklore Society, 1975

Smith, John Holland. *The Death of Classical Paganism*. New York: Charles Scribner, 1976

Squire, Charles. *Celtic Myths & Legends*. New York: Portland House, 1997

Straffon, Cheryl. The Earth Goddess: Celtic and Pagan Legacy of the Landscape. London: Blanford, 1997

Stephens, John L. *Incidents of Travel in Yucatan*. New York: Dover Publications, Inc., 1963 (A reprint of the Harper & Brothers 1848 edition)

Stewart, R.J. *Celtic Gods Celtic Goddesses*. London: Blandford, 1990, 98

Stucky, Frederick James. *The Holy Groves of Britain: Vol 1. King Arthur was a Londoner*. Devon: Merlin Books Ltd., 1995

Swan, James A. Sacred Places: How the Living Earth Seeks Our Friendship. Santa Fe: Bear & Co., 1990

Thomas, Keith. *Religion and the Decline of Magic.* London: Penguin Books, 1971

Tompkins, Peter. *Mysteries of the Mexican Pyramids.* New York: Harper & Row, 1976

Trevelyan, Marie. *Folk-Lore and Folk-Stories of Wales.* London: Elliot Stock, 1909

Varner, Gary R. "Sacred Symbols: The Fish," in *Bright Blessings*, Vol. I, Issue 7, September 2000

Varner, Gary R. *The Gods of Man: Gods of Nature – God of War.* Morrisville: Lulu Press Inc. 2007

Västrik, Ergo-Hart. "The Waters and Water Spirits in Votian Folk Belief," in *Folklore*, Vol. 12, December 1999. Institute of the Estonian Language

Walker, Barbara G. *The Women's Encyclopedia of Myth's and Secrets.* Edison: Castle Books, 1983

Wall, Dr. J. "Extract of a Letter of J. Wall, M.D. to the Rev. Dr. Lyttelton, Dean of Exeter, and F.R.S. concerning the good Effects of Malvern Waters in Worchestershire," in *Philosophical Transactions of the Royal Society*, Vol. 50, December 1757, 23-24

Walters, R. C. Skyring. *The Ancient Wells, Springs, and Holy Wells of Gloucestershire.* Bristol: St. Stephen's Press, 1928

Westervelt, William D. *Hawaiian Legends of Old Honolulu.* Rutland: Charles E. Tuttle Company, 1963

Westwood, Jennifer. *Albion: A Guide to Legendary Britain.* London: Paladin/Grafton Books, 1987

Whetton, Chris. "The mysterious underworld," in *Hydrocarbon Processing*, Journal of the Society of Hydrocarbon Engineers, February 2000, Vol. 79, No. 2, www.hydrocarbonprocessing.com/archive_00-02/00-02_she.html

Wilde, Lady. *Irish Cures, Mystic Charms & Superstitions.* New York: Sterling Publishing Company, Inc., 1991

Willetts, R. F. *Cretan Cults and Festivals.* Westport: Greenwood Press, Publishers, 1980, (A reprint of the 1962 edition published by Routledge & Keegan Paul Ltd.)

Woodbury, Richard B. and Ezra B.W. Zubrow. "Agricultural Beginnings, 2000 BC–AD 50," in *Handbook of North America n Indians: Vol.9-Southwest*, edited by Alfonso Ortiz. Washington: Smithsonian Institution, 1979

INDEX